5

Peachpit Press

Visual QuickPro Guide
FileMaker Pro 5 Advanced for Windows and Macintosh
Cynthia L. Baron and Daniel Peck

Peachpit Press

1249 Eighth Street
Berkeley, CA 94710
(510) 524-2178
(510) 524-2221 (fax)

Find us on the World Wide Web at: http://www.peachpit.com

Peachpit Press is a division of Addison Wesley Longman

Copyright © 2001 by Cynthia L. Baron and Daniel Peck

Editor: Becky Morgan
Production Coordinator: Kate Reber
Copy Editor: Doug Clark
Technical Editors: Tim Flynn, Julian Nadel
Compositor: Owen Wolfson
Indexer: Cheryl Landes

ISBN: 0-201-70472-2

0 9 8 7 6 5 4 3 2 1

Printed and bound in the United States of America

♻ Printed on recycled paper

To Cos and Bis, for appreciating and supporting.

To Shai, again and always.

And to Dan, for a friendship with legs.

—Cyndi

Thanks to:

Sarah Boslaugh, my wife, for love and forbearance.

Cyndi Baron, my friend and co-author, for guidance and friendship.

Henry Sapoznik, mein bruder un banje rebbe.

Delfina Davis and Kevin Mallon at Filemaker Inc.

—Dan

Acknowledgements

Cyndi:

Thanks to our Peachpit team:
Marjorie Baer for starting us out,
Becky Morgan for keeping us going and
Kate Reber for bringing us down the home
stretch. And a thank you to Nancy Davis,
the occasional editorial lurker.

Dan:

For their inspiration and challenges:
Richard Cohen, Linda Hammell, Nancy
Senken, Kathy Dolan, AnnMarie, Jim & Terry
Rogers, Ginger Cemelli, Carolyn Kostopoulos,
Roz Goldfarb, Jessica Goldfarb, Daniel
Kestenbaum, Ron Marx, Jeff Cohen,
Marianne Carroll, Rob Getlan, Leon Ablon,
Stacy Kartegener, Craig Cohen, Stacey
Snyder, Cheryl Schneider, Lorin Sklamberg ,
Jessica Kligman, Laurie Winfrey and Kirsten
Odegard, Kate Reber and Marjorie Baer and
our editor Becky Morgan at Peachpit Press.

For tunes and sanity, my bandmates in the
Buck Mountain Band: Bob & Sue Taylor and
Carl Kirby and in the Corn Family: Phil Levy,
Sarah Carlton and Jason Sypher.

For friendship, good times and the occasional
glass of wine: John Hatton, Ellen White and
Elizabeth White-Hatton at Cleff'd Ear
Productions. Warren Argo, Cindy Hartman,
Joy LaSalle, Maggie Brown and Joan Green at
the Festival of American Fiddle Tunes. And
everyone at Divers City in Key Largo.

And Andy Cemelli, whom I miss every day.

TABLE OF CONTENTS

TABLE OF CONTENTS

About

FileMaker Pro 5.0

Welcome to the Visual QuickPro Guide to FileMaker Pro 5.

FileMaker is hands-down the simplest database program to pick up and use. You already know this, because you've benefited from its clarity and accessibility. You know and are comfortable with the FileMaker interface and its terminology (like fields, requests, lookups, and relationships). You can input records at lightning speed. You don't need the Help file to create and edit new fields and layouts, or to run effective finds and sorts. But if any of the above sounds like a foreign language to you, put this book down and pick up *FileMaker Pro 5 for Windows and Macintosh: Visual QuickStart Guide*, by Nolan Hester, which will give you a solid grounding in the basic features and capabilities of FileMaker 5.

Now that you've been creating useful FileMaker projects, you've reached the point where you've realized that you don't know everything you'd like to know about FileMaker, and database development in general. You could be doing more, and maybe doing it better. We hope this book helps you to break through to the next level of FileMaker mastery. It offers tips, techniques, and examples of little-known features to help you to perform remarkably sophisticated database tasks.

FileMaker 5.0: Highlights of New Features

FileMaker 5.0 incorporates a host of enhancements. Some of them are immediately obvious to the casual user. Others will only become important as you join the ranks of the experienced.

Layout/Report Assistant

If you're familiar with Microsoft's Wizards, you'll recognize FileMaker's Layout/Report Assistant as the same idea with a different name. When you choose New Layout/Report and select anything other than Blank layout (the manual step-by-step layout creation method), the Assistant will step you through layout creation. Although the Assistant will be most appreciated by newbies to FileMaker, even experienced users will find this feature a terrific shortcut to building standard layouts.

Besides automating the creation of several standard layout types, the Assistant also includes layout themes—template, color and text styles (**Figure 1.1**) for on-screen display and printed reports. Themes are simply XML code, so if you want to create something special you can modify them in a text editor like BBEdit (**Figure 1.2**).

Table View

Instead of requiring you to waste time setting up layouts just to view your data in a useful way, the new version of FileMaker provides three customizable layouts for quick data examination. You can view and print any database in Form, List or Table View. Table View is particularly important, because it operates dynamically like a spreadsheet. You can reorder and resize columns. When you widen a column, the columns to its right automatically move over to make room for it (**Figure 1.3**). You can do anything in Table View that you could in any other layout in Browse or Find mode, including sorting and entering data.

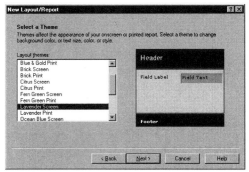

Figure 1.1 The Layout/Report Assistant displays a sample of the Theme when you highlight its name.

Figure 1.2 Open a theme in the text editor you use to create Web pages to alter an existing theme.

Figure 1.3 Widen a column in Table View by grabbing its border and dragging it to the new size.

Direct formatted Web access to FMP files

As usual, FileMaker has taken what can be a complicated process and made it breathtakingly simple. Once you have your information displayed in a database layout, you're one minute away from a Web page and a live back-end database. Because the new version of FileMaker supports Cascading Style Sheets, your FileMaker information is automatically transferred into Web pages in a style you choose from supplied templates. The templates are limited in number, but they correspond to some of the layout themes, making it easy to maintain a consistent look on the Web and on a local computer.

Although the Instant Web Publishing feature is tremendously useful, it does limit how much control you can have over the look and feel of your database Web pages. You'll need the Developer's Edition to add interactivity or other Web page enhancements.

Microsoft Office compatibility

Most people who need to put together a database also use Office applications, so FileMaker has changed its interface to be very Office-friendly. This is great if you already know Office well, but not so much of a plus if you've been using FileMaker for years and were already comfortable with its interface. On the other hand, this compatibility goes well beyond look-and-feel issues. You can drag and drop Excel spreadsheets directly into FileMaker and open them as databases. We think this is a reasonable trade-off for having to break some old FileMaker habits.

ODBC/SQL support

If you have to share information with non-FileMaker databases, this addition alone is reason enough to upgrade to version 5.0. Most big corporate or Web-based databases are rooted in SQL (Structured Query Language), a programming language specifically created for relational databases. ODBC (Open Database Connectivity) is the common ground between these databases and desktop applications. FileMaker 5.0 includes an ODBC driver, which means that you can not only attach to an Oracle or NetObjects Fusion server to find or offer information, you can communicate easily with other desktop applications that also support ODBC, like Microsoft Office and Microsoft Access.

Importing scripts

Experienced database developers know that scripts are the most powerful part of FileMaker. Until now, you could create a complicated script in one file, but you had to recreate it step by step if you wanted to use it in another. Now you have to write a script only once. When you need all or part of it again, just cut and paste. You'll still have to edit the script to allow for differences in field names, relationships or other specifics, but you'll find this a real time-saver.

Conditional value lists

Conditional value lists dynamically show different values depending on the data in another field. To the uninitiated this may seem like a small enhancement, but anyone who has ever tried to create a form with drop-down lists for a Web page knows its necessity. This is a really valuable feature that easily accomplishes what used to demand great script trickery.

FILEMAKER 5.0: HIGHLIGHTS OF NEW FEATURES

FileMaker 5.0 Editions

The folks at FileMaker have made a big change in how they license the software. There are now four versions of FileMaker: the standard FileMaker Pro 5.0, the Unlimited version of the standard, FileMaker Server, and the DE (Developer's Edition).

FileMaker Pro 5.0 and FileMaker Pro 5.0 Unlimited are identical except for one key feature. The standard version has a user limit of ten. A user is defined by the computer's IP address, not the user's log-in name, and the limit is in force for a 24-hour period.

FileMaker DE includes a standard version of FileMaker along with some utilities for advanced development work (like a program that can rename files and update all references in other files to the new name). It also includes a vast array of technical information and documentation, particularly on Web integration and CDML. (A utility to help you create CDML steps for HTML is included as well.) Version 5.0 includes an update to its run-time module, which allows you to create an application-independent version of a FileMaker database.

Unlike the other FileMaker products, FileMaker Server 5.0 is not a development tool. It is a dedicated file server application for multi-user databases. We cover it in depth in Chapter 14. However, this new release can host only version 5.0 files, not earlier database versions.

About Upgrading to FileMaker 5.0

Upgrading to FileMaker 5.0 is quite painless. FileMaker automatically detects the fact that the database was created in an earlier version and prompts you through the very short sequence of steps. We do, however, have to warn you about two significant problems before you move all your old databases to the new version. First, a newly created database or one transferred from an earlier version of FileMaker Pro to the latest one isn't backward-compatible. That is, an .FM5 file can't be read in an older version and there is no way to re-save it in one of the earlier formats. There's no going back. Keep copies of your files in the older format, and don't upgrade to FM5 at all if your database must be accessible on a computer that's not up to FileMaker 5's system requirements.

Second, because the standard FileMaker Pro version has some significant licensing restrictions for Web databases, you may need to make a choice between FileMaker Pro 5's enhanced usability and direct Web connections, and the limited access it provides. If you are a single user who wants to make your database accessible to a large number of people over the Internet, you should either stick with the earlier version you have, or upgrade to the more powerful FileMaker Pro 5.0 Unlimited.

Using This Book

We hope you're no stranger to Peachpit's Visual QuickStart series. This book shares the QuickStart format, but differs in intent and material. QuickStart guides offer comprehensive feature-by-feature coverage of a software program. In this book we assume that you're familiar with how the program works because you're already using it. We also assume that you're a user who has the potential to become a FileMaker developer, but needs some guidance in making the jump between basic features and hard-core corporate development. Instead of exhaustive coverage of features, we concentrate on the practical ins and outs of situations you might run into while you work.

Because we're covering more complicated information, this book has some tasks that are a little longer than the QuickStart usual. We occasionally use sidebars to give you a little background on a topic, because we believe that when you have background knowledge it's easier to apply general instructions to your specific situation.

Windows and Macintosh

Although we've tended to use a lot of Windows screen shots to illustrate this book, it really doesn't matter what platform you use with FileMaker Pro. Except for an occasional dialog box and things (like saving files and printing) that are different because of the operating system, everything in FileMaker is exactly the same everywhere.

With very few exceptions, any FileMaker Pro database will transfer seamlessly back and forth between the platforms, and can be updated over a network by people working on either type of computer. When one of these exceptions crops up (as they will in a few places) we'll point them out to you so you can be prepared.

ORGANIZING
DATA EFFICIENTLY

2

To get the most out of any set of data, that data must be organized. Although this seems like an obvious statement, executing it is trickier than may initially appear. For every set of information there are dozens, maybe even multiple dozens of ways that information can be categorized, broken into pieces, and connected. Adding more complexity to the process, more than one of those ways may be the "right" way... depending on your goals. Almost every database can be made cleaner, more flexible, and easier to manipulate. Even if you've been creating FileMaker database files for some time, you can benefit from reexamining your process and structure for ways they can be augmented and improved.

About Relational Databases

FileMaker is a relational database program. That means two important things. First, it's a tool for taking a collection of information items and imposing a formal organization on them. (That's the part that makes it a database program.) All the earliest computer databases shared this characteristic, as, to some degree, do modern spreadsheet programs. Second, FileMaker allows you to fluidly retrieve, add to, and dynamically assemble that information in separate but connected database documents, without having to modify the initial database structure or create duplicate data entries. (That's the relational part.) Relational database programs are more flexible, sophisticated and powerful than simple flat database programs.

Just because FileMaker allows you to create relational databases doesn't mean that every database you create using FileMaker will take full advantage of these features. In fact, most beginning users of FileMaker understand the database part of its capabilities long before they understand (and effectively use) the relational parts.

Dynamic data

One of the primary principles behind a relational database is that data should never be duplicated. If you create a file with one set of information, you shouldn't need to copy or re-enter any of the field entries to create a new file. At most, you need a single duplicated field to act as the place where two sets of information "join." That join is also referred to as a *key field*, a category of unique information that identifies which records in one database refer to a particular record in another database. You can use this key field to display the data from the other database on a layout alongside the data in the first database.

A classic example used by database mavens to illustrate relational databases is a college course registration. Colleges can have thousands of students and hundreds of courses, so it would be really impractical to duplicate all the student information for each course roster. Instead, a course roster is created from a database of students, a database of faculty, and a database of courses. The course roster is the place where these separate entities join, with the course number serving as the field where the connections are made. We'll examine that scenario in greater detail later in this chapter.

Gathering Information

Database design can be enormously gratifying, particularly in its initial creative stages. As a developer, you can be equal parts designer and detective. You get to see information both globally and very specifically, as you speak to individual users and examine broad strategic issues. The decisions you make in structuring data can make an organization more efficient, its staff more comfortable and less frustrated in their work, and in some magical instances, can even lead to tangible business breakthroughs.

Of course, database developers don't always have the luxury of a clean slate. Every living database branches, grows, and can end up in desperate need of pruning—or even uprooting and replacing. Whether you're starting a database from scratch or retrofitting an existing one, the life expectancy of your database will be longer if it begins with careful and logical planning, based on solid research and discovery.

Before you begin to create fields and files, you should know:

- ◆ **The goal of the database**. Why is it needed or what problems will it solve? Here's where logic and common sense are most important. You want to create a database structure that provides not only a solution to the immediate problem, but also some room for growth. If there's already some form of database in place, examine how it began and developed. The history of an organization and its data can often provide clues to what the organization's future needs will be.

continues on next page

◆ **The people who will use the database.**
Unless this database is your personal
project, others will need to work with the
information. What do they want to be
able to do with the files? If there's an
existing system in place, you should ask
people what they would like to change to
avoid perpetuating existing problems.
Observe users as they work with the data
as well. Sometimes people are unaware
of how many unnecessary steps they
perform, simply because they're so used
to the old system that its shortcomings
are not apparent to them. Your job is not
only to organize data, but to make that
data easy to read and access.

◆ **What information is important.**
By using your own knowledge and/or
interviewing the users, you should develop
a list of required information categories.
Within those categories, you will want to
create a list of information specifics.

◆ **How your database will relate to
other office systems.** Although some
databases remain specialized islands, an
organization's database is more likely to
relate to several functions and business
activities. Will users need to fax or email
database information? Will the data be
accessible over the Internet? Will the
finance department want to use information from sales and marketing?

By examining all the facts and artifacts that
show how information moves through the
real world, you eventually develop a good
concept of what your database will cover
and how it will be structured.

Many databases are a replacement for existing systems. Functioning systems always
depend on forms, records, and flat files, and
so can you. Sometimes the only failing of
the current system is that it's not computer-
ized. If so, you can and should ground your
structure firmly on a method that people
already know. Base your initial categories
and field headings on the existing format,
then expand by looking for data that isn't
yet being captured or presented successfully.
For example, an organization may already
track sales by individual but not by region.
Capturing this information would enable
them to have a better sense of the effectiveness of their sales force, and their regional
sales management.

Even if you're starting from scratch because
the organization is new or this is the first
attempt at capturing the information, you're
probably not really breaking new ground.
Others have likely created similar databases
before. Ask around to discover what methods
are being used in organizations similar to
your own. One great source for templates or
inspiration is the various sample files available at several FileMaker Internet sites. See
Appendix B for specific URLs.

Creating a Field List

Once you have a collection of raw paper data and the input from anyone contributing information or requests you can implement, it's time to determine which major information topics you need to include in the database. In some cases, you'll already know how this information should be organized because you're copying an existing format. If so, you can skip directly to your data structure strategy. Otherwise, you need to list every data topic that might be important.

This sounds like a tall order, and indeed it is. Breaking down the data into its smallest parts is one of the hardest and most critical aspects of creating a good database. All too many files are flawed by a developer's tendency to lose patience or run out of time before breaking out the data sufficiently.

For example, one of the classic database errors is to create a field called Name, and to enter the person's entire name into it instead of breaking the information down into two or three fields (Last Name and First Name/MI or Last Name, First Name and a separate middle initial field). It doesn't take too long before this error comes back to haunt you, because it prevents you from searching and sorting on the last name and denies you all sorts of elegant FileMaker tools for creating form letters. Fixing this error requires a rather complex script (see Chapter 12) and some additional tweaking to clean it up.

Looking at a field list

Although every field list is different, what they all share if done properly is a surprising length. A database can begin with a very limited field list, but as it becomes a tool you depend on, more and more fields get added.

Each time you add a field and enter more data into it, it's harder to be sure that every record contains parallel information and that this information has actually been input into the correct record. If you create a clear, well structured core that begins with all your most important field categories, you and the database users will have less work utilizing it later.

In our college database example, a quick listing of important information would look like this.

Student Last Name	Instructor Teaching Course
Student First Name	Credits per Course
Student Address	Instructor ID
Student City	Instructor Department
State	Instructor Last Name
Zip	Instructor First Name
Year Enrolled	Instructor Address
Birth date	City
Student Major	State
Student ID Number	Zip
Courses Taken	Phone
Credits Accumulated	Date Hired
Student Grades	Courses Taught
Course Numbers	Classes Running
Course Names	IDs of Students in Classes
Course Descriptions	Student Last Names
Course Prerequisites	Student First Names
Dept(s) Offering Course	Grades Earned in Class

Though this is a pretty long list, it still doesn't include everything the college would want to know. Even so, it's more than enough material to break into the categories that will become the actual database structure.

Developing a Data Structure Strategy

The most important part of creating a relational database is determining how you'll organize the data you've listed. The easiest way to visualize the task is to imagine your database as a series of spreadsheets. Each spreadsheet is a logical grouping of fields that belong together. Each individual column heading is a major category of information. Each row is a set of fields with entries in the columns. The column headings become the field headings in your database. Your mission is to match up the right set of column headings for each spreadsheet.

The best way to start this process is to segment the information into categories, and avoid putting too many columns in each category so you don't go crazy working with too many variables at once. Look for modules of information that can be logically grouped (**Figure 2.1**).

Let's continue with the college database. We have a class of data called Students. In the Student table listing, we'd certainly have the student name. But there are so many other pieces of information about the student to consider! The key thing to remember is that, although all this information is important, not all of it belongs in the Student spreadsheet table. For example, the Dean's office

Student Data	**Faculty Data**	**Class Data**
Student ID number	Instructor ID number	Student ID number
Student Last Name	Department	Student Last Name
Student First Name	Instructor Last Name	Student First Name, MI
Student Address	Instructor First Name	Student Major
Student City	Instructor Address	Course Number
State	City	Course Name
Zip	State	Credits
Phone Number	Zip	Instructor ID number
Major	Phone	
Year Enrolled	Date Hired	
Birthdate	Course Numbers	**College Data**
High School Graduated	Course Names	
Region/Country		Departments
Course Numbers		Majors
Course Names	**Course Data**	Course Numbers
Credits Accumulated		Student ID numbers
Grade Point Average	Course Numbers	Instructor ID numbers
	Course Names	
	Course Descriptions	
	Course Prerequisites	
	Credits	
	Department	

Figure 2.1 The original list of possible data has been organized into logical groups.

probably already has a list of majors the college offers, broken out by the department that offers them. The Registrar's office certainly needs a separate database of courses for the student to choose from, as well as prerequisites for each class to prevent students from registering for a course they're not prepared to take. So these types of information are related to students, but aren't part of their primary information.

What does belong? Only the information that will remain intrinsic to the student no matter what happens during his or her college career: ID, birth date, addresses, phone numbers. Course-related information

belongs in a different table, grade and credit information might belong in another. It's easier to create a lookup or a relationship between two tables to bring sets of information together than it is to separate information you've crammed together in one table. For example, although you'll need to know the courses students take and their grade point averages, the course information itself should be separate from the student records. The grade point average can be found by creating a calculation and a summary field that links to the database where final class grades are kept (**Figure 2.2**).

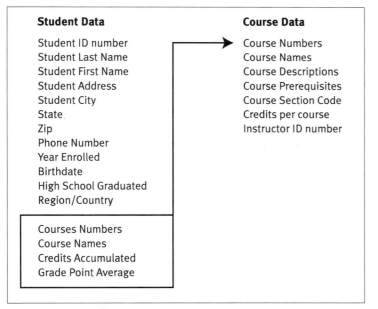

Figure 2.2 Although the circled data is part of the student information, it logically belongs in a separate file in the database.

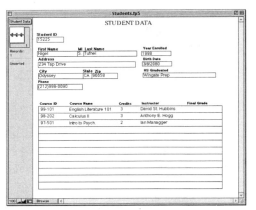

Figure2.3 The Student Data file has a layout that includes a portal listing all the courses in which the student is currently enrolled.

Since one student will take many courses, you'll want to create yet another file that contains the Student ID and the Course ID for each course in which the student enrolls. This is known as a "one-to-many" relationship (one student/many courses). In Chapter 6, you will see FileMaker techniques to create such relationships. For example, we could create a portal to list all of the courses for that student on a layout in the Student database, and use a summary of related fields to total the number of credits each student has earned (**Figure 2.3**).

FIELDS CREATED WITHIN INDIVIDUAL FILES

Student Data	Faculty Data	Course Data	Class Data
Student ID number	*Instructor ID number*	*Course Numbers*	Course Number
Last Name	*Last Name*	*Course Names*	*Grades*
First Name	First Name	*Credits*	Date
Major	Address	Descriptions	Student ID number
Address	City	Prerequisites	
City	State	Department	
State	Zip	Instructor ID number	
Zip	Phone		
Phone	Date Hired		
Year Enrolled			
Birthdate			
High School			
Region/Country			

FIELDS CREATED WITH LOOKUPS & RELATIONSHIPS

Student Data	Faculty Data	Course Data	Class Data
Course Numbers		Instructor Last Name	Course Name
Course Names			Student Last Name
Credits Accumulated			Student First Name
Grade Point Average			Student Major
			Instructor ID number
			Instructor Last Name
			Credits

Figure 2.4 No fields should have to be input twice in a well-designed database. The fields in italics will appear in other databases by setting up relationships or using lookups.

Creating a Data Structure Chart

In our college database example, we've progressed through information gathering and categorizing data into fields, and have assigned the fields to categories that will be separate files in the database. Now we need to figure out what relationships each file should have to each of the other files in the database. The best way to visualize the relationships is to create a series of charts that represent the individual categories of information, then determine the relationship these groups should have to each other.

We have several files that will have a variety of relationships. The main ones are Students, Faculty, Courses, and Classes:

◆ **Students:** Contains the data related to each individual student. Except for grade-related information, this data should remain relatively static once it is input.

◆ **Courses:** Contains the data related to each course offered. Course information changes infrequently, so this is also a fairly stable file.

◆ **Faculty:** Contains the data related to each member of the faculty. Faculty can be added or deleted but, like the student and course files, will not change on a regular basis.

◆ **Classes:** Contains a list of running courses, along with the list of students taking them and the instructor who teaches each course. This list changes every semester and requires a separate record for each class taken by every student.

Note that we have begun to divide our list into fields that will contain records in the individual databases and fields that will depend on lookups or relationships to other databases. All of our duplications are here, as well as those fields that are unique but depend on data from other files—like the students' grade point averages and their accumulated credits, which will be calculated from their class data (**Figure 2.4**). We can use these organized field charts as blueprints for creating our database fields.

Field Design Tactics

The final step before moving to FileMaker and creating your database files is determining the fine points of your fields and relationships. A good strategy can be undermined by errors in tactical details—those important decisions that lead to a FileMaker implementation that's clear, flexible, and scalable.

Identifying key fields

Not all data is created equal. Certain types of information will be needed almost everywhere, while other types will rarely appear. Column headings that appear in multiple spreadsheet tables are good candidates for database key fields.

For example, in our imagined university database, a student's name or ID number will appear in many places: on the course roster, on the student's grade listing at the end of the term, and on the bursar's office listing of course payments. On the other hand, the student's phone number, while important in some situations, will hardly ever be needed outside the Student file listing itself. The name or ID number are good candidates for use as key fields; the phone number, which could easily change and is less useful, would not make a good key field. In your own database, you should always look for the most stable data to use as an identifier.

Choosing unique key fields

In our example, we've noticed that both the students' names and their ID numbers appear on multiple forms. They aren't, however, equally good candidates for use as a key field. For one thing, which part of the student name would you use? You certainly couldn't use the last name alone. Even first and last names are likely to be repeated.

Adding a middle initial can help, but any large college or university will have some duplications even using all three pieces. So, despite the constant recurrence of this information, it's not unique. The ID number, on the other hand, although not the first column in any spreadsheet list, is the only portion of the student data that can't be duplicated by any other student record. We use the same reasoning to choose our unique key fields for the other files in our database (**Figure 2.5**).

✔ Tip

- If a person's Social Security number is available, it is an ideal key field since only one person can have that number. To minimize input errors, always make sure that you specify the Social Security field as number, rather than text.

Student Data	Faculty Data	Course Data	Class Data
■ *Student ID number*	▲ *Instructor ID number*	● *Course Numbers*	● *Course Number*
Last Name	Last Name	Course Names	Grades
First Name	First Name	Credits	Date
Major	Address	Descriptions	Course Name
Address	City	Prerequisites	■ *Student ID number*
City	State	Department	Student Last Name
State	Zip	▲ *Instructor ID number*	Student First Name, MI
Zip	Phone		Student Major
Phone	Date Hired		Instructor ID number
Year Enrolled	Course Numbers		Instructor Last Name
Birthdate	Course Names		Credits
High School			
Region/Country			
Course Numbers			
Course Names			
Credits Accumulated			
Grade Point Average			

Figure 2.5 The key fields for each database are marked in this chart. The symbols identify which set of files will be connected by their key fields.

Using global fields

Most database fields have different information for every record. Global fields, on the other hand, always contain the same information no matter which record or layout you are viewing. As you will see in Chapter 3, global fields are the best way to insert universal container data, like form letter text and graphic elements (logos, signatures, or special symbols). They're also the way to hold the information needed for data variables in calculations and scripts. As you examine your flowcharts, look for unchanging data elements that you can place into global fields.

In our college example, the school logo or a boilerplate affirmative action text disclaimer would do well as global fields. If you plan to create scripts that will require a loop counter, a global field would serve this purpose nicely.

✔ Tip

■ Even if you don't have an immediate need for a global field, you can create one (or more) and hold it in reserve. This may save both time and inconvenience later, since FileMaker doesn't allow you to create new fields when multiple users are actively accessing a file. The same logic can apply to any types of fields, whether they be text, number or container.

Using repeating fields

Generally speaking, you shouldn't. Whenever possible, build your database by creating relationships between files, and list your multiple entries in a portal. Repeating fields in FileMaker are leftovers from when it was a flat file database, not a relational one. Because repeating fields can contain multiple entries in the same field, they are fairly inflexible, can't be individually searched or used in a relationship, and don't work well calculations.

In Chapter 6, we examine some of the few instances when a repeating field can be useful.

✔ Tip

■ One of the first things that you should notice in your field list is that some categories are duplicated, sometimes in more than one place. Once you've built the skeleton for one database (the simpler one, like the Faculty database in our example), you can copy the file, rename it, and update the field names for other similar files (like the Student file in our example). Then you can continue by adding the extra fields and relationships the second file requires.

Tracking fields

Depending on how active your database is and how many people use it, you might want to create fields that track the date and time changes to it were made. Creation and modification fields (created with Auto-Enter options), although not part of the data structure per se, can be invaluable tools for tracking records, as can a field that automatically enters the name of the database user who input or modified the record. In your courses and classes database, for example, you might have a kiosk-type setup with your database set to Entry Only so students could register themselves for classes. By time- and date-stamping these entries it would be easy to determine which students should be given precedence for a seat in a class with limited enrollment.

Implementing Relationships

When you created your flowchart of relationships, you outlined the most obvious places where the data in individual files would intersect. When it comes to implementing these relationships, you need to consider not just what the relationships will be, but how you want to express them in layouts and where you want them to join.

Thinking ahead about sorting and searching

When planning your database, you should be thinking about which pieces of information will be used to find certain records and which may be used to sort data. Then you can make sure that those pieces of data are in separate fields.

For example, you will probably want to sort and search using such criteria as Last Name (for alphabetical listings) or Zip (for mailings). That is why it is critical that these sets of data be in separate fields, and not combined with the first name or the city and state.

Another useful field is one listing the high school that a student graduated from, because you can generate reports that let you track them as alumni later. These fields should be included from the outset, so that you don't have to go back and laboriously enter the data later.

✔ Tip

- If you don't want your finds and sorts to take forever, look at your data relationships for likely search combinations before you break data into different files. Indexing is the key to a speedy search. Fields that are in portals can't be indexed, so FileMaker will take a lot longer to locate this related information.

IMPLEMENTING RELATIONSHIPS

Using key fields and relationships

Once the databases are created, you need to establish the relationships among them. In this example, we noticed early on that the Class data contained very little unique information. Therefore, it will have two main relationships: to the Student database (using the Student ID as the key field), and to the Course ID. The bulk of the data found in the Class database will be a result of lookups from the other related files. (The link to the Faculty database is indirect, since the Instructor ID field in Courses can be used to connect faculty information to the Class database.)

The Student ID will look up the rest of the student information and copy it into the class roster. At the end of the class, grades and credits earned will flow back to the Student database so that you can list which courses a student has taken, and summarize how many credits have accumulated. When you enter the Course ID in the Class database, the Course ID relationship will copy the course information (name, description and credits) into the lookup fields (**Figure 2.6**).

Using lookups vs. relating data

By definition, building a relational database is based on the idea of using related data. Ordinarily, relating data is a much better strategy than relying on lookups, even though lookups are initially easier to create on the fly. One major problem with lookups is that they defeat one of the main purposes of a relational database, which is to avoid duplication of effort. Because you copy information from one file to another in a lookup, you freeze that data in the second file. Unless you update your lookup each time you change the original file (and we can hardly think of a worse waste of time), it's not long

before the information is incomplete, flawed, and ultimately useless.

Despite these negatives, there are a few situations where you should plan to relate data using lookups. When a database entry needs to display related information that shouldn't be constantly updated, lookups are perfect. In our college example, once a course roster has been completed and the time period during which a student can drop or add a course elapses, data from the roster should become part of the student's historical information. That's why the Classes database is important: It combines selected student, course, and instructor information. When you create a new record in this database, the student ID number and course number are entered. By using a lookup from the Courses database to the Classes database for information like the instructor name and course credits, you have an archive from the time that the student took the course.

Testing Your Database

Now that you've divided your information into databases, figured out which fields belong in which files, and strategized the relationships and lookups, you're finally ready to create the FileMaker files themselves. Resist the temptation to think that your project is done. Once you have the architecture of the database set up, don't forget to test your decisions with some representative users before your structure is set in stone. You may discover that, although your structure makes perfect logical sense, it works at cross-purposes to some person's established workflow. Listen carefully to feedback, even it means reconsidering some aspect of your structure. No matter how experienced you are, you always have something to learn from the people who will work with your creation every day.

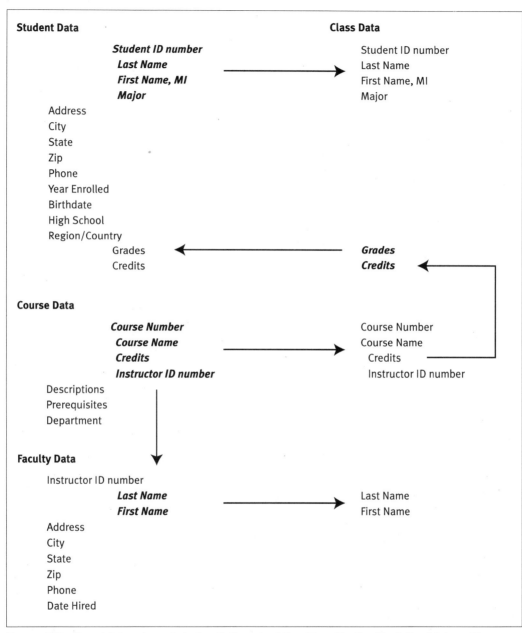

Figure 2.6 The Class database is created primarily through relationships with other files in the database. The arrows indicate the flow of information as lookups copy data to and from the Class database.

LAYOUT
ENHANCEMENTS

FileMaker layouts are the connection between you, the database developer, and the users who will actually work with the database you've designed. An elegantly designed database with awkward layouts will lead to input errors that eat away at efficient use. Such a database can actually be less useful than a beginner's effort whose layouts are clear and carefully created. In this chapter, we'll explore several tools like pop-up lists and check boxes to facilitate data entry and viewing, as well as advanced techniques to create properly constructed layouts, speed up data entry, eliminate entry errors, clarify the meaning of the data, and make the data easier to read.

Usability, Legibility, and Logical Grouping

Although a database developer doesn't have to be a graphic designer, it doesn't hurt to know a little bit about how people read and use information. When planning your layouts, consider how they can be optimized to avoid confusion. A few minutes of extra work on your part can save database users hours of frustration.

If you've planned your database with care, you've examined existing business forms and talked with people to find out how they use them. Once you've figured out what type of information you need to cover in a database, spend some time considering how that information should be visually arranged. For data entry layouts especially, your field arrangement can be critical. Group fields of similar or sequential information together. Whenever possible, arrange fields to match the order of the raw material that people using the database will work from. If you don't, the data inputter is certain to miss or transpose information. For example, if a sales department uses contact sheets that provide phone numbers in order of voice, then fax, then mobile, so should the layout you create.

People in western-language countries read from left to right and top to bottom. If you need to create a layout with fields broken into two columns, separate the columns widely if the flow of information will fill one column before moving to the next. The opposite is true if your tab order will move left to right, then top to bottom (**Figure 3.1**).

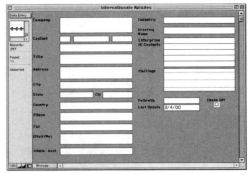

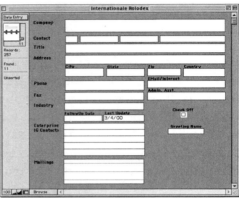

Figure 3.1 These layouts contain essentially the same fields, but present their information differently according to how the data will be added. The top layout information fills the left column, then moves to the right. The bottom layout moves left to right, then down line by line.

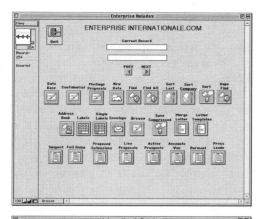

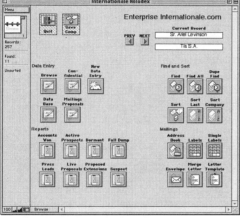

Figure 3.2 In the bottom main menu layout, reports and functions are organized by function. Use the Arrange > Set Alignment command to help you lay out your groupings on a menu page.

Although FileMaker Pro gives you the useful option of changing the tab order of fields in a layout, use this feature sparingly. People take breaks in the tedium of inputting, and it's much easier for them to lose their place in a layout whose tabs jump around the page.

If you've made several types of layouts and reports for a database, it's always a good idea to provide a menu of buttons linked with scripts to each of the layouts and reports. Just as you would in organizing fields, group similar types of button actions together, and provide headings for the groups to make it easy to recognize their functions (**Figure 3.2**). Organizing the main menu like this makes it easier to train new people and speeds up information processing even for accomplished users. We explore menu and button options in Chapter 9, "Extending the Interface with Scripts."

✔ Tip

- Avoid typing labels and other important information in all capital letters. Not only do they take up more space, but they're much harder to read than labels in upper- and lowercase, particularly if the labels are fairly close together (**Figure 3.3**).

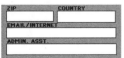

Figure 3.3 It takes people longer to recognize letterforms when they're typed in all capital letters.

USABILITY, LEGIBILITY, AND LOGICAL GROUPING

Cross-Platform Issues

Since FileMaker Pro is a multi-platform and multi-user program, the same database may be running simultaneously on both Macintosh and Windows machines. A layout created on a Macintosh will look similar on a Windows machine, but some aspects, like fonts and colors, will display with slight variations. To make sure that people on both types of computers will be able to view and work comfortably with the database, you should consider screen sizes, font usage, and layout colors and graphics in designing a cross-platform database.

Although the Macintosh OS 8.1 and newer and Windows 95 and newer operating systems both support longer file names, there are still a surprising number of people who continue to work with older computers and operating systems. In order to assure compatibility across platforms, file names should adhere to the DOS/Windows 8.3 format, which limits a file name to only eight alphanumeric characters (no punctuation or spaces), and doesn't recognize any difference between capital and lowercase letters. It also requires Macintosh users to add a file extension to the file name itself in order for the file or database to be recognized as valid on a Windows computer (**Figure 3.4**). If you don't follow this naming convention you may have to change the file name later on. Renaming a file can have serious consequences. Any relationships, scripts, and portals you've created with the old name will have to be recreated using the new one.

Cross-Platform Fonts

To ensure that your FileMaker database will read nicely on machines other than your own, use the fonts that are standard on most computers. Standardizing allows you to create a dependable look for your database no matter where it's running, and saves you the extra work and aggravation of having to change the fonts later. If you absolutely need to use fonts other than the standards, make sure that these fonts are installed on every machine that will use your database. If the font you use is not available on a computer running your database, another font will be substituted by the system software (see sidebar).

✔ Tip

■ Avoid using the Outline and Shadow font styles available on the Macintosh. These type styles have no equivalent in Windows.

Figure 3.4 The correct form for naming a FileMaker Pro 5 database to use it on both platforms looks like this:

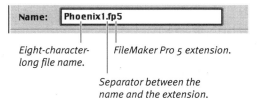

Eight-character-long file name.

Separator between the name and the extension.

FileMaker Pro 5 extension.

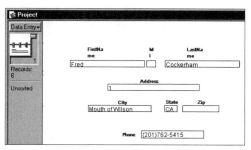

Figure 3.5 Text blocks created on a Macintosh can display incorrectly in Windows if the typeface used isn't stored in the user's system.

Even when you use the standard fonts, some differences between Mac and Windows will still be obvious on screen. Fonts display somewhat larger in Windows than they do on the Mac. This means that the descenders (lower parts of the letters like g and q) and the first and last letters of a text block or field may be cut off (**Figure 3.5**). If you make your fields and text blocks slightly longer and higher you can avoid this problem. Setting text blocks (like field labels and other layout text) to Center alignment will also help avoid display problems, although that often makes for a less attractive print document. If the appearance of your output is important to you or your users, you should create two versions of your layouts—one for each operating system.

Font Equivalents

Every Windows or Macintosh operating system installs some basic fonts in its system folder. Some of them are only meant to be used in menus or for screen display. These are called system fonts. It's a bad idea to use system fonts (like the Mac's Geneva) in a cross-platform database because they have no equivalent font on the other side. Besides system fonts, each platform also includes some typefaces that are meant for print output. These fonts have equivalents that FileMaker will automatically substitute when the database is viewed on the other platform. These equivalents are:

Macintosh Fonts	Windows Fonts
Helvetica	Arial
Times	Times New Roman
Monaco	Courier
Courier	Courier

If you're working on a Macintosh but are creating a cross-platform database, you should install Microsoft TrueTypefonts (downloadable from www.microsoft.com) and use Arial and Times New Roman to build your database rather than Helvetica and Times. Although FileMaker Pro will automatically substitute Arial for Helvetica, the two fonts just aren't the same. Labels you created in Helvetica will run longer in Arial, and your nicely designed layouts and letter text will become a patchwork of badly broken lines.

Cross-Platform Colors

You will use colors in FileMaker layouts to shade the background of a layout, or to highlight or contrast fields against the background. If the computers running your database can display 16,000 or more colors, the colors you use will appear essentially the same across platforms. Windows will render colors slightly darker than on a Macintosh, and colors chosen in Windows will appear lighter and slightly washed-out on a Mac. Simply avoid using the darkest and lightest shades in the color palette to get around this problem.

To use your database on older computers whose video capabilities are limited to 256 colors or to ensure color compatibility across platforms, set the color preference to the Web "color-safe" palette of 216 colors.

To set the Color Palette:

1. Choose Edit > Preferences > Application.

2. When the Application Preferences dialog box appears, click the Layout tab.

3. Select Web palette (216 colors) in the Color Palette box (**Figure 3.6**) and click OK to close the dialog box.

✔ Tip

■ Although it is possible to add custom colors to FileMaker, doing so increases the file size and slows the display redraw. As a rule, it's a bad idea.

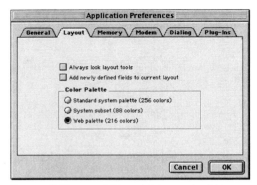

Figure 3.6 All cross-platform databases should have their document preferences set to Web palette to prevent using an unpredictable color by mistake.

Using Graphic Text

One method for displaying non-standard fonts on a layout is to create the text in a paint program. The text can be pasted into your layout as a graphic and will display identically on any computer. This isn't a very efficient way to work if you have lots of text, but it's just fine for logo type or other graphics.

There are three ways to bring over graphic type—one if you are creating the type yourself, another if you have no paint programs and are inserting a graphic provided by someone else, and a third if you don't want the graphic shape to be editable on the layout. This last option, which relies on a container field, is particularly useful if you're dealing with a logo that must look exactly as it was designed. Copied or inserted graphics are all too easy to stretch and compress without your realizing it. Graphics placed in a container field stay put.

To copy a graphic from a paint program into a layout:

1. Open your graphics program and create your type or open the document that already contains it.

2. Select the graphic, then copy it to the Clipboard (in Windows: Ctrl+C/on the Mac: Command-C).

3. Return to FileMaker and switch to Layout mode (Ctrl+L/Command-L). Paste the graphic onto the layout (Ctrl+V/Command-V).

✔ Tip

- If you will need to print the logo or graphic text, create the original art at a print resolution of at least 300 dpi. Otherwise the outlines of your text or logo will look jagged and rough on paper.

To import graphic text from a file:

◆ Switch to Layout mode (Ctrl+L/Command-L). Choose Insert > Picture and navigate to the graphics file you want to insert. Once you find it, click Open.

Your graphic will appear as a free-floating box. You can move or scale it like any other layout object.

To import uneditable graphic text:

1. Make sure you already have a graphic saved in one of the formats FileMaker can import, then go to the layout where you plan to add the graphic. Choose File > Define Fields (Ctrl+Shift+D/Command-Shift-D).

2. When the Define Fields dialog box appears, type the name of your new field into the Field Name text box.

3. In the Type area of the dialog box, select the Container radio button, then click Create (**Figure 3.7**). The new field is added to the field list. Click Done.

continues on next page

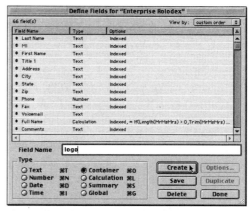

Figure 3.7 To place an uneditable graphic into a layout, create a new field, select Container as the field type, and click Create.

4. Switch to Layout mode (Ctrl+L/ Command-L). From the layout tools on the left, choose Field and drag the field to its new position.

5. From the Specify Field dialog box that appears (**Figure 3.8**), choose the name of the container field you just created, uncheck the Create field label check box and click OK.

6. Resize the field box to fit the graphic you'll be placing there.

7. Switch to Browse mode (Ctrl+B/ Command-B). Select the container field on your layout.

8. Choose Insert > Picture (**Figure 3.9**)and navigate to the graphics file you want to insert. Once you find it, click Open. The graphic will be positioned in the center of your container field (**Figure 3.10**). If you don't like its position, return to Layout mode and move or resize the container field.

The text will now be a graphic on your layout. Keep in mind that the letters aren't really text. You can't edit or change them, except by returning to the graphics program.

✔ Tip

■ If you are working on a Macintosh with FileMaker Pro 5 and use the Insert > Picture command, you may receive an error dialog box that says "Error –2804 occurred during initialization of Claris XTND system." If this message appears, you won't be able to insert graphics in FileMaker fields. This can happen if you (or a software installation program) have turned off the XTND Power Enabler in the Extensions folder. FileMaker needs this Macintosh extension to process graphics in container fields. Just go the Extensions Manager, turn the extension back on, restart your machine and try again. Your graphic should appear without a problem.

Figure 3.8 Uncheck Create field label when you put the field on your layout to avoid having a label on your graphic.

Figure 3.9 To place a graphic into a container field choose Insert > Picture.

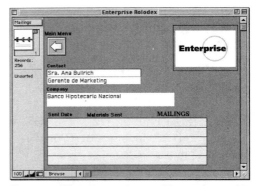

Figure 3.10 When you use Insert > Picture, the graphic is positioned in the center of the container.

Figure 3.11 This button makes it clear that you'll leave the FileMaker program if you click it.

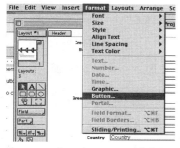

Figure 3.12 To make any graphic into a button, choose Format > Button.

Figure 3.13 The Specify Button dialog box has a scrolling list of button actions, and can offer various options depending on the action chosen.

Formatting Elements as Buttons

FileMaker's Button Tool allows you to create a simple rectangular button and assign a command to it. But virtually any item on a layout can be formatted as a button (including fields). Creating a recognizable graphic for a custom button can help you quickly identify what the button does (**Figure 3.11**).

To use a graphic as a button:

1. Go to the layout where you'd like to place a button. Go to Layout mode (Ctrl+L/ Command-L). Follow the instructions in "To import graphic text from a file" on page 29 for copying or inserting a graphic in Layout mode.

2. Select the graphic you've copied or inserted into your layout, and choose Format > Button (**Figure 3.12**).

3. When the Specify Button dialog box appears, choose the command in the list that you wish to assign to the button, then click OK.

✔ Tip

■ When you choose a command for your button, the Options box on the right will display check boxes or a drop-down list (**Figure 3.13**) if there are more choices for you to make. Otherwise, the Options area will be blank.

One of the most helpful interface enhancements allows you to use a field as a button. By making the Name field into a button that switches to an individual record layout, you can click a name and be switched directly to the details layout.

To make a field into a button:

1. Go to the layout you'd like to add a field button to, and enter Layout mode (Ctrl+L/Command-L).

2. Click on the field you want to make into a button.

3. Choose Format > Button.

4. When the Specify Button dialog box appears, click on Go to Layout (**Figure 3.14**) in the Navigation section of the scrolling list.

5. In the Options section, choose the layout you want to switch to from the drop-down list, then click OK.

   When you click on the field button in Browse mode, the layout will switch and the data for the record you clicked on will be displayed (**Figure 3.15**).

✔ Tips

■ When a field is formatted as a button, you can't edit the contents by just selecting the field. If you want to be able to edit the field when you click on it, you'll need to make that option part of a script you assign to the button. See Chapter 9 for more about attaching scripts to buttons.

■ If you would like to use some FileMaker graphics without having to create your own, refer to Appendix A for information about commercially available button sets.

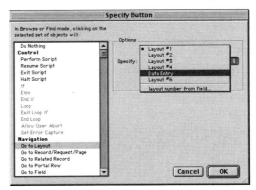

Figure 3.14 Selecting Go to Layout from the command list brings up a drop-down list of all the layouts in your current database.

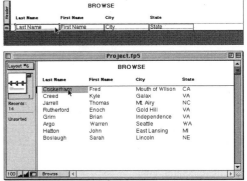

Figure 3.15 To switch to an individual record from a columnar layout, make one of the fields a button, then click on the field in Browse mode to go to the individual record.

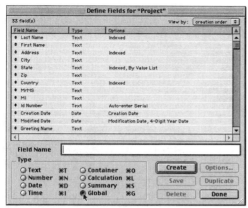

Figure 3.16 To make a global container field, be sure to choose Global as your field type, not Container.

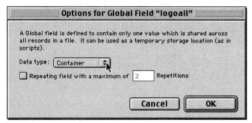

Figure 3.17 When you create a global field, FileMaker will ask you to choose the field data type.

Figure 3.18 Use Insert > Picture in Browse mode to place a graphic into a global container field.

Reusing Graphics

If you need to use the same graphic on multiple layouts, the most convenient approach is to create a global field as a container. You can then use the graphic on any layout in the database.

To create a global container field:

1. Choose File > Define Fields (Ctrl+Shift+D/Command-Shift-D).

2. When the Define Fields dialog box appears (**Figure 3.16**), name the field and choose the Global radio button from the Type section. Click Create.

3. When the Options dialog box appears, choose Container from the Data type drop-down menu (**Figure 3.17**). Click OK, then click Done.

4. Switch to Layout Mode (Ctrl+L/ Command-L), then switch to the layout where the container field will be displayed.

5. From the layout tools, choose Field and drag the field to its new position.

6. From the Specify Field dialog box that appears, choose the name of the global container field you just created and click OK. Resize the field box to fit the graphic you'll be placing there.

7. Change to Browse mode (Ctrl+B/ Command-B). Select the container field on your layout.

8. Choose Insert > Picture and navigate to the graphics file you want to insert. Once you find it, click Open.

The field now contains the graphic. Since it is a global field, it will display and print the same graphic in every record (**Figure 3.18**).

REUSING GRAPHICS

Entering Data in a Standard Layout

Although you or someone else will have to type in most of the data for a FileMaker database, there a few ways to streamline the process. Not only will these shortcuts speed up data entry, but they will also help eliminate typing errors. Two of the most useful short-cuts are the Insert > From Index command and the Value list.

To use Insert > From Index, you'll first need a field whose options have been set to index its records. When you set a field to be indexed, FileMaker keeps track of the data every time you add a record to the field. Then, when you search for data, it checks the index rather than looking up the records themselves.

Indexing is a time-saving device, but it can have one little downside. Because an index file may contain a lot of data, if you're running FileMaker on a computer with a small hard drive you could run into space problems. If you have lots of storage space to burn, use the indexing function with confidence, because the search time it saves you definitely makes it worthwhile. ·

The Insert > From Index command lets you access the Index file directly. You can choose from a list of all entries that have already been entered into a specific field and paste the entry you want directly into the field. You can use this command to verify that your input is phrased identically to other records, and to decrease the trailing or initial spaces that can confuse an alphabetical sort. Insert from Index is particularly useful when using the Find Mode to search for data, since by definition the data you're searching for already exists in that field.

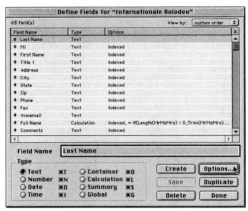

Figure 3.19 Choose Options to access the indexing options for a field.

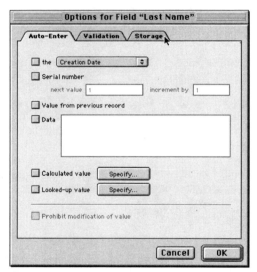

Figure 3.20 The Storage tab holds the indexing options.

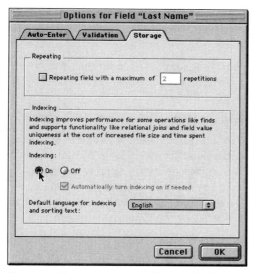

Figure 3.21 Choose On to start indexing a field.

Figure 3.22 The field's options automatically update to show that the field is indexed.

Figure 3.23 To search for an existing entry without having to type it into a field, use Insert > From Index.

Figure 3.24 Only entries appropriate to the field you've chosen will appear in the View Index dialog box.

To index an existing field:

1. Go to File > Define Fields.

2. In the Define Fields dialog box that appears, click the field name that you'd like to index and click Options (**Figure 3.19**).

3. When the Options dialog box appears, click the Storage tab (**Figure 3.20**).

4. In the Indexing section of the dialog box, click the On radio button, then click OK (**Figure 3.21**).

    The field list will update to show that the field is now indexed (**Figure 3.22**). Click Done to close the Define Fields dialog box.

To paste an entry from the index:

1. Make sure you're in Find mode (Ctrl+F/Command-F). Click inside the data entry field that you want, then choose Insert > From Index (Ctrl+I/Command-I) (**Figure 3.23**).

    A list of each entry already made in that field will appear (**Figure 3.24**).

2. Double-click the desired entry to insert it into the data entry field.

ENTERING DATA IN A STANDARD LAYOUT

Creating and Formatting Value Lists

One of the most convenient ways to speed up data entry and eliminate mistakes is the value list. You can format a field to display a pop-up menu, pop-up list, radio buttons or check boxes. These formats are strategies to narrow your users' choices, since they present only those options that you consider valid actions. Once a value list is created, it's available for every field in your database. For example, if you have several fields that will contain a Yes/No, you only have to create one Y/N value list.

Choosing a value list style

The value list style you choose should match the type of data you want to present. Styles are more than aesthetic or arbitrary choices. They affect how long it takes a user to figure out what they should do next, and how easily they can do it. Choosing the wrong format negates the efficiency of creating a value list and leads to mistakes.

Radio Buttons

Use radio buttons when the choices you offer are both mutually exclusive and limited. For example, a radio button format is a good choice for a field containing the type of credit card used in a transaction.

Check Boxes

Use check boxes when the user can choose multiple items in field. A check box is also a good format to turn a choice on or off or as a confirmation (like a check box next to Yes). Remember that the text next to the check box or radio button is the contents of a field, not the X or bullet that appears. In other words, you can't count, add or otherwise manipulate the checks or radio buttons themselves. They're only a format to help the user navigate the field options you've set. If you change a check box field back to a standard field,

you'll only see the selected values for the record, not the whole group of choices (**Figure 3.25**).

Pop-up List

Use pop-up lists when the number of choices in the value list is very long. When the user clicks into a field with a pop-up list, they see a scroll bar. The user can either click on the scroll bar to advance the list or type the first letter or two to jump to an item.

Pop-up Menu

Use pop-up menus when there are more than three or four mutually exclusive choices, but few enough not to cover up something important beneath them when the pop-up menu opens.

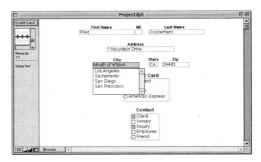

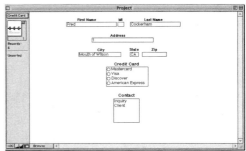

Figure 3.25 In this layout, the Contact section on the left has five possible entries. When you change it back to a standard format, only the entries that had checks next to them still appear.

Figure 3.26 To create a new value list, choose File > Define Value Lists.

Figure 3.27 Choose New to define a new value list.

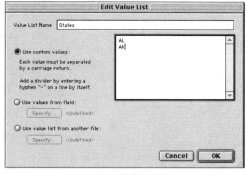

Figure 3.28 Every value must be typed on a separate line in a value list.

Figure 3.29 Choose "Use values from field" and then click Specify to select a field in the current database for your value list.

Validating Formats with Value Lists

People often use the pop-up menu format when another choice would be much more appropriate. If you have ever filled out a form on a Web page, you have probably seen a pop-up list with the abbreviations for all 50 states. Unless you live in Alabama, Arkansas or California, you probably find this format *less* convenient than if you simply typed in your state's two letter abbreviation. If you release the mouse on the wrong choice you have to repeat the process. A scrolling pop-up list might be a good solution, or you can use a value list to validate user entries. If you create a value list with all the state abbreviations, it will compare the list against the entry to minimize errors.

To use a value list for validation:

1. Go to the layout you'd like to format. Choose File > Define Value Lists (**Figure 3.26**).

2. When the Define Value Lists dialog box appears, click New (**Figure 3.27**).

   When the Edit Value list dialog box appears, give your value list a name.

3. Click inside the input box and type the items in your value list. Press Return (Mac) or Enter (Windows) between each value (**Figure 3.28**).

Notice that you don't have to input every choice if you already have a field with this list in your database, or if you're using FileMaker Pro 5 and have typed the entries into a different database as a value list. If you have an existing value list you'd like to use, in the Edit Value List dialog box, choose either "Use values from field" or "Use value list from another file" and click Specify to navigate to the existing field or value list (**Figure 3.29**).

continues on next page

4. After you've typed the last entry or specified an existing value list, click OK and then Done.

5. Choose File > Define Fields (Ctrl+Shift+F/Command-Shift-F).

6. In the scrolling list in the Define Fields dialog box, double-click the field you want to validate (**Figure 3.30**) and click Options.

7. When the Options box appears, click the Validation tab.

8. Choose the value list you just created from the drop-down list next to Member of value list (**Figure 3.31**).

9. Click OK and then Done.

Now when you input data in the chosen field, FileMaker will check the input against the value list. If the value doesn't match the list, you'll see a dialog box (**Figure 3.32**) that alerts you to the error.

✔ Tips

■ If you have a file that will have many value lists or if you wish to use the same value list in several different files, you can create a database that contains just value lists and use them in any other file.

■ If you specify a value list in a different database and move the primary file to another computer, remember to move the database file whose value lists you specified as well. If you don't, FileMaker won't be able to locate the value list to validate your input.

■ If you have a database with lots of value lists, check the scrolling list first before naming your new value list to avoid similarities that might lead to confusion.

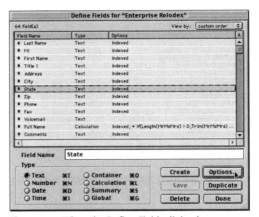

Figure 3.30 When the Define Fields dialog box appears, choose the field you want to validate from the field list.

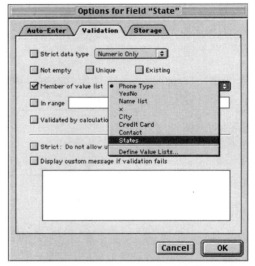

Figure 3.31 When you choose a value list, the check box next to Member of value list is automatically checked for you.

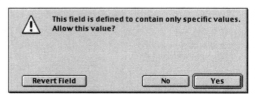

Figure 3.32 This dialog box allows the user to deliberately accept an error. You can eliminate this option by choosing strict validation from the Options box when you define the field.

Figure 3.33 To connect a value list to a field, choose File > Define Relationships.

Figure 3.34 Choose New to define a new relationship.

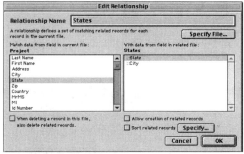

Figure 3.35 Select one field from the main database on the left, and a second field from the related field that will become the value list on the right.

Working with Conditional Value Lists

Value lists are an excellent tool in the battle against data errors, but they have some inherent limitations. The more possible entries you have, the less useful value lists become. FileMaker 5 enhances value lists by allowing you to use fields in your database to dynamically alter the value list display.

Imagine you're creating a database of store branches for a nationally franchised company. They have offices in major cities in each state. Although the number of cities is limited, it still averages 15 per state, and some of them have similar names with different spellings (like Charleston and Charlestown), making the entries difficult to validate. To solve this problem, you could begin by creating a file with two fields: the states and their cities. Using this file as a value list, you can create a relationship between the state and city fields of the store branches. When you enter a state, only its cities would appear as entry values.

To use a conditional value list:

1. Choose File > Define Relationships (**Figure 3.33**).

2. When the Define Relationships dialog box appears, click New (**Figure 3.34**).

3. In the Open File dialog box, select the file and click Open.

   The Edit Relationship dialog box will appear, and the name of your file will be inserted in the Relationship Name line. You can change it to something else, but it's a good idea to maintain the same name for your relationship and value list so you'll remember what the relationship is for.

4. Choose one match field from each of the two lists (**Figure 3.35**).

continues on next page

5. Click OK, then click Done to close the Define Relationships dialog box.

6. Choose File > Define Value Lists.

7. When the Define Value Lists dialog box appears, click New.

8. In the Edit Value List dialog box, type a name for the value list and click "Use values from a field."

9. When the Specify Fields dialog box appears, click "Only related values" and choose the relationship you defined above from the drop-down list (**Figure 3.36**).

10. In the left value column, click the field you'll want to display the subset of values. Click OK twice and then click Done.

11. Make sure you're in Layout mode (Ctrl+L/ Command-L), then go to the layout where the field you just selected is displayed.

12. Click on the field that will display the value list subset and choose Format > Field Format (**Figure 3.37**).

13. When the Field Format dialog box appears, click on Pop-up list in the Style section and choose the list to be used (**Figure 3.38**). Click OK.

When you switch back to Browse mode and enter a value into the first field, the pop-up list will display only the subset of value options appropriate to that field.

✔ Tip

■ This technique will also work with pop-up menus, radio buttons, and check boxes. If there is no entry in the first field, the list in the second field will be blank.

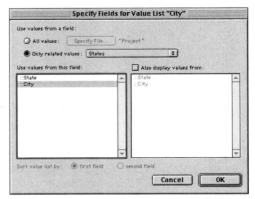

Figure 3.36 Be careful to specify the second field (the one that's dependent on the first input) when setting up the value list.

Figure 3.37 To make your value list subset appear as a group of choices in the correct layout field, choose Format > Field Format.

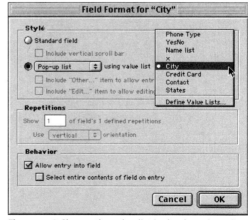

Figure 3.38 Choose the value list in the drop-down list.

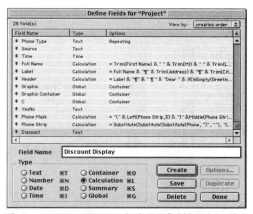

Figure 3.39 You create a calculation field by giving the field a descriptive name, selecting the Calculation radio button, and clicking Create.

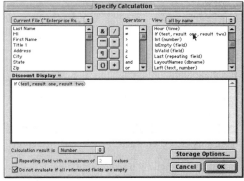

Figure 3.40 To place a function in the calculations text box, double-click it in the functions scrolling list. Functions are followed by parameters in parentheses, each of which needs to be specified.

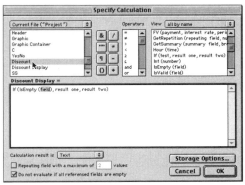

Figure 3.41 To specify what field to use in a calculation, double-click it in the field list on the left.

Using Calculated Field Labels

When you design a layout, you usually include all fields that might be needed, even if some aren't always used. Major changes are best handled by creating another layout, but there can be times when you only need to include (or exclude) a specific field. For instance, you might have designed an invoice layout that includes a discount field. You would only want that field and its label to appear if there *is* a discount. (Otherwise the customer will want to know why they didn't get one.) By creating a calculated field that contains both the value and the label, you can customize the layout to automatically display or hide the field.

To create a calculated field label:

1. Choose File > Define Fields (Ctrl+Shift+D/Command-Shift-D).

2. When the Define Fields dialog box appears (**Figure 3.39**), type a name into the Field Name text box. Choose Calculation as the type, and click Create.

3. When the Specify Calculation dialog box appears, double-click If in the functions list on the right (**Figure 3.40**).

4. In the Discount Display area, replace "test" in the If calculation by double-clicking it to make it the only highlighted parameter, then double-clicking IsEmpty in the Functions list.

5. With "field" highlighted in the calculation, double-click the field you want to designate in the fields list on the left side. This example uses the Discount field (**Figure 3.41**).

continues on next page

6. Double-click to select "result one," then click the quotes button in the Operators keypad (**Figure 3.42**).

7. Double-click to select "result two," then click the quotes button again. Type the name of your label between the quotes. In this example, the label is "Discount."

8. Move your cursor between the last quote and the parenthesis and click the ampersand button. Add the NumToText function by double-clicking it in the right functions list.

9. With "number" highlighted in the calculation, double-click the same field you chose in step 5. This example uses the Discount field.

10. Move your cursor between the two close parentheses. Click the ampersand (&) button, the quotes button and type % between the quotes.

11. Click OK to save the calculation (**Figure 3.43**), then click Done to close the dialog box.

12. Go to the layout where the new field will be displayed and switch to Layout mode (Ctrl+L/ Command-L).

13. Add the new field to the layout.

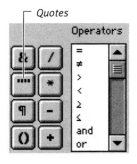

Quotes

Figure 3.42 The most frequently used operators are controlled by the keypad. In this example, Quotes is indicated on the keypad.

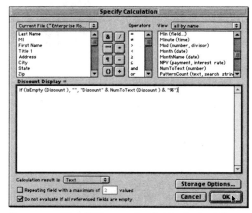

Figure 3.43 Click OK to save the finished calculation.

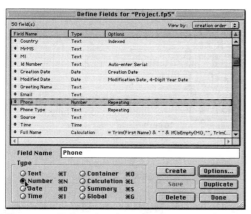

Figure 3.44 To format a phone number, it must be a number field.

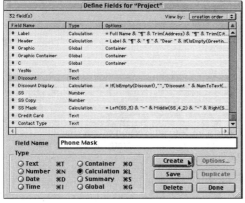

Figure 3.45 After you've verified that your Phone field is a number, create a new field for your mask by choosing calculation as the type and clicking Create.

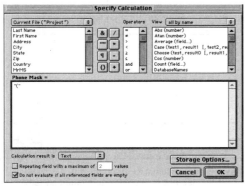

Figure 3.46 To make a parenthesis appear before the phone number, type it between quotes.

Creating Field Masks

Many database programs have the ability to format data like phone numbers and Social Security numbers automatically. If you enter 2125551234 in the phone field, you'll see (212) 555-1234 instead. FileMaker Pro does not offer this feature, but you can mimic it on a layout. If you place a locked, formatted display field directly over an unlocked entry field, you mask the bottom field while still leaving it active. Connect the two fields with a calculation, and whatever value you enter displays properly in the field above it.

To create a field mask:

1. Go to a layout with a field you'd like to mask. Choose File > Define Fields (Ctrl+Shift+D/Command-Shift-D).

2. When the Define Fields dialog box appears, select your existing field and change its type to Number if it was created as a Text field. This example uses the Phone field (**Figure 3.44**).

3. Create a new field with the word Mask in the Field Name line (like Phone Mask or Credit Card Number Mask), select Calculation as the Type and click Create (**Figure 3.45**).

4. When the Specify Calculation dialog box appears, click the quotes button and type (between the quotes (**Figure 3.46**).

continues on next page

5. Click to the right of the quotes and then click the ampersand button (**Figure 3.47**). Double-click Left in the Function list on the right to add it to the calculation in the formula builder window (**Figure 3.48**).

Left will format the area code of the phone number by separating the first three numbers from the rest of the contents of the field.

6. Double-click "text" in the Left calculation to highlight it, then double-click Abs in the Function list. Abs will replace "text" in the calculation (**Figure 3.49**).

If the user enters a parenthesis at the beginning, FileMaker will assume that the number is a negative. The Abs function will return the entry as a positive.

Figure 3.47 Click the ampersand (&) operator button to link functions together.

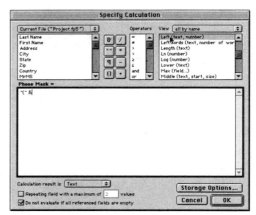

Figure 3.48 The Left function counts characters from the left of the field to separate them from the rest of the field contents.

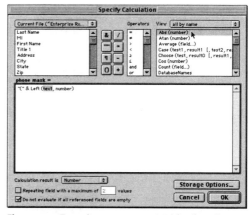

Figure 3.49 To replace a parameter with a function, select the parameter in the formula builder, then double-click the function in the function list.

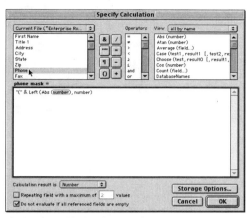

Figure 3.50 With the Abs "number" parameter highlighted, select the field you want to connect to your mask.

7. With the first "number" highlighted in the formula builder, double-click Phone in the Field list (**Figure 3.50**).

8. Highlight the remaining "number" and type 3 (**Figure 3.51**).

   The number parameter specifies how many numbers the Left function should put inside the parentheses. Since this is an area code, you type 3.

9. Move your cursor to the end of the formula. Click the & operator button, then the quotes operator button and type) inside the quotes.

10. Move your cursor to the end of the formula and click the ampersand button. Add the Middle function by double-clicking it in the right Functions list (**Figure 3.52**).

    The Middle function works like the Left function, but instead of counting from the far left, begins counting at whatever character number you type in the "start" parameter, for the number of total characters you specify in the "size" parameter.

continues on next page

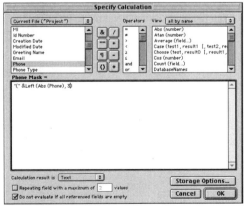

Figure 3.51 To specify how many numbers should display after the first parenthesis, replace the parameter with that number. (For an area code, you type "3.")

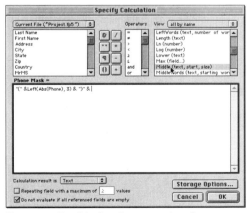

Figure 3.52 To add a function to a series of calculations, click the & button and then double-click the formula from the function list.

CREATING FIELD MASKS

11. Use copy and paste to replace "text" in the Middle function with "Abs(Phone)" from the first part of the calculation.

12. Double-click "start" and replace it by typing 4, then select "size" and replace it by typing 3 (**Figure 3.53**).

To specify the second part of the telephone number, the 4 represents which number in the sequence begins after the area code. The 3 represents how many digits will follow.

13. Move your cursor to the end of the formula. Click the ampersand button and then the quotes button. Type a hyphen (-) between the quotes

14. Move your cursor to the end of the formula, then click the ampersand button. Add the Right function by double-clicking it in the function list.

15. Replace "text" with "Abs(Phone)" again, then double-click "number" and replace it by typing 4.

16. Click OK (**Figure 3.54**) and then Done to close the Define Fields dialog box. You've finished creating the Mask field.

17. Go to the layout where you want the formatted field and switch to Layout mode (Ctrl+L/Command-L).

18. Select your Phone field, or create one if necessary.

19. Duplicate the field by clicking and dragging it while holding down the Alt (Windows)/Option(Mac) key.

20. In the Specify Field dialog box, uncheck Create field label and select Phone Mask from the list (**Figure 3.55**), then click OK.

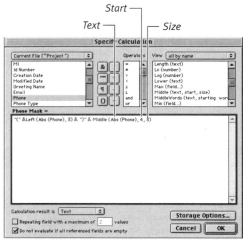

Figure 3.53 To specify the second part of the telephone number, replace "start" with 4 and "size" with 3.

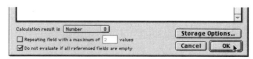

Figure 3.54 After completing your formula, click OK.

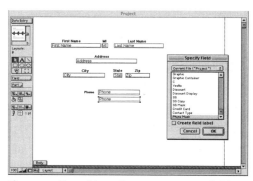

Figure 3.55 To avoid creating an unnecessary field label, uncheck the Create field label check box when you make the Mask field.

Figure 3.56 Lock a field by unchecking Allow entry into field.

Opaque icon

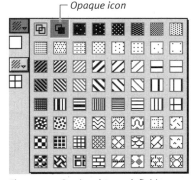

Figure 3.57 Setting the mask field to Opaque prevents the entry field beneath it from showing through.

21. While the Phone Mask field is selected, choose Format > Field Format (Ctrl+Alt+F/Command-Option-F) .

22. When the Field Format dialog box appears, uncheck Allow entry into field, then click OK (**Figure 3.56**).

This prevents data from being entered into the Mask field. When the user clicks on this field, the cursor will actually go into the entry field behind it.

23. Make sure that the Fill for the Mask field is set to Opaque (**Figure 3.57**).

24. Drag the Phone Mask field so that it is squarely on top of the Phone field.

When you switch to Browse mode and click on the Phone Mask field, the cursor will actually be in the Phone field.

✔ Tips

■ Although the example puts parentheses around the area code, you can use the same strategy to separate numbers with periods, hyphens or slashes instead.

■ You can set validation for the Phone field to length(phone)=10. This tells FileMaker that there should be exactly 10 characters in the field. If you forget to enter an area code or try to enter an extra number, FileMaker will alert you.

Copying Layouts

You'll frequently want to duplicate an existing layout. If the layouts are in the same database, this is quite simple, but it may well be that the layout you want to duplicate is in another database. For example, you might have created an invoice layout for one client, and now you're building a database for a completely different company that has also asked for an invoice form. FileMaker does not have the capability to import layouts. But by using Copy and Paste, you can recreate most of a layout in another database.

Figure 3.58 Set the layout parts to match the layout you are copying from.

To recreate a layout in another database:

1. In the database that will contain the layout, create a new layout, but don't add any fields.

2. Set up the blank layout so that it contains the same layout parts (Header, Body, Footer, etc.) as the layout to be copied (**Figure 3.58**) and, using the rulers, make sure it has the same vertical size as the original layout.

3. Switch to Layout mode (Ctrl+L/ Command-L) and open the database containing the original layout.

4. Choose Edit > Select All (Ctrl+A/Command-A).

5. Choose Edit > Copy (Ctrl+C/Command-C) and switch back to the new database.

6. Make sure that you are still in Layout Mode and choose Edit > Paste (Ctrl+V/Command-V). All fields and text from the original layout will appear.

   The pasted items (fields and text) will still be selected, so you can click and drag everything to line them up in the new layout.

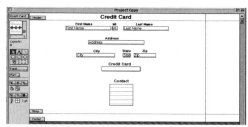

Figure 3.59 Copied layout fields with no exact duplicate names will be blank, like Credit Card and Contact in this layout.

If any of the field names differ from the original database, those fields will be blank on the new layout (**Figure 3.59**). You can double-click on the blank field boxes and the Specify Field dialog box will appear, allowing you to choose the correct name for that field.

✔ Tip

■ Sometimes you may want to select just the fields (or text) on the original layout. Rather than individually selecting each item, try this:

1. Click on one field (or text block).

2. Press Command-Option-A (Macintosh) or Control+Alt+A (Windows).

3. All of the fields (or text) will be selected, but nothing else.

COPYING LAYOUTS

CALCULATION FIELDS

When you create a database, you break data into many separate fields because smaller bits of information are more flexible and easier to search. In layouts, however, you want to regroup these fields to recreate the original flow of text. With a calculation, you can combine the individual fields into a single element that formats the data exactly the way that you want.

Although a calculation field may seem like a lot of trouble initially, it's actually an elegant time saver. Calculation fields offer powerful formatting capabilities for everything from labels and envelopes to form letters. If you combine them with FileMaker's text capabilities, you can frequently avoid having to use a separate word processor for standard letters and other types of bulk mailings.

Once you have created a calculation field you can place it on a layout like any other type of field. But that's where the similarities end. In a normal layout made up of many small fields, you have to laboriously select each field to change type size, font or positions. Then, if one of the fields will sometimes be blank, you need to use the Sliding command to close up the space the blank field leaves behind. You can forget all that with a calculation field. Its combined information can be formatted as easily as it would be in Microsoft Word or AppleWorks. (In fact, considering Word, probably even easier.)

For frequent bulk mailings like monthly statements or special price promotions, a calculation field can make FileMaker a considerably better choice than other programs. Because a calculation field always refers back to the original fields for its information, addresses, area codes and other all-too-changeable data will always update automatically once edited into the original record.

Merging Fields Using Calculations

Calculations provide an easy way to create a new field that's a collection of information from existing fields. Once you've merged the separate fields into one "super field," creating layouts gets much easier. Compare the ease with which you can align and reposition a calculation field to how you work with the individual fields, and we think you'll be convinced (**Figure 4.1**).

In these steps the calculation field Full Name combines the First Name, Middle Initial and Last Name fields (with spaces in between) into a single field that you can place on any layout instead of the three separate fields. It also leaves out the Middle Initial (and the extra spaces around it) if a name doesn't contain one.

To merge fields:

1. Choose File > Define Fields (Ctrl+Shift+D/Command-Shift-D).

2. When the Define Fields dialog box appears, type the name of your field in the Field Name text box, select the Calculation radio button, then click Create (**Figure 4.2**). In this example, we use Full Name.

3. The Specify Calculation dialog box appears. From the function list on the right, double-click the Trim function to begin the calculation in the formula box.

   Trim seeks out initial and trailing spaces that surround other text and "trims" them away from the text or number. The parameter "text" will be highlighted in the formula box (**Figure 4.3**).

Figure 4.1 The layout on the top uses three text fields, the one on the bottom uses one calculation field. The printed document looks the same either way.

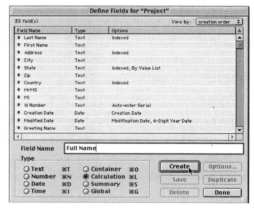

Figure 4.2 Create a calculation field and call it Full Name.

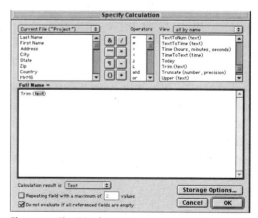

Figure 4.3 The Trim function removes any extra spaces entered before or after the text in a field.

MERGING FIELDS USING CALCULATIONS

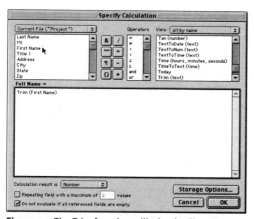

Figure 4.4 The Trim function will trim the First Name field in this example.

Figure 4.5 Choose the ampersand (&) symbol to combine functions.

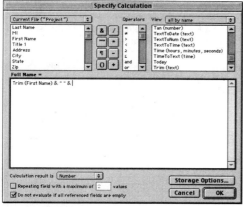

Figure 4.6 Type a space within the quotes in the formula box to add a space to the text.

4. The Trim function acts on the field that replaces its parameter. From the field list on the left, double-click the first of the fields you want to combine. This example uses First Name (**Figure 4.4**).

5. Click to the right of the parentheses. From the formula operators keypad, click the ampersand button (&) to add it to the formula box (**Figure 4.5**).

6. The quotes operator is used to add text characters to a calculation. From the formula operators keypad, click the quotes button and type a space inside the quotes. Click to the right of the quotes and click the ampersand button again (**Figure 4.6**).

continues on next page

MERGING FIELDS USING CALCULATIONS

7. To leave out a field and its extra space when that field is empty, double-click If to choose it from the function list (**Figure 4.7**).

If the name has a middle initial, you'll need to add it with a space after it. But some names don't have middle initials. You need a function that will allow for both possibilities. The If statement checks the field to see whether or not a situation exists. It can have two results: result one (if test is true) and result two (if test is not true).

8. In the formula box, double-click the "test" parameter in the If statement to select it. From the function list, double-click IsEmpty (**Figure 4.8**).

9. From the field list, double-click the next field you want to add to the calculation field.

This example uses the MI field (**Figure 4.9**). The IsEmpty function looks at this field to see if there is data in it.

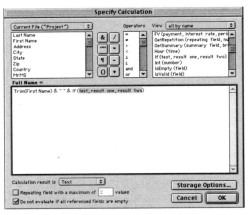

Figure 4.7 Use an If statement to test whether or not a field contains data.

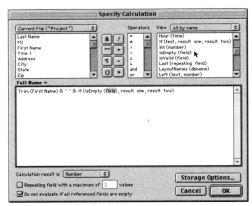

Figure 4.8 To test if a field is empty, use the IsEmpty function as the test parameter.

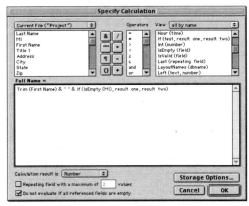

Figure 4.9 The IsEmpty function looks to see if a field has data in it.

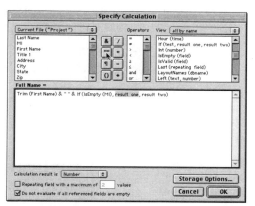

Figure 4.10 To eliminate the field if it's empty, replace the "result one" parameter with the quotes operator and don't type anything inside the quotes.

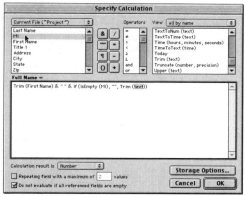

Figure 4.11 To insert the field if it has data and trim any extra spaces around it, choose the Trim function and the field name.

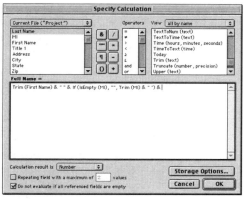

Figure 4.12 To add a space to the field text, put it between the quotes.

10. In the formula box, double-click to highlight "result one." From the operators keypad, click the quotes button to add a set of quotes to the calculation (**Figure 4.10**).

By replacing the "result one" parameter with the quotes operator without typing anything inside the quotes, you eliminate an empty field. (Much nicer than using the Sliding command!)

11. In the formula box, double-click to highlight "result two." From the function list, double-click Trim. The "text" parameter is highlighted in the formula box (**Figure 4.11**). Since you'll want to trim the second field if it has data in it, double-click the same field you chose in step 9 above.

This example uses the MI field, so Trim will cut away any extra spaces around the middle initial if the full name has a middle initial in it.

12. In the formula box, click between the two parentheses, then click the ampersand button from the operators keypad.

13. From the operators keypad, click the quotes button. Type a space between the quotes, then click to the right of the parentheses and select the ampersand button from the operators keypad (**Figure 4.12**).

This adds a space after the middle initial if a name has one.

continues on next page

14. In the function list, double-click Trim. With "text" highlighted in the formula box, select the next desired field from the field list.

This example uses the Last Name field (**Figure 4.13**). In this case, you use the Trim function to eliminate leading spaces.

15. Set the Calculation result to Text because this calculation field won't contain any numerical calculations. Click OK (**Figure 4.14**). When you're finished, click Done.

Now you have a completed formula in a field. When you place this field on a layout, it will display the full name on a record in Browse mode and also on a printout.

✔ Tips

■ When you select a function, FileMaker highlights its parameter in the calculation input box to prompt you to choose a field.

■ This example can be customized to add fields at the beginning (like Dr. or Mrs.), or a title field (like Chair or Accounts Payable) at the end. Remember to add a comma to the space between quotes before the ending title field.

■ As calculations grow in complexity, they become increasingly difficult to read in the formula box. You can insert returns in long formulas to make them easier to read. FileMaker ignores the returns when evaluating the calculation (**Figure 4.15**).

■ If you want to insert a return into the text result of a calculation, click the paragraph button in the operator keypad (¶). Like all other characters you want to display as text, the paragraph marker must always be surrounded by quotes in the formula.

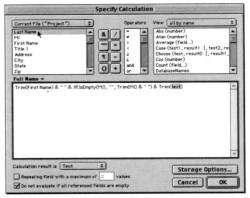
Figure 4.13 In this case, the Trim function eliminates leading spaces in Last Name.

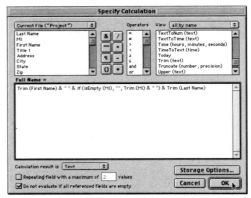
Figure 4.14 Use the drop-down menu to change the Calculation result to Text .

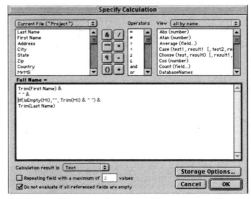
Figure 4.15 The same formula in Figure 4.14 with returns inserted for readability.

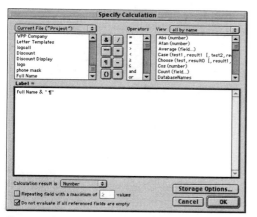

Figure 4.16 To put the first field on a line of its own, put a paragraph symbol between quotes.

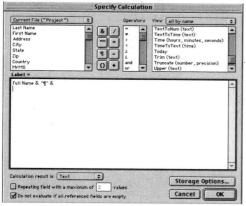

Figure 4.17 Just like in a word processing program, typing a return breaks the formula line.

Formatting Labels or Envelopes

Calculation fields can be combined with other fields to build more complex formulas. For example, once you have a Full Name calculation field, you can combine it with the address data to create a Label field. This field can become a building block for every layout that requires these fields to be used together. Not only will it make a label easy to position for printing, but the same field works nicely as a letter header or "sold to" field in an invoice as well. Just adjust the field fonts and sizes on each layout.

To create a label field:

1. Choose File > Define Fields (Ctrl+Shift+D/Command-Shift-D).

2. When the Define Fields dialog box appears, type the name you'll use for your label field in the Field Name text box, select the Calculation radio button, then click Create. We use Label as the field name in this example.

3. When the Specify Calculation box appears, double-click on the name of the full name calculation field you created in "To merge fields" on page 52—in our case, Full Name. From the operators keypad, click the ampersand button.

4. From the operators keypad, click the quotes button and then the paragraph (¶) button (**Figure 4.16**).

5. Click to the right of the quotes, then click the ampersand button and press Return (Mac) or Enter (Windows) (**Figure 4.17**).

6. From the function list on the right, double-click Trim.

continues on next page

7. With the text parameter highlighted in the formula box, double-click the next field to be used in the calculation.

This example uses the Address field.

8. Click to the right of the parentheses (**Figure 4.18**).

9. Next you want to put the Address field on its own line in the label. Click to the right of the quotes, then click the ampersand button and press Return (Mac) or Enter (Windows).

10. From the function list, double-click Trim. Replace the text parameter by double-clicking City in the field list.

11. Click the quotes button and type a comma and a space inside the quotes. Click to the right of the quotes and click the ampersand button (**Figure 4.19**).

12. From the function list, double-click Trim. Replace the text parameter by double-clicking State in the field list. Click to the right of the quotes, and from the operators keypad click the ampersand button.

13. Click the quotes button and type a space inside the quotes. Click to the right of the quotes and click the ampersand button to add a space before the next field.

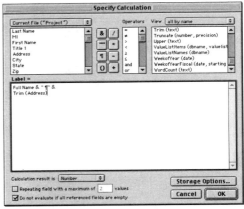

Figure 4.18 Use the Trim function to delete extra spaces around the address line.

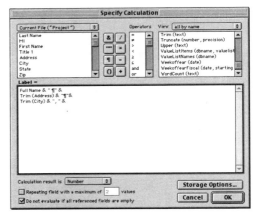

Figure 4.19 To insert a comma between two fields, use the quotes button and type a comma and a space inside the quotes.

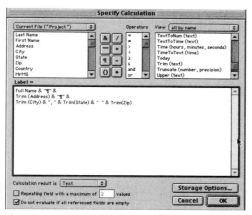

Figure 4.20 To string City, State and Zip together on one line, use ampersands (&) between functions and don't insert the paragraph symbol.

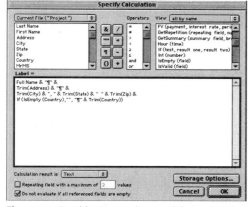

Figure 4.21 To add a Country line to a label, select the If function, and use IsEmpty to test the results. If the field contains data, the calculation will add a paragraph marker and the field contents. If it is empty, no extra line is inserted.

14. From the function list, double-click Trim. Replace the text parameter by double-clicking Zip in the field list (**Figure 4.20**).

15. Set the Calculation result to Text and Click OK. When you're finished, click Done.

Now you have a completed formula in a field. When you place this field on a layout, it will display three lines of text: the full name and two address lines.

✔ Tip

- If your addresses will sometimes include a country but not always, use the If function combined with IsEmpty to add the Country field as the last line of the formula. For information on how to do this, see Steps 7 through 11 in "To merge fields" on page 52 (**Figure 4.21**).

Formatting Form Letter Modules

If you've created form letter layouts before, you know that it's relatively easy to use merge fields to personalize a standard letter. However, if you depend heavily on form letters, you still end up repeating the same tasks over and over when you use this tactic. Form letters usually follow the same basic concept—a salutation (Dear), a courtesy title (Mr., Ms., General or Exalted Leader) and a last name. Then comes the body of the text, followed by a sign-off (Sincerely) and a signature name. Replace many of these form letter elements with calculation fields and you can minimize duplications.

If you're clever about creating options with the all-purpose If function, you can trim the number of different layouts and letters you need to create as well.

For example, if you have a Greeting Name field, you can set your salutation to automatically create either a formal or informal heading. You'd still use If and IsEmpty functions to check for text in a field (like the MI field), but substitute the Greeting Name field instead. If there is no text in the Greeting Name field, the salutation would default to the standard formal format (Dear Mrs. Jones). If it is supplied, the less formal greeting name (a first name or a nickname) would be used (Dear Karen).

One of the most useful next steps in putting the Label calculation field to work is to put it on a letter layout. Most well-composed letters include the addressee's name and address as a block of text (just like the label). Following the block of text is a greeting line, and occasionally a date. Since the elements and their positions are standard, they're a prime target for another modular calculation field.

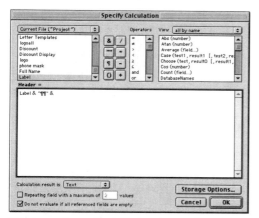

Figure 4.22 To create a letter header, use the existing Label field, then add paragraph markers to separate the addressee information from the rest of the letter.

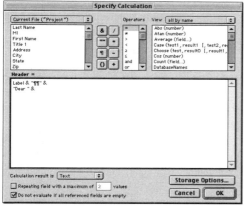

Figure 4.23 Put different portions of the header calculation on different lines so you can read them easily later.

You can adapt the techniques below to create layouts such as business forms, statements, invoices and other printouts that combine global and standard fields.

To create a standard letter header:

1. Follow the steps in "To create a label field" on page 57.

2. Choose File > Define Fields (Ctrl+Shift+D/Command-Shift-D).

3. When the Define Fields dialog box appears, type the name of your header field in the Field Name text box, select the Calculation radio button, then click Create. We use Letter Heading as the field name in this example.

4. When the Specify Calculation box appears, double-click on the name of your label calculation field—in our example, Label. From the operators keypad, click the ampersand button.

5. From the operators keypad, click the quotes button and then the paragraph (¶) button two or three times to create enough space between the header address and the letter salutation. Click to the right of the quotes and click the ampersand button from the operator keypad (**Figure 4.22**).

6. From the operators keypad, click the quotes button. Between the quotes type Dear followed by a space. Click to the right of the quotes. From the operator keypad, click the ampersand button (**Figure 4.23**).

continues on next page

FORMATTING FORM LETTER MODULES

7. From the field list, double-click your courtesy title field.

This example uses MrMsMrs.

8. From the operator keypad, click the ampersand button, then the quotes button. Type a space inside the quotes.

9. Click to the right of the quotes and click the ampersand button again (**Figure 4.24**).

10. From the function list, double-click Trim. With "text" highlighted in the formula box, double-click your Last Name field in the field list.

11. Click to the right of the parentheses. From the operators keypad, click the ampersand button, then the quotes. Type a colon inside the quotes.

12. Make sure your Calculation result is set to Text, click OK, then Done.

You now have a standard letter header and greeting in one field.

✔ Tip

■ Once you get the hang of the concept, you can start combining modules of calculation fields to help you streamline your layout creation. For example, many invoices have two address sections: the ship-to address and the bill-to address. Sometimes these addresses are the same, but occasionally they're not. If you created one calculation field for the shipping address (usually the same as the label field), you can create another for a bill-to address. If the bill-to address exists, it would be inserted on the layout. If the bill-to calculation field is empty, the shipping address could be inserted instead.

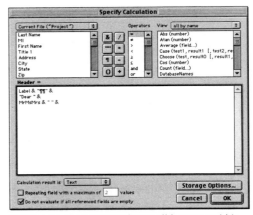

Figure 4.24 Always remember to add a space within quotes whenever you are merging several text fields on one printed line.

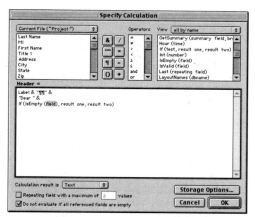

Figure 4.25 To create a formula to choose between two options depending on whether there's data in a field, select the If function, then select IsEmpty as its test parameter.

To create a customizable letter heading:

1. Follow the steps in "To create a label field" on page 57.

2. Choose File > Define Fields (Ctrl+Shift+D/Command-Shift-D).

3. When the Define Fields dialog box appears, type the name of your header field in the Field Name text box, select the Calculation radio button, then click Create.

   We use Letter Heading as the field name in this example.

4. When the Specify Calculation box appears, double-click on the name of your label calculation field—in our example, Label. From the operators keypad, click the ampersand button.

5. From the operators keypad, click the quotes button and then the paragraph button two or three times to create the visual space you'd like between the header address and the letter salutation. Click to the right of the quotes again and click the ampersand button from the operator keypad (**Figure 4.22**).

6. Click the quotes button. Type Dear followed by a space between the quotes. Click to the right of the quotes. From the operator keypad, click the ampersand button (**Figure 4.23**).

7. Double-click If to choose it from the function list. In the formula box, double-click the "test" parameter in the If statement to select it. From the function list, double-click IsEmpty (**Figure 4.25**). The IsEmpty function looks at a field to see if it contains any data.

   continues on next page

8. With the "field" parameter highlighted in the formula box, double-click Greeting Name in the field list (**Figure 4.26**).

9. In the formula box, double-click to highlight "result one."

10. Double-click the courtesy title field in the field list.

11. In the operator keypad, click the ampersand button, then the quotes button. Type a space inside the quotes.

12. Click to the right of the quotes and click the ampersand button.

13. Double-click Trim in the function list, which highlights "text" in the formula box, then double-click your Last Name field in the field list (**Figure 4.27**).

14. In the formula box, highlight "result two" and double-click the Trim function. With "text" highlighted in the formula box, double-click Greeting Name in the field list (**Figure 4.28**). Click to the end of the line.

15. From the operator keypad, click the ampersand button, then click the quotes button and type a colon between the quotes.

16. Make sure your calculation is set to Text, then click OK. When you're finished, click Done.

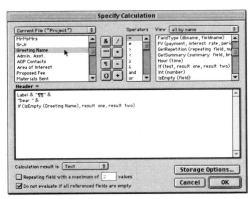

Figure 4.26 To use a Greeting Name if one exists, select it as the test parameter for IsEmpty.

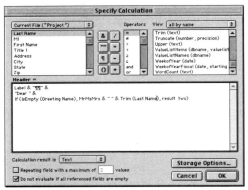

Figure 4.27 If the Greeting Name field is empty, the calculation will use the standard formal greeting of Mr/Ms/Mrs plus a space and the Last Name.

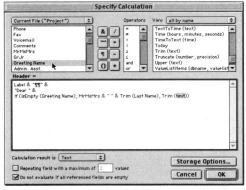

Figure 4.28 Choosing Greeting Name as the field for "result two" inserts it instead of the formal greeting whenever you want to use an informal name for the addressee.

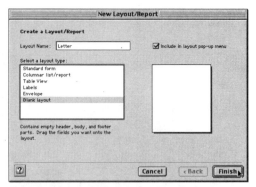

Figure 4.29 Choose Blank layout from the options in the New Layout dialog box.

Augmenting a Form Letter

If you have a letter header calculation field, you can use it on a form letter layout. In fact, if you create the parts of the letter as separate fields, you'll have modules that will make future layouts increasingly easy to develop.

If you're using printed letterhead sheets for your form letters, skip step 1, and steps 8 through 11, since you won't need a global container field if the logo is already printed on the paper.

To create a form letter with modular fields:

1. Go to the file where you want to create your new layout. First create a text global field to hold the body of your form letter and a container global field for the letterhead logo if you have one

   We cover creating container global fields in Chapter 3, "To create a global container field."

2. Choose View > Layout Mode (Ctrl+L/Command-L), then choose Layouts > New Layout (Ctrl+N/Command-N).

3. In the New Layout/Report dialog box, type the layout name (in this case Letter) in the Layout Name box and select Blank layout from the layout type list (**Figure 4.29**). Click Finish to create the layout.

   An empty layout with Header, Body and Footer tabs will appear. You create a blank layout to avoid adding unnecessary parts that you'll have to delete later.

   continues on next page

4. Go to View > Graphic Rulers to turn on the horizontal and vertical rulers. Rulers will make it easier to set up your letter.

5. Click on the Header part tab to select it. Drag it down until the header equals the margin you want at the top of your letter (**Figure 4.30**).

In our example, we've left enough room to add a container field with our letterhead logo and some comfortable white space above it (**Figure 4.31**).

6. Click on the Body tab and drag it down until it's at the 10¹/₂ inch (or 760 point) vertical mark. You'll see the dashed line indicating that you've reached the bottom of the page (**Figure 4.32**).

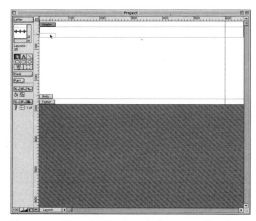

Figure 4.30 Drag the Header tab down to resize the part.

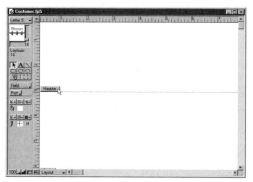

Figure 4.31 This header part is three inches deep to allow for a margin and a letterhead logo.

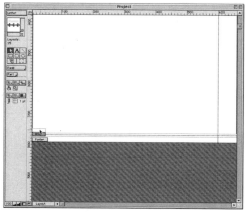

Figure 4.32 Drag the Body tab down to the bottom of the page.

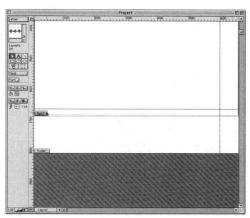

Figure 4.33 Drag the Body tab up to make room for the footer.

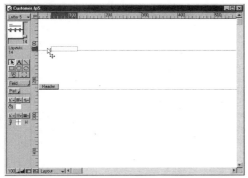

Figure 4.34 Drag the field tool to the header to place your container field on the layout.

Figure 4.35 Choose the global container field from the field list in the Specify Field dialog box.

7. If you don't need a footer, select it and press Ctrl+Z/Command-Z to delete it. (For most letters, you don't need a footer unless you have a letterhead design that has something printed at the bottom of the page.) Otherwise drag the Body tab back up the layout until you have enough room for the footer (**Figure 4.33**).

8. Scroll to the top of the layout. If you are going to use the global letterhead field, click the field tool in the tool area on the left and drag it into the Header part (**Figure 4.34**).

9. When the Specify Field dialog box appears, uncheck the Create field label box.

10. Choose the global letterhead field you created in step 1 and click OK (**Figure 4.35**). In our example, the field is called "gLogo."

11. Resize the field so it's big enough to display the entire letterhead or logo.

12. Click the Field tool and drag it onto the Body part. When the Specify Field dialog box appears, choose Letter Heading.

continues on next page

13. Now you need to know how much room to leave for the records in your database. To see a sample record, choose View > Show > Sample Data (**Figure 4.36**).

14. The first record in your database will appear in the Letter Heading field in the Body part on your layout (**Figure 4.37**).

Unless you're sure the sample is the longest record, resize the field to allow for the longest and deepest address. You don't have to be precise, since you can always go back and change the layout later.

15. Click the field tool and drag it onto the layout below the Letter Heading field.

16. Choose your global letter field in the Specify Field dialog box. Resize the letter field to fill the rest of the Body part (**Figure 4.38**).

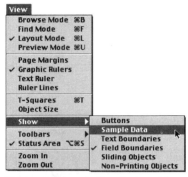

Figure 4.36 To make it easier to set the field sizes for your form letter, choose View > Show > Sample Data.

Figure 4.37 Show Sample Data makes setting the proper size of a field much easier by displaying the data instead of the field names.

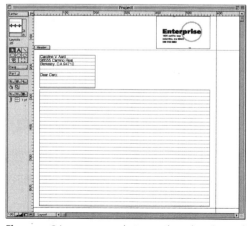

Figure 4.38 Leave a space between the salutation and the body of the letter.

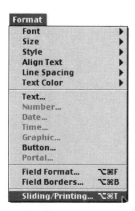

Figure 4.39 To get rid of unused extra space you've left in your layout, choose Format > Sliding/Printing.

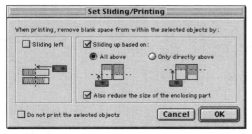

Figure 4.40 Sliding up will get rid of blank lines on the layout.

17. Shift-click to select both the Letter Heading and Letter fields on the layout, then choose Format > Sliding/Printing (**Figure 4.39**). Sliding will get rid of blank lines on the layout.

18. When the Set Sliding/Printing dialog box appears, click the "Sliding up based on" check box to prevent extra vertical spacing from being inserted because of differences in field record lengths, and the All Above radio button to take the longest body part into account when aligning fields vertically below it (**Figure 4.40**).

19. Switch to Browse Mode (Ctrl+B/Command-B). Click in the letter field and type the text of the letter.

✔ Tips

- The dashed line on a layout indicates the page break. Watch for it when you create a new layout! If the Body part extends past the end of page break line, every letter will produce a blank page when you print it.

- It's a good idea to put a "g" at the beginning of a global field name as a reminder of its field type.

- To further automate your form letters, create a global container field for the signature. Scan a signature, add it to the Global field, and place the field below the letter text.

- The fields that are set to slide will only do so when the layout is printed or in Preview Mode (Ctrl+U/Command-U) In Browse Mode, the fields will show where they were placed on the layout.

CREATING DATA REPORTS

No matter how carefully you design a database or how accurately data is entered into it, your database remains an underutilized resource unless you can mine it for the precise information you need. Performing this effective information retrieval is a two-step process, covered in this chapter.

The first step is to isolate the set of information you need. You already know how to search on one field so that information will be organized in a specific way. Any time you need to see a mailing list by state or city, instead of alphabetically or in the order names were entered, you're performing a simple search. You may also know that you can add more criteria to a search in order to narrow down this information. For example, if you want to find which customers in Newport, Rhode Island received mailings in April and June but not in May, and whether they purchased anything in response, a simple search is not enough. Fortunately, FileMaker Pro offers search tools for zeroing in on this exact set of information (known as the found set) and sort tools for organizing the found set in the most effective manner.

Once you have chosen a found set, you need to summarize it on a layout to display it for yourself and others. A summary report can show how many customers in the group responded, tell you how much they spent by month, and total the sales per individual—giving you quick feedback for decision-making.

Using Search Operators

FileMaker uses search operators to extend the power of Finds. "And" and "Or" searches are "big gun" tools that allow you to pull out large categories of data based on field names. Search operators are more like precision instruments: Using them, you can search for information that's more deeply buried in the database records themselves. These search operators are also very useful if you're not exactly sure what you're looking for but you know it has to be there. Mistyped entries, variant spellings, a checkbook discrepancy in the February balance—they can all be located with a well-chosen search operator.

The range operator is most often used to find a series of dates or numbers, but it's equally useful for an alphabetic search. In fact, most operators allow you to use letters in the same manner as numbers in finds. Try this with the range, greater than and less than operators to search for items in different parts of the alphabet.

To use a search operator in a data search:

1. Switch to the layout you want, then choose View > Find Mode (Ctrl+F (Windows) /Command-F (Mac).

2. Click the field you wish to search. Type the first letter of the range.

3. In the status area on the left, click the Symbols arrow to choose the range operator from the drop-down menu (**Figure 5.1**). Type the last letter of the range, then click Find.

   In this case, typing A…M in the Last Name field will find all of the records where a check was paid to a supplier whose name begins with a letter in the first half of the alphabet (**Figure 5.2**).

Figure 5.1 You don't have to search for operators on the keyboard; they're all listed in the Find status area.

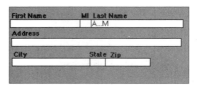

Figure 5.2 The range operator can be used to find ranges of letters, as well as dates or numbers.

Figure 5.3 To find all entries with an ampersand (&) or other search operator in them, place quotes around the operator to change it from an operator to a plain text character.

Figure 5.4 By combining the "any character" wildcard (*) with the ampersand in quotes, you can find all entries with an ampersand in them no matter where the ampersand appears.

✔ Tips

■ Another way to search for a range that begins or ends at an end of the alphabet would be to type <=M in the Last Name field.

■ You can recreate or modify your last find by using the Records > Modify Last Find command (Ctrl+R/Command-R). This switches back to Find Mode and puts the same criteria into the appropriate fields. You can make any desired changes to the Find criteria before you click Find.

■ If you need to find an entry that includes one of the search operators (like an ampersand) place quotes around it. Quotes change an operator into a plain text character for search purposes (**Figure 5.3**). The combination of operators in this example will find all the entries with an ampersand anywhere in their name (**Figure 5.4**).

Search Operators

<	Finds values that are less than the search criteria
<=	Finds values less than or equal to the search criteria
>	Finds values greater than the search criteria
>=	Finds values greater than or equal to the search criteria
=	Finds values that exactly match anywhere in the field
...	Finds values that fall within a range (1/1/2000...1/31/2000)
!	Finds records that have duplicate values in a field

//	Finds records where the field contains today's date.
?	Finds records that have an invalid character in a date field
@	Substitutes for a single character in search criteria (J@nes will find Jones, Janes or Junes)
*	Substitutes for any number of characters in search criteria (J*nes will find Jones, Jarones or Jinones)
""	Criteria in quotes will be found if the criteria is the phrase between the quotes. ("John Jones Jr.")
==	Finds values that exactly match the search criteria

Creating an "Inverted" Search

You probably know that you can omit records from an existing found set. However, you can also use the process of elimination to create a found set made up only of records that don't match the Find criteria. Imagine that you're projecting your average monthly sales for a bank loan. You don't necessarily want to include the month you closed up shop and snorkeled in the Bahamas, so you'd want to create a report that omitted that period from the found set.

You can even create a single search that selects certain records and omits others. This combination lets you eliminate your vacation period while selecting only corporate purchase orders from the rest of the year's records.

To omit records from a search:

1. Switch to the layout you want to use for the search, then choose View > Find Mode (Ctrl+F/Command-F).

2. Enter the search criteria you want to eliminate from the found set in the appropriate fields.

3. In the status area, check the Omit box (**Figure 5.5**), then click Find.

   The records that meet the search criteria will be omitted from the found set. In our example, the result would be a list of sales that excluded activity in the month of April.

To select and omit at the same time:

1. Switch to the layout you want to use for the search, then choose View > Find Mode (Ctrl+F/Command-F).

2. Enter the search criteria for the records you want find into the appropriate fields.

3. Choose Requests > Add New Request (Ctrl+N/Command-N). Enter the search criteria for the records you want to eliminate into the field, then click the Omit box. Click Find.

The found set will display the records that meet the first search criteria (purchase orders, for example) but won't contain the records that meet the criteria in the second request.

✔ Tips

- Watch the order of your combinations when you combine criteria that you want with criteria you want to eliminate.

- If a record meets the first criteria but also meets the omit criteria, it won't appear in your found set. For example, if your company doesn't accept purchase orders below $1,000, it would be useless to select purchase orders as the first criterion and then omit amounts below $1,000 from the set.

- If you create a complex Find combination or one that you will use frequently in the future, you can create a Perform Find (Restore) script to restore the last Find. We cover scripts in detail in Chapter 7.

Figure 5.5 Click the Omit box to omit records instead of finding them.

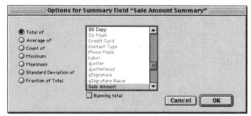

Figure 5.6 In the Options for Summary Field dialog box, you choose both the field to summarize and the form the summary will take.

Creating Summary Layout Parts

Once you have a found set, you can summarize it in a variety of ways. Using summary fields, you can count how many records were found and print the count in a report. You can create totals, averages, minimums and maximums of number fields. If you are statistically inclined you can even create standard deviations.

Layouts with summary fields require a little more planning than those without them. A summary field is unique in that the same field will display different values, even in the same layout, depending on which part it appears in. A summary field defined as a total in the Trailing Grand Summary will display the total of that field for the entire found set. But the same field in the sub-summary layout part will only display the total for the sub-summary field.

To create summary fields:

1. Choose File > Define Fields (Ctrl+Shift+D/Command-Shift-D). In the Define Fields dialog box, click on the field to be summarized.

2. Change the field name by adding "Summary" to the end of it.

3. Click the Summary radio button.

4. Click Create (*not* Save).

5. When the Options for Summary Field dialog box appears, choose the type of summary you want (**Figure 5.6**). Click OK.

✔ Tip

■ A summary field set to Count will return the number of records that have an entry in the summarized field.

To create a layout with summary parts:

1. Choose View > Layout Mode (Ctrl+L/Command-L). Choose New Layout (Ctrl+N/Command-N).

   This automatically starts up the Layout Assistant. Based on the choices you make, the Layout Assistant creates the layout parts you need and places fields and their labels in a logical place within the parts.

2. In the New Layout/Report dialog box that appears, type a name for the layout and choose Columnar List/Report as the layout type (**Figure 5.7**). Click Next.

3. Click the Report with Grouped Data radio button. Check the Include Grand Totals box if you want to have totals for the entire report appear at the end (**Figure 5.8**). Click Next.

4. In the Specify Fields dialog box, double-click on each available field to be included in the Body part of the report in order to place it in the Layout fields list. This example uses the Full Name and the Sales Amount, Sales Tax and Sales Total fields (**Figure 5.9**). When you're done, click Next.

5. In the Organize Records by Category dialog box, just click Next.

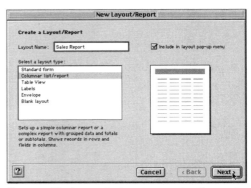

Figure 5.7 The Layout Assistant automates the process of creating a new layout.

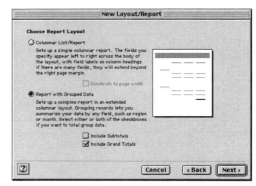

Figure 5.8 This layout example will include Grand Totals at the end of the report.

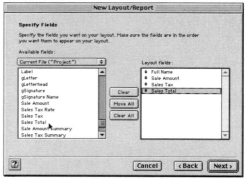

Figure 5.9 Add the fields that are not summaries to the Body part of the report.

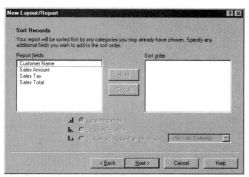

Figure 5.10 If you want to sort the report by one or more fields, choose them from the Report fields box.

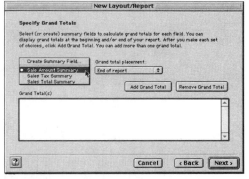

Figure 5.11 This step adds the Summary fields that will display the Grand Totals in the Grand Summary part.

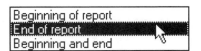

Figure 5.12 Choose the layout position for the summary totals from the Grand total placement drop-down menu.

6. If you wish to sort by any of the Report fields listed in the Sort Records dialog box (**Figure 5.10**), double-click to select them. If you don't want to sort the report or if you are going to sort by other fields, leave the Sort order box blank. Click Next.

7. If you haven't yet created your summary fields, you can do so by choosing Create Summary Field from the Summary Field drop-down menu in the Specify Grand Totals dialog box.

8. Select each of the summary fields you want to use, then click Add Grand Total to put each one into the Grand Total listing.

We use summary fields that total Sales Amount, Sales Tax and Sales Total (**Figure 5.11**).

9. From the Grand total placement drop-down menu, choose the position on the layout where you want the Grand Totals to appear (**Figure 5.12**).

In this case, the totals will appear as a Trailing Grand Summary at the end of the report because we chose End of report from the drop-down menu. Click Next.

continues on next page

10. In the Select a Theme dialog box, choose a color scheme for your report.

If you are going to print the report on a black and white printer, the best choice is generally Default (no colors) (**Figure 5.13**). Click Next.

11. In the Header and Footer dialog box, add any items like page numbers and data stamps that you wish to include in a specific place on the report by selecting them from the drop-down menus (**Figure 5.14**). Click Next.

12. To automatically create a script that will recreate the Sort order you used for this summary and display the report in Preview, click the "Create a script" radio button and type a name for the script. (If you don't type a name, FileMaker will insert the layout name here) (**Figure 5.15**). If you don't want a script or plan to create your own, click "Do not create a script." Click Next.

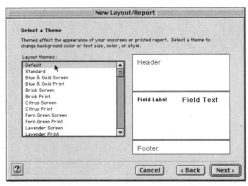

Figure 5.13 You can specify a color scheme for the report. If the report is to be printed on a laser printer, choose the default (no colors).

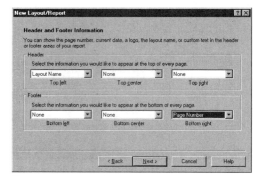

Figure 5.14 For a multiple-page report, you can add footer or header page numbers and titles.

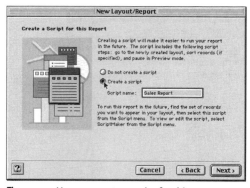

Figure 5.15 You can create a script for this report automatically.

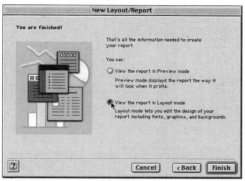

Figure 5.16 In Layout mode, you can fine-tune your report by reformatting fields and adding text.

13. If you want to see the report immediately, click the "View the report in Preview mode" radio button. If you want to fine-tune the layout, click "View the report in Layout mode" (**Figure 5.16**).

14. Click Finish to close the dialog box. Depending on which choice you made, your layout will display in either Preview or Layout mode.

✔ Tips

■ If you'd like your totals to display at the beginning of a report instead of at the end, choose Beginning of report in step 9 above.

■ If you have already created a report with a Trailing Grand Summary part, create a Leading Grand Summary part in Layout mode and place it at the top of the report, between the Header and Body parts. Then drag the summary fields to it and delete the Trailing Grand Summary.

Using Counts and Averages

Using an existing report with summary fields as a basis, you can easily add counts and averages. For example, if you have summary fields that track individual sales, total sales and state sales tax, you can duplicate the summary total fields, rename them and change their calculation result to add a summary field that counts the number of sales and the average sale amount.

To create counts and averages with a summary layout:

1. Choose File > Define Fields (Ctrl+Shift+D/Command-Shift-D).

2. Duplicate the summary field that holds the total amount of the field you want to average (in this example, it's the Sale Amount Summary field). Change its name to something unique. Click Save (**Figure 5.17**).

3. Double-click on the new field. When the Options dialog box appears, click the Average of radio button (**Figure 5.18**). Click OK.

4. To create another summary field that counts the number of sales, repeat steps 1 and 2. This time click the Count of radio button in the Options dialog box. Click Done to close the dialog box.

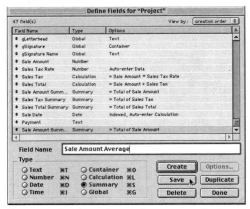

Figure 5.17 Duplicate the existing summary field, rename it and change its calculation result from Total of to Average of.

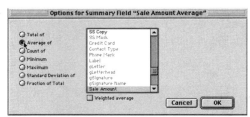

Figure 5.18 Duplicating an existing field and changing the calculation saves time in creating a summary field.

Using Counts and Averages

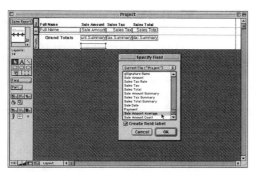

Figure 5.19 Add the Sale Amount Average to the Trailing Grand Summary part to display the average of all sales in the report.

5. In Layout mode, choose the layout that will display the new fields. If it doesn't already have a Trailing Grand Summary part, create one by dragging the Part tool to the layout and choosing the Trailing Grand Summary radio button from the Part Definition dialog box. If this part already appears in the layout, click the bottom of the part and drag down to make room for the new fields.

6. Drag the Field tool to the Trailing Grand Summary part and add the Average field to display the average of all sales in the report (**Figure 5.19**). Click OK.

7. Drag the Field tool to the Trailing Grand Summary part again, and add the Count field to display the number of individual sales in the report. Click OK.

✔ Tip

■ It's always a good idea to put the field type somewhere in the name of a summary field, so you can easily recognize its purpose.

Creating Running Totals

If you create a database to manage your checkbook, it is convenient to see the balance after each entry. This incremental update is called a running total. You can use a running total summary field to display a total for each record instead of just the total for all records.

To create running totals:

1. Choose File > Define Fields (Ctrl+Shift+D/Command-Shift-D).

2. In the Define Fields dialog box, enter a name, choose Summary as the type, and click Create.

3. When the Options dialog box appears, choose the Total of radio button and check the Running total box below the list of fields (**Figure 5.20**). Click OK.

4. Repeat steps 2 and 3 for as many running total fields as you need.

   In our example, we create two summary fields: one for deposits and one for withdrawals.

5. To display the running balance, you need to create a calculation field that subtracts the withdrawal field from the deposit field. Open the Define Fields dialog box, type a name in the field name box, click the Calculation radio button and then click Create.

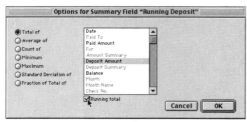

Figure 5.20 To add running total summaries for a field, check the Running total box when you create the summary field.

6. In the Specify Calculation dialog box, double-click the first field (in this case, Running Deposit) from the field list on the left, click the minus button in the operators keypad, then double-click the second field (in this case, Running Withdrawal) (**Figure 5.21**). Click OK and then click Done.

7. In Layout mode, switch to the layout where you want the running total to appear. Add the Running Balance field to the Body part of a column layout or to a standard layout (**Figure 5.22**). Switch to Browse mode to see the balances.

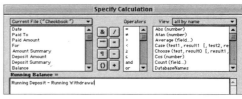

Figure 5.21 For a running checkbook balance, create a calculation field that subtracts the total withdrawals from the total deposits.

Running Balance field

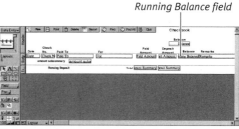

Figure 5.22 The Running Balance field displays the current balance for each record.

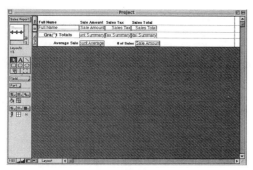

Figure 5.23 Drag the Part tool to the place on the layout where the total field should appear.

Figure 5.24 In the Part Definition dialog box, choose the field name from the scrolling list.

Trailing Grand Summary

Sub-summary

Figure 5.25 When you add a new part to the layout, the part below it will shrink.

Creating Sub-summary Reports

FileMaker has the power to take you beyond simple totals. Using the Sub-summary layout part, you can produce reports that display subtotals for any field. For example, you can create a report that shows sales totals broken out by state and, within each state, broken out by payment type.

You'll need to manually add a Sub-summary part to a layout. Although you can create a Sub-summary part with the Layout Assistant when you first design a layout, the Assistant can't be used to modify existing layouts.

To add a Sub-summary part to a layout:

1. Choose View > Layout Mode (Ctrl+L/ Command-L). Switch to the layout where you want to add sub-summaries.

   This example uses the Sales Report layout created in "To create a layout with summary parts" on page 76.

2. Click the Part tool and drag it onto the layout. In this example we add the sub-summaries to the Trailing Grand Summary (**Figure 5.23**).

3. When the Part Definition dialog box appears (**Figure 5.24**), click the "Sub-Summary when sorted by" radio button, then choose the field name for which you want subtotals from the scrolling list. This example uses the State field. Click OK.

4. The Sub-summary part is now on the layout, but the Trailing Grand Summary part is too small and the fields that were in it are now in the Sub-summary part (**Figure 5.25**). Resize the Trailing Grand Summary part to accommodate the moved fields.

continues on next page

5. Select the totals fields and their text labels. Hold the Ctrl (Windows)/Option (Mac) key and drag them back down where they belong (**Figure 5.26**).

This strategy keeps the fields aligned, as well as duplicating them so they appear in two different layout parts. In the Sub-summary part, they will display subtotals for each state. In the Grand Summary part they will display totals for the entire report.

6. Delete any field labels or other text you duplicated but don't need in one of the parts.

7. Drag the Field tool to the Sub-summary part. When the Specify Field dialog box appears, choose the first field you want the sub-summaries to be sorted by. In this example, we chose State (**Figure 5.27**).

✔ Tips

■ To add more subtotals, repeat steps 2 through 6, changing the field you specify for the sort and duplicating the summary fields on the new sub-summary parts.

■ To make a report easier to read, you can add horizontal lines below the Header text and the sub-summaries. Click on the Line tools, hold down the Shift key (to keep the line straight) and draw the lines in the Header and Sub-summary parts (**Figure 5.28**). You can use the Ctrl/Option-drag technique to duplicate the horizontal lines (or any other layout element).

Figure 5.26 Drag with the Ctrl/Option key to copy the summary fields and position them in both the Sub-summary and Trailing Grand Summary parts.

Figure 5.27 Add the field that the summary fields will be sorted by to the Sub-summary part.

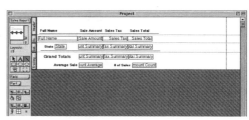

Figure 5.28 The report will be easier to read with horizontal lines separating the sections.

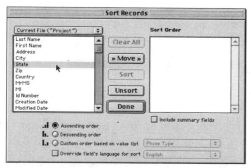

Figure 5.29 Choose as your first Sort field the one for the first Sub-summary part on the layout.

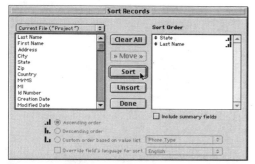

Figure 5.30 After you sort the sub-summary field(s), you can choose the sort order for the records in the Body part.

Sorting Data for Sub-summary Reports

If you go directly to Preview mode after adding Sub-summary parts to a report, the subtotals will *not* appear. Before you preview, you must sort the database to match the order of the sub-summaries in your layout.

The key to using sub-summaries is sorting the database in the right order. In this example, the database must be sorted first by State, then by Last Name.

To sort data for sub-summary reports:

1. Since you can't sort records in Layout mode, switch to either Browse or Preview mode. Choose Records > Sort (Ctrl+S/Command-S).

2. When the Sort Records dialog box appears, double-click on the first field you want to sort by, which should be the first sub-summary in the layout. (You could also highlight the field, then click Move.) This example uses the State field for the first sort (**Figure 5.29**).

3. If you have added more than one sub-summary, double-click these fields in the order that the parts appear on the layout.

4. Select a radio button to determine how your sort will be arranged (ascending or descending order), and click Sort.

5. After sorting the sub-summary fields, you can sort the fields that appear in the Body part (**Figure 5.30**).

Exporting Summary Data

The report described above may be useful to you printed out. But suppose you want to use the totals in another program?

Using the Export Records command, you can create a file that contains the same information that is in the printed report, including the subtotals. This file can be opened in a spreadsheet or word processor, or imported into your accounting software for invoicing. Once you have it in another application, the data is completely editable. It can be used to create quarterly or annual reports in a layout program like QuarkXPress, or to define charts in Excel or PowerPoint.

To export summary data:

1. Make sure you've sorted your data properly by following the procedure in "To sort data for sub-summary reports" on page 85.

2. Choose File > Export Records. When the Export Records to File dialog box appears, choose a file type from the Save as type drop-down list (**Figure 5.31**). In this case, it will be a spreadsheet, so we'll choose WK1(Windows) or WKS(Mac). Type a name for the file, choose a destination folder and click Save.

3. When the Specify Field Order for Export dialog box appears, double-click the names of all the fields you want to export. This moves the fields into the Field Order list. Remember to choose the Summary fields as well (**Figure 5.32**).

   Windows users will need to make a selection from the Character Set drop-down list if they're exporting to a file that will be read in another operating system. If you're working on a Mac, your Specify Field Order dialog box won't have this list.

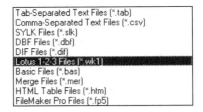

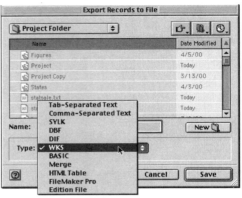

Figure 5.31 For exporting to spreadsheets, choose WK1 (Windows) or WKS (Mac).

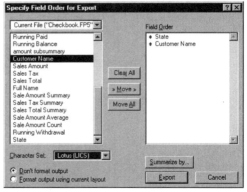

Figure 5.32 The first fields should be the fields that are used in the sort, followed by the summary fields.

Figure 5.33 Make sure that the check mark appears to left of the field name.

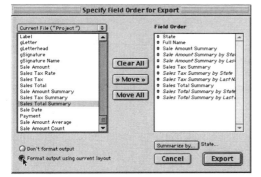

Figure 5.34 You can choose to format the numbers in the export file as they are in the current layout

Figure 5.35 Add column headers to an exported FileMaker spreadsheet file.

4. Click Summarize by; the Summarize by dialog box lists the sort fields. Click to the left of the field names so that a check mark appears—don't just click on the field name (**Figure 5.33**). Click OK to return to the Specify Field Order dialog box.

5. All the sub-summary fields will have joined the fields you chose in step 3. If you wish to have the numbers formatted like the current layout, click the "Format output using current layout" radio button (**Figure 5.34**). Click Export to save the exported file.

6. If you open the WKS/WK1 export file in Excel, it won't display column headers. You'll have to add them manually (**Figure 5.35**).

✔ Tips

■ If you are going to use the export file in a word processor, choose TAB (Windows)/ tab-separated (Mac).

■ If you are working on the Mac, add the right extension to the exported file name if you'll need to use it in Windows. (The Windows version of FileMaker adds the extension automatically.) For a spread-sheet, add .WK1. For a word processing document, add .TXT.

■ As with Finds, if you create an export file, you can create an Export Records (Restore Export Order) script to recreate the same export fields in the future.

■ If you need to maintain the field labels as column headings in your exported file, try exporting your files in either Merge (MER in Windows) or DBF formats. If you use one of these formats, be sure to check the labels carefully once you open the exported file. Merge brings over the labels, but replaces any spaces with underscores. DBF maintains the spaces, but has a maximum 10 character limit per label.

CREATING RELATIONSHIPS

6

Every file starts its life as a free-floating entity, managing a specific set of data and separate from other files. This is fine if the file meets all your database needs, but frequently it doesn't. As you discover new information to track, you create additional files to contain it. The time inevitably comes when you realize that some of the information in one file could be profitably used in another one.

Perhaps you've planned out all the possible connections your files could make and have built them to share data. Hats off to you if you have! In reality, such clarity usually comes with experience. You're probably working with files that were created before you discovered all the ways they might interconnect.

FileMaker doesn't require you to own a crystal ball. In fact, a database file that's too full of fields becomes cumbersome to update and takes too long to search. By creating relationships between files, you can painlessly join multiple sets of data without having to duplicate information. Once connected, the merged information can be displayed and manipulated as if there was only one database file.

About Relationships

The concept of a database relationship can seem more complex than it really is. FileMaker relationships are based on one very down-to-earth concept: that information can be shared in many ways. It can flow one way (like a TV station broadcasting the news) or two ways (like a reporter interviewing someone by phone), or use some combination (like the interviewee talking to the reporter at the same time she's using a videocam to broadcast to the Internet).

In a group of database files, you might have a mailing list containing names and addresses, and a second file that tracks customer invoices. You want to display the name and address information from the mailing list in the invoice file. Like the broadcasting station, the mailing list is the information source. The invoice file, like the TV, is the information destination. It's receiving information but not giving anything back.

Using FileMaker, there's nothing to prevent the receiving file from opening a two-way communication, or becoming the information source for another file. All FileMaker files have a peer-to-peer relationship, meaning that they're all capable of being sources or receivers of information, or both.

In FileMaker terminology, when a file is playing the role of a receiver, it's called a *master file*, because it's the focus of the information transfer. The file broadcasting its information is called the *related file*. Although we'll use these terms when necessary, they tend to confuse the issue because they aren't descriptive of what's actually going on. Instead, we'll refer to the master file as the *receiver* or *destination file*, and the related file as the *source file*.

The examples in this chapter are based on two model files. One is a customer file containing each client's name and address data. The other is a sales file with one entry for each client's purchase. The sales file (the master file or receiver) will use the data from the customer file (the related file or source).

Defining a Master File

To define a file as either source or receiver, you need to create a key field—which FileMaker calls the *match field*—that is common to both files. Each record in the source file must have a unique match field, so that the receiving file can identify which record is which.

There can only be one instance of a match field in the source file, while there could be any number of occurrences of it in the master. This is referred to as a One-to-Many relationship.

There are two common methods for creating a match field. The easiest is to create a serial number field, using the Auto-Enter field option to assign a sequential number to every new record you create.

To create a serial number match field:

1. In the source file, choose File > Define Fields. When the Define Fields dialog box appears, type a name for the match field, click the Number radio button, then click Create. In this example, the field name is Key Serial. When you're done, double-click on the new field name.

2. When the Options dialog box appears, click the Auto-Enter tab. Click the check box for Serial number. If this is a new database without any existing records, click the box for "Prohibit modification of value" to prevent anyone from altering this field by mistake (**Figure 6.1**). If this is a database with existing records, leave this box unchecked for now. Click OK and then Done.

Figure 6.1 Prohibit Modification prevents the auto-entered value from being changed.

Figure 6.2 Add the serial match field to the layout so you can update existing records.

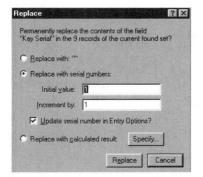

Figure 6.3 The Replace command allows you to update the beginning number in the auto-entry sequence.

3. If this is a new database without existing records, you've finished. If you are adding this field to a database that already has records in it, you'll have to add serial numbers to the existing records before you can enter new ones. To do so, choose View > Layout Mode (Ctrl+L/Command-L).

4. Drag the Field tool to the layout and choose your serial number field name from the scrolling list in the dialog box (**Figure 6.2**).

5. Choose View > Browse Mode (Ctrl+B/Command-B).

6. Click in the serial number field. Choose Records > Replace (Ctrl+=/Command-=).

7. When the Replace dialog box appears, click the "Replace with serial numbers" radio button (**Figure 6.3**). Click Replace. The existing records now have sequential numbers in the serial number field, and the field definition has been updated to enter the next serial number with one higher than your last record.

8. Return to File > Define Fields and double-click the serial number field name.

9. When the Options dialog box appears, choose the "Prohibit modification of value" check box. Click OK and then click Done.

✔ Tip

■ Not all types of fields can be used as match fields. Container fields can't ever be match fields. Global and Summary fields can be used as match fields in the destination file, but not in the source.

Creating a Match Field in a Master File

To use data from the source file you've created a match field in, you also need a match field in a master (destination) file. Once you have both match fields, you define a relationship that links the master to the source.

Figure 6.4 Define a relationship in the master (receiver) file, not the source file.

To create a match field in a master file:

1. In the destination file, go to File > Define Fields.

2. Define a new number field and name it. This example is named Key Serial to match the source field of the same name. Click Create, then Done.

3. Choose File > Define Relationships.

4. When the Define Relationships dialog box appears, click New (**Figure 6.4**).

5. In the Open File dialog box choose the source file by either double-clicking or selecting it and clicking Open. In this example the file is Customers.FP5 (**Figure 6.5**).

6. In the Edit Relationship dialog box, Relationship Name already displays the name of the file chosen in step 5. (You can change it if you want.) In the "Match data from field in current file" scrolling list, click the serial field. In our example, it's Key Serial (**Figure 6.6**).

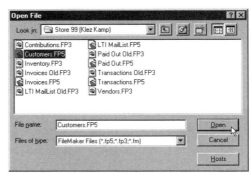

Figure 6.5 To define a new relationship, begin by choosing the source file.

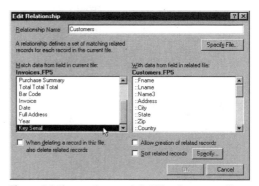

Figure 6.6 Choose the match field for the master file from the left scrolling list.

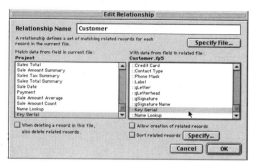

Figure 6.7 Choose the related source field from the right scrolling list.

7. In the "With data from field in related file" scrolling list, choose the name of the serial field in the source file (**Figure 6.7**). Click OK and then Done.

✔ Tips

■ To create a relationship using a calculated field, repeat the steps in "To create a match field in a master file," substituting the name of the calculated field for the serial match field.

■ Give the match field in the master file the same name as the match field in the source. The names don't *have* to be the same to create a relationship, but it makes it easier to remember which fields are related.

■ Watch your field types! Match fields must be the same type of field.

Lookup vs. Related Fields

Once you've established a relationship between files, you can choose between two methods for using the source file data. With the first method, you use the Lookup function to copy the actual data from a field in the source file to a field in the receiver file. Alternatively, you can display the source file data directly by placing its fields on a layout (or using them in a calculation) in the receiver file.

If you choose Lookup, when you enter a value in the source file's match field, the data in the specified fields is copied into fields in the receiver file. Once you've copied the files, however, if the data in the source changes, the data in the receiver file won't update. This might be useful if, for example, you want to maintain the customer's shipping address at the time of the sale.

If you choose to display the source data in the master file layouts without copying it, any changes made to the source *will* be reflected in the master file. The fields displayed in the layout are the *actual* fields in the source database, not a copy. If a customer moves and you update your records, all the entries in both databases will show the new address, no matter when the entries were originally made.

To create lookup fields:

1. Open your master file and choose File > Define Fields.

2. When the Define Fields dialog box appears, type a name for the first field, make it a text or number field (depending on what you need), and click Create.

Figure 6.8 To copy data from the source file into a field in the current database when a new record is created, check the Looked-up value check box.

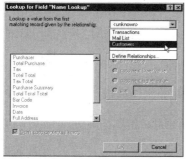

Figure 6.9 Choose a relationship from the Lookup dialog box list, or choose Define Relationships to create a new one.

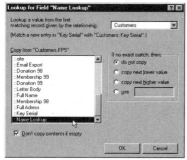

Figure 6.10 In the Lookup field list, choose the field in the source file from which the data will be copied.

3. Repeat step 2 for every field from the source database that you need to duplicate. These fields will hold the data that will be copied from the source file. Use the same field names for these destination fields that you used in the original source file.

4. When you've finished creating the new fields, double-click on the first field name.

5. The Options dialog box appears with the Auto-Enter tab displayed. Check the Looked-up value check box (**Figure 6.8**). This brings up the Lookup dialog box.

6. From the drop-down list, choose the relationship you created for the two files.

In our example, it's Customers, which we created in "To create a match field in a master file" on page 92 (**Figure 6.9**).

7. The Copy from field list will become active. Choose the field to be copied from the source file (**Figure 6.10**). Click OK, then click OK again to close the Options box.

8. Repeat steps 3 through 6 for each field that will contain looked-up data, then click Done.

✔ Tip

■ You can update data in the master file that you entered with a Lookup. To do this, click in the match field in the layout and choose Records > Relookup. The database will copy the related data from the source into all lookup fields using that match field for the relationship. If you only want to update certain records, do a search for those records and then choose Records > Relookup. Only records in the Current Found Set will be updated.

LOOKUP VS. RELATED FIELDS

To use related fields on a layout:

1. Go to the layout on which you want to display the related fields. Choose View > Layout Mode (Ctrl+L/Command-L).

2. Drag the Field tool onto the layout to bring up the Specify Field dialog box.

3. From the drop-down list above the field lists, choose the relationship you wish to use (**Figure 6.11**).

4. The field list will display the fields in the source database (**Figure 6.12**). Choose the field name you want and click OK.

5. Repeat steps 2 through 4 for each field you want to use.

   The related fields on the layout will have field names preceded by two colons (::) (**Figure 6.13**). The double colons indicate that the fields are from a relationship, not from the current file.

✔ Tips

- A database can have many relationships. You can use a field from any relationship on a layout. Just choose the relationship in the Specify Field dialog box before choosing the field name.

- The source match field can have multiple entries, separated by returns. As long as the match field in the destination field is the same as any of the entries in the source match field, the relationship will work.

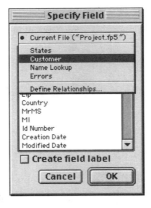

Figure 6.11 Choose the relationship that will be used to display the data for this field.

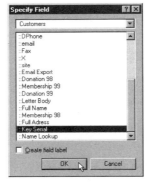

Figure 6.12 After you choose a relationship, the Specify Field list changes to display the source file's field list.

— Double colon before field name

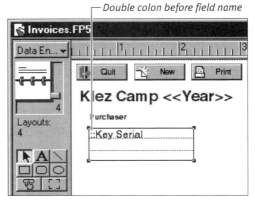

Figure 6.13 Every field on a layout that depends on a relationship will have a double colon in front of its name.

Figure 6.14 Enter the value in the match field for the related record.

Figure 6.15 The related data won't appear until you click another part of the layout or press the Enter/Return key.

Using a Match Field to Choose a Related Record

Once you have a relationship between two files and have created lookup fields (or added related fields to the layout), you can bring data from the source to the receiver file.

The simplest (though not necessarily the best) way to transfer data is to type the serial number value directly into the match field.

To use a match field to choose a related record:

1. Go to a layout that has a related field on it and switch to Browse Mode.

2. Create a new record (Ctrl+N/Command-N).

3. Type the customer's serial number (from the Customer file) into the serial number field. In our example, the field is Key Serial (**Figure 6.14**).

4. Click someplace else on the layout or hit Enter/Return. The related data will now appear in all the fields (**Figure 6.15**).

✔ Tip

■ Related values will change if another value is entered in the match field. To update a single record, change or clear the serial number value and then re-enter it.

Using Calculated Match Fields

A serial number match field assures that you won't create duplicate key values. However, it's much more useful for establishing a relationship between existing records than for new ones. In fact, it can be downright irritating if you try to use it for a new invoice. To create a new customer record, you have to know (or manually look up) the customer's serial number. Although you could look up serial numbers in the database, this is obviously not very efficient.

As an alternative, you can create a calculated match field that uses the data in the source file to uniquely identify which record is being chosen. The following example may need a little tweaking for your individual needs. If you have a very large database, for example, you may have to add the street address or phone number field to create a unique record for each customer.

To create a calculated match field:

1. In the source file, choose File > Define Fields (Ctrl+Shift+D/Command-Shift-D).

2. When the Define Fields dialog box appears, type a name for the field, make it a Calculation and click Create.

   In this example, we call the field Name Lookup (**Figure 6.16**).

3. When the Specify Calculation dialog box appears, enter the following formula in the Specify Calculation dialog box (**Figure 6.17**). If necessary, substitute your own field names for the ones in our example calculation.

   ```
   Trim (Fname) & " " & Trim(Lname) & "
   "& Trim(City) & " " Trim(Zip)
   ```

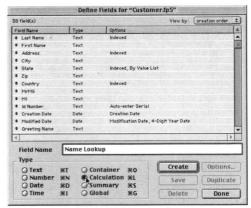

Figure 6.16 Name Lookup will be the unique match field for each customer record.

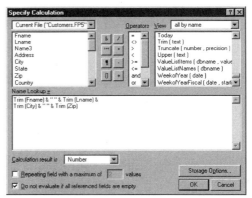

Figure 6.17 Enter returns between calculation elements to make reading the formula easier.

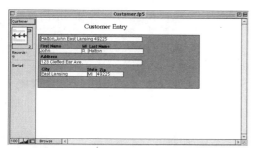

Figure 6.18 This calculated lookup field will contain the Last Name, First Name, City and Zip code with punctuation.

Notice that there are spaces between the quotes of the formula, and that we've added returns to make the formula easier to read.

4. Click OK, then click Done. Add this new field to a layout. It will contain a First and Last Name, City and Zip code, all correctly separated by spaces and punctuation (**Figure 6.18**).

✔ Tips

■ For more details, see "Merging Fields Using Calculations," in Chapter 4.

■ To create a relationship using a calculated field, repeat the steps in "To create a match field in a master file" on page 92, substituting the name of the calculated field for the serial match field.

■ When you create a calculated key field, keep in mind that FileMaker only indexes the first 20 characters of each word in the text that results from the formula (for example, "Dick Tracy, Metropolis 07307"). The maximum total characters the program indexes is 60, including spaces. So if the total amount of characters goes above the limit and two fields share the same first 20 characters, you could easily have errors in your lookup. You can avoid this problem by using only those fields that are most likely to provide a unique result. Eliminate the ones (like the State field if you're using a Zip field) that you don't need.

Field Formatting with a Calculated Match Field

Using the calculated field technique combined with a drop-down list format allows the user to choose the customer from a list of names rather than numbers. You will need to make one change to the relationship as it was shown in "To create a calculated match field" on page 98. It's more efficient to list the customers in alphabetical order by last name, so you'll want to re-sort before you create the drop-down value list.

To add a drop-down list to a match field:

1. Go to the receiver file and switch to the layout that holds your calculated match field. Choose File > Define Relationships.

2. When the Define Relationships dialog box appears, double-click the relationship that you established by creating a calculated field.

   In this example, we use Name Lookup (**Figure 6.19**).

3. When the Edit Relationship dialog box appears, click the "Sort related records" check box (**Figure 6.20**).

4. In the Specify Sort dialog box, double-click a field to define the sort criteria.

   In this example, we use Last Name (**Figure 6.21**). Click OK, and then OK again, then click Done.

Figure 6.19 Double-click to choose the relationship that uses your calculated match field from the Define Relationships listing.

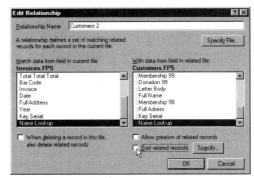

Figure 6.20 Choose Sort related records to organize the files in the match field.

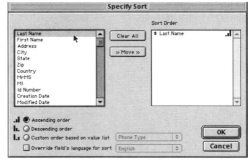

Figure 6.21 To choose the way a match field will be sorted, select the field you want to sort on from the Specify Sort list.

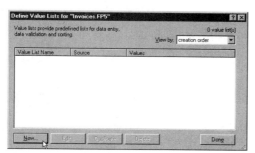

Figure 6.22 The Define Value Lists dialog box will be empty if you have never used it in the file before.

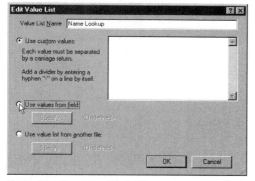

Figure 6.23 Give the value list the same name as the calculated field to make it easy to remember their connection.

5. Choose File > Define Value Lists. When the Define Value Lists dialog box appears, click New (**Figure 6.22**).

6. When the Edit Value List dialog box appears, give the value list the same name as your calculated match field and click the "Use values from field" radio button (**Figure 6.23**).

7. The Specify Fields for Value List dialog box will appear with the name of your master file in quotes at the top. Click Specify File (**Figure 6.24**).

8. From the Open File listing, navigate to the source file and double-click to select it.

9. The Specify Fields for Value List dialog box will appear again. From the list on the left, click to select the calculated match field. In our example, the file is Name Lookup (**Figure 6.25**). Click OK, then OK again and then Done.

continues on next page

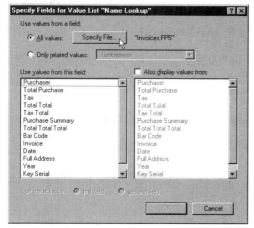

Figure 6.24 Click Specify File to choose the source database.

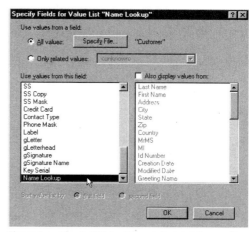

Figure 6.25 The field list of the related database will display in this scrolling list.

FIELD FORMATTING WITH A CALCULATED MATCH FIELD

10. Go to the data entry layout and switch to Layout Mode (Ctrl+L/Command-L).

11. From the tools on the left, choose the Field tool and drag it onto the layout to add the calculated match field to the layout (**Figure 6.26**).

12. Click this field to select it and choose Format > Field Format (Ctrl+Shift+M/Command-Shift-M).

13. When the Field Format dialog box appears, click the Pop-up list radio button and choose the calculated match field from the "using value list" pop-up on the right (**Figure 6.27**). Click OK.

14. If you are using lookup fields, verify that they are defined to copy data using the Name Lookup relationship. (See "To create lookup fields," page 94.) If you are displaying related data, make sure that the fields are from the correct relationship.

15. Return to Browse mode and create a new record (Ctrl+N/Command-N).

16. Click in the match field. It will display a list of names from the source field of the same name in the Customer database. Click on the name you want (**Figure 6.28**).

All of the related (or lookup) fields will fill with the values from the related record of the name you chose (**Figure 6.29**).

✔ Tip

■ In a pop-up list, you can type the first letter or two to go right to the first item that begins with those letters.

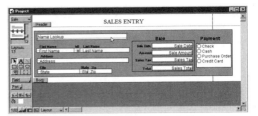

Figure 6.26 Use the calculated match field to choose the related record.

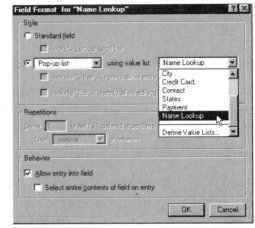

Figure 6.27 The list of values from the match field in the related source database will display in the pop-up.

Figure 6.28 The list of customer names will appear in alphabetical order by Last Name.

Figure 6.29 When you choose a name in the Name Lookup list, all of the related fields display the values from the source database.

Figure 6.30 A repeating field for phone number can contain all of the numbers for a particular person in a single field.

Figure 6.31 A related field with the same number of repetitions as a typical phone field can contain the designations for each number, yet allow you to search or collect the entries individually.

About Repeating vs. Related Fields

Many FileMaker users are excited when they discover the FileMaker repeating field. It seems to save time while you're defining fields—a boring stage for many in creating a database. A repeating field allows you to group multiple entries into one field, but have them appear on a layout as if they were separate entries. One practical use for a repeating field might be for people with more than one email address. Repeating fields allow you to avoid the tedium of making several fields labeled "email 1", "email 2", etc.

On the other hand, most accomplished FileMaker developers use repeating fields sparingly or not at all, because you can accomplish many of the same things much better through the use of related fields. Repeating fields have significant disadvantages. In general, they are treated as one indivisible unit. You can only sort repeating fields by their first entry and you can't create subtotals for particular entries. Although there is a calculation formula to pry out a particular repetition from the rest (GetRepetition), in general individual items in repeating fields are very difficult to extract for a report.

For all of these reasons, whenever you're considering using a repeating field, ask yourself whether a related database makes more sense. (It usually does.)

✔ Tip

- Phone numbers are a frequent use for a repeating field because you can enter all of the numbers for a particular person in one place (**Figure 6.30**). On the other hand, instead of creating a repeating field, you could create a text match field as both a relationship and a label for each phone number (**Figure 6.31**).

About Portals

Portals are a tool for accessing multiple files in another database without having to actually copy the data. They are a supercharged alternative to creating a relationship and placing a source field on a receiver field's layout.

Using a portal, you can display fields from all of another file's records without duplicating information or bloating a database with information that lives in another place. Take our two example files, Customer and Sales. You could create a portal in the Customer file to list all of the purchases made by each customer (**Figure 6.32**). Once you have a portal, you can even use it to create new records in a related field. (See "Creating Related Data" below for more details.)

To create a portal:

1. Go to the master file layout where the portal will be added and switch to Layout Mode (Ctrl+L/Command-L).

   Make sure the layout has enough room for the portal (**Figure 6.33**). If it doesn't, drag the Body tab down to resize the part.

2. Click the Portal tool. Click on the layout and drag the pointer out and down to size.

3. In the Portal Setup dialog box that appears, click the drop-down list and choose the relationship for this portal (**Figure 6.34**).

4. If you haven't yet created a relationship, choose Define Relationships from the drop-down list and follow the instructions in "To create a match field in a master file" on page 92 and then return to the Portal Setup.

5. In the Format section of the Portal Setup dialog box, type in the number of rows you want to display.

ABOUT PORTALS

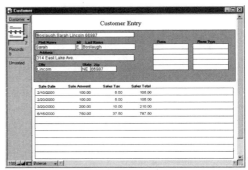

Figure 6.32 A portal can be used to show a list of all related records contained in another file.

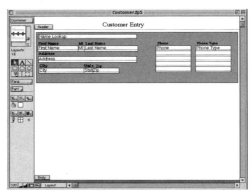

Figure 6.33 If you need more room on a layout to add a portal, drag the Body tab down to enlarge the part.

Figure 6.34 You can either choose an existing relationship or create a new one using the Portal tool.

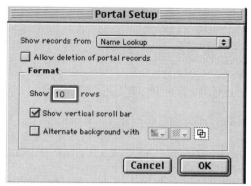

Figure 6.35 Add a scroll bar so the user can access all records regardless of the number of portal rows you choose.

Figure 6.36 The portal lists all purchases found in the source file that were made by this customer.

6. Click the "Show vertical scroll bar" check-box (**Figure 6.35**). Doing this allows the user to access all the records if there are more records than rows. Click OK.

7. With the portal selected on the layout, follow the steps in "To use related fields on a layout" on page 96 to add fields to the top row of the portal with the Field tool.

You only need to add fields to the top row, since the portal will repeat them for as many related records as there are in the source file.

8. Switch back to Browse mode to see the records in the portal (**Figure 6.36**).

✔ Tip

- When you add fields in a portal, make sure that your field labels are outside the portal or they will be repeated with every related record that appears in the layout list instead of appearing only once as headings.

Creating Related Data With Portals

When you create a relationship, one of the options is "Allow creation of related records" (**Figure 6.37**). If this option is checked, you can use the source file to create new records in the destination file.

To enter data in related files using portals:

1. Go to the master file layout where the portal will be added, and switch to Layout Mode (Ctrl+L/Command-L).

2. Make sure the layout has enough room for the portal. If it doesn't, drag the Body tab down to resize the part.

3. Click the Portal tool. Click on the layout and drag the pointer out and down to size.

4. Go to File > Define Relationships.

5. When the Define Relationships dialog box appears, double-click the relationship to bring up the Edit Relationship dialog box.

6. Make sure that "Allow creation of related records" is checked. Click OK and then Done.

7. Switch to Browse Mode (Ctrl+B/ Command-B) if you aren't there already.

8. Click in a field in the first blank row of the portal (**Figure 6.38**). Enter data in any of the fields in that row.

   The data you entered is contained both in the master file and in a new record in the related database.

9. You can switch to the related database to see the new record (**Figure 6.39**).

   The key field in the new record of the related file is automatically filled in with the data in the current record of the source.

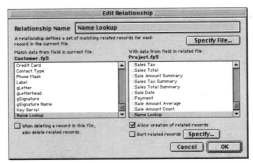

Figure 6.37 Check "Allow creation of related records" to use the source file to create new records in the destination file.

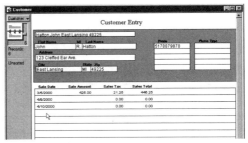

Figure 6.38 When the first blank row in a portal is clicked, a new record is created in the related database and the new data you enter is added to the record.

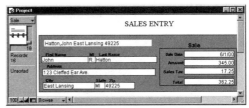

Figure 6.39 You can go to the related database to see the contents of the new record.

✔ Tip

■ Portals make serial number key fields very useful. Instead of having to manually input a serial number to bring up a customer record, a portal will enter the serial number automatically. Just be sure to create serial number match fields (as shown on page 90 in "To create a serial number match field") before you create the portal on your layout.

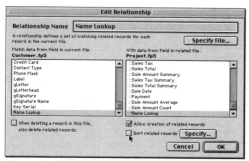

Figure 6.40 Click "Sort related records" to choose a field to sort the portal records.

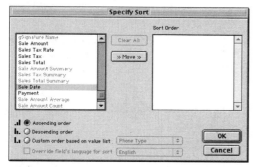

Figure 6.41 You can specify Ascending, Descending or a Custom order for each sort field.

Sorting Data in Portals

There is no way to specify a sort method in a portal once you're in a layout. If you want to view the portal data sorted by one of its fields, you need to specify this option in the relationship itself.

To sort data in portals:

1. Choose File > Define Relationships.

2. When the Define Relationships dialog box appears, select the relationship your portal uses and click Edit.

3. When the Edit Relationship dialog box appears, click "Sort related records" (**Figure 6.40**).

4. In the Specify Sort dialog box, double-click the field(s) to sort (**Figure 6.41**). You can specify Ascending, Descending or Custom sort for each field. Click OK.

   Portals based on this relationship will now display the related records sorted by the criteria and the order you specified.

Summarizing Related Data

Summary functions work on related fields in a layout just as they do on the non-related fields in the database. You can summarize the contents of a portal's data using a calculation field to create an account statement for individual clients, for example.

To summarize related data:

1. Open your master file and go to the layout that holds your portal. Choose File > Define Fields.

2. When the Define Fields dialog box appears, type a name for the field, click the Calculation radio button, then click Create.

   In this example, the field name is Sales Summary (**Figure 6.42**).

3. In the Specify Calculation dialog box, double-click an aggregate function from the function list on the right.

   Depending on what type of information you want, you can use Sum, Average, Count, Max, Min, StDev or StDevP. In our example, we've chosen Sum because we want to add all of the records.

4. Click the drop-down list above the field list on the left and select the relationship for the field you want to summarize (**Figure 6.43**).

   The field list will change to display the fields in the source file. Because they're related fields, their names begin with a double colon.

5. In the field list, double-click the field you want to summarize (**Figure 6.44**).

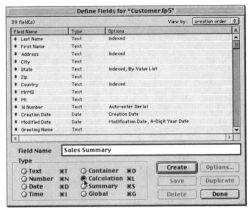

Figure 6.42 Related fields can be summarized with a calculation field.

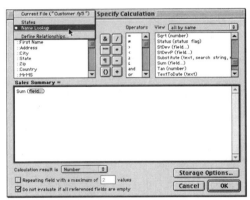

Figure 6.43 Before you choose a field, choose the relationship from the drop-down list to switch the field listing to the source file.

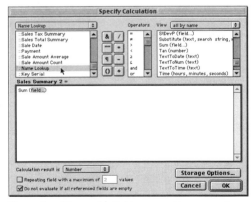

Figure 6.44 Choose the field you want to summarize from the field list on the left.

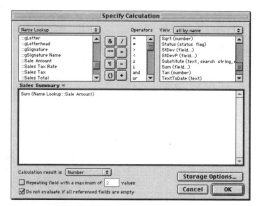

Figure 6.45 Enter the related field in the function between the parentheses.

New summary field

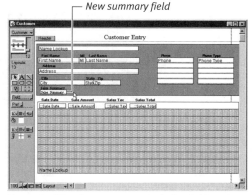

Figure 6.46 Put the summary calculation field on the layout body, not in the portal.

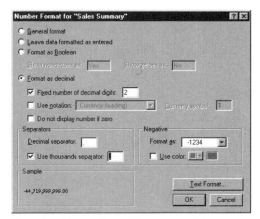

Figure 6.47 You can format the summary field to display in any standard number format.

6. The two related field names (the one in the master file and its related field in the source) will appear in the formula box (**Figure 6.45**).

7. Leave the calculation result set to Number. Click OK and then Done.

8. Switch to Layout Mode (Ctrl+L/Command-L) and add the field to the layout outside the portal.

In our example, we've added a Sales Summary field (**Figure 6.46**).

9. Go to Format > Number.

When the Number Format dialog box appears, you can specify exactly the format in which you want the summary information to appear (**Figure 6.47**).

In this case, we chose the Format as decimal radio button and set it to display the number to two decimal places. We also used a comma to set off the thousands column.

10. Switch to Browse mode to see the total for that record in the summary field (**Figure 6.48**).

Figure 6.48 The summary calculation field displays the total for the current record.

About Self-Relationships

Not only can you relate one file to another, you can also relate records within a file to each other. This is called a self-relationship. There are lots of situations where self-relationships are useful. If you have a database of contact names, many of whom work for the same company, you can create a self-relationship in a portal to list everyone working for the same company on each individual employee's record. Self-relationship portals can be defined as buttons to switch between records. You can also use a self-relationship to do simple finds, create summary fields and even create lookups to speed up data entry.

To create a self-relationship:

1. Choose File > Define Relationships.

2. When the Define Relationships dialog box appears, click New.

3. In the Open File dialog box, double-click the name of the current file (**Figure 6.49**). In this case, the file is called Contacts.fp5.

4. In the Edit Relationship dialog box, enter a relationship name.

   In this example, we use the Company field, so we've named the relationship Company.

5. Click the same field in both field lists (**Figure 6.50**).

6. If it's not already checked, click the Sort related records check box. Click Specify to bring up the Specify Sort dialog box.

7. In this example, we'll set the Sort criteria to Last Name by double-clicking to choose it (**Figure 6.51**). Click OK, OK again and then Done.

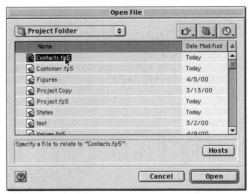

Figure 6.49 To create a self-relationship, choose the current file name in the Open File dialog.

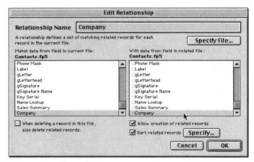

Figure 6.50 Choose the same field name in both field lists.

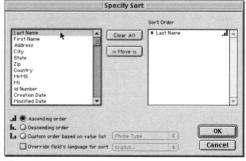

Figure 6.51 You can choose any field to sort the relationship.

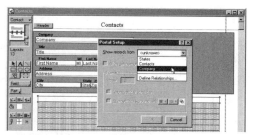

Figure 6.52 Choose the relationship that the portal will use to choose records.

Figure 6.53 Add fields into the first row of the portal using the Field tool.

Fields from the self-relationship

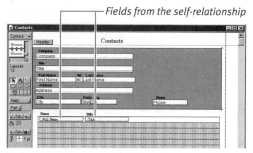

Figure 6.54 Choose the self-relationship you want to display from the drop-down menu.

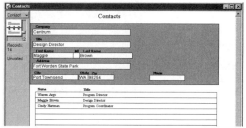

Figure 6.55 In Browse Mode, the portal will display the fields from the related records.

To display and access self-relationship data:

1. Switch to the layout where you will display the related data and choose View > Layout Mode (Ctrl+L/Command-L).

2. Make sure the layout has enough room for the portal. If it doesn't, drag the Body tab down to resize the part.

3. Click the Portal tool. Click on the layout and drag the pointer out and down to size.

4. In the Portal Setup dialog box that appears, click the drop-down list and choose the relationship for this portal (**Figure 6.52**).

5. Select the Field tool and drag it to the portal to add a field.

6. When the Specify Field dialog box appears, make sure you use the right relationship to choose the fields (**Figure 6.53**).

   In this case, we'll add Full Name and Title (**Figure 6.54**).

7. Switch to Browse Mode to view the portal with the related data (**Figure 6.55**).

   The names listed in the portal are from the records where the company name is the same as the current record.

✔ Tip

- Once a self-relationship has been created, you can use the "Go to Related Record" command in the Navigation portion of the Specify Button dialog box to jump to a specific related record. You can also choose just the related records as if you had done a search for the contents of the match field in the current record.

ABOUT SELF-RELATIONSHIPS

Using a Portal for Navigation

By making a portal field into a button, you can quickly switch between records by just clicking the field.

To use a portal for navigation:

1. Go to a layout with the self-relationship portal and switch to Layout Mode (Ctrl+L/Command-L).

   In this example, we use the company portal we created in "To display and access self-relationship data" on page 111.

2. Click one of the self-relationship portal fields. In this example, we use Full Name (**Figure 6.56**). Chose Format > Button.

3. In the Specify Button dialog box, scroll down to the Navigation section and select the type of location you want to connect your button to (**Figure 6.57**).

4. In the Options section on the right, select the relationship in the Specify drop-down list (**Figure 6.58**). Click OK.

5. Switch to Browse mode. Click on a Name field in the portal. You'll now see the record for the name you selected.

✔ Tip

- When you make a field into a button, you can no longer use the field to edit data. However, once you click the field/button, FileMaker brings you to the related record where you can make changes.

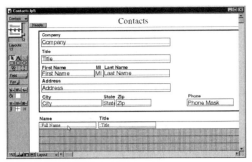

Figure 6.56 Select a field in the portal to make into a button.

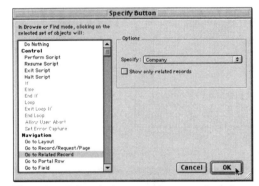

Figure 6.57 Select the button address type from the Navigation section. We choose Go to Related Record.

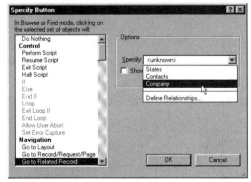

Figure 6.58 Connect the Full Name field to the related source file.

Button tool   *Button being created*

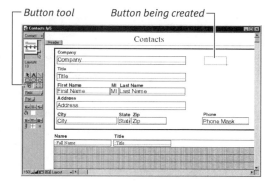

Figure 6.59 Use the Button tool to create a button on the layout.

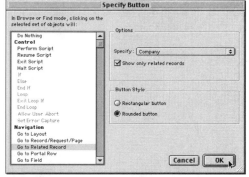

Figure 6.60 "Show only related records" acts like a Find command.

Searching for Self-Relationship Data

Instead of using a portal field as a button, you can create a separate button in the portal and use it to perform a search in the self-relationship records.

To search for self-relationship data:

1. Go to a layout with the self-relationship portal and switch to Layout Mode (Ctrl+L/Command-L).

2. Click the Button tool, then click and drag on the layout to size and place the button (**Figure 6.59**). The Specify Button dialog box appears.

3. From the list on the left, scroll to the Navigation section and select the Go to Related Record command.

4. In the Options section on the right, choose the relationship (we use Company).

5. Check the "Show only related records" box (**Figure 6.60**). Click OK.

6. At the flashing cursor, type a title for the button. You can also resize and add color if needed.

   When you switch to Browse mode and click the button, the found set of company records will appear in the portal.

Creating a Lookup with a Self-Relationship

By using a self-relationship to do a lookup, you can save yourself lots of repetitive input and decrease typing errors. Many types of information, like a Zip code and the city and state combination it represents, must always be the same. If you use the most specific information (in this case, the Zip code) to define the relationship, you can automatically insert the other two fields contents.

To create a lookup with a self-relationship:

1. Choose File > Define Relationships.

2. When the Define Relationships dialog box appears, click New.

3. In the Open File dialog box, double-click on the name of the current file. In this case, the file is called Contacts.fp5.

4. In the Edit Relationship dialog box, type in a relationship name.

   Since we're looking up records based on the Zip code, that's what we've named our relationship.

5. Click the same field in both field lists. In this example, we've chosen the Zip field (**Figure 6.61**).

6. Leave the Sort related records check box unchecked because you don't need to specify a sort. Click OK and then Done.

7. Choose File > Define Fields.

8. In the Define Fields dialog box, double-click the first field you want to look up. In our example, it's City.

9. The Options dialog box appears with the Auto-Enter tab in front. Click the Looked-up value checkbox (**Figure 6.62**).

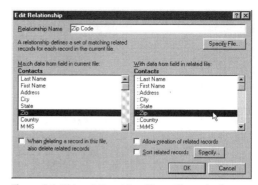

Figure 6.61 This relationship will use Zip as the key field.

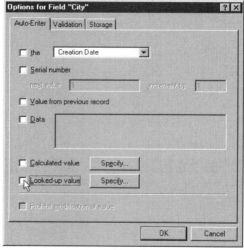

Figure 6.62 To create a lookup based on a field, choose Looked-up value from the Options dialog box.

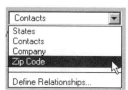

Figure 6.63 Use the Zip Code relationship to do the lookup.

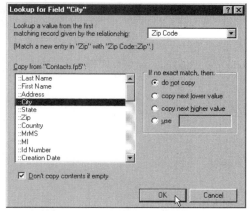

Figure 6.64 Don't copy the values for City and State if the zip code isn't exactly the same.

Figure 6.65 You can choose to create a new tab order, or edit the existing one.

10. When the Lookup dialog box appears, click the drop-down list at the top to choose the self-relationship you just created (**Figure 6.63**).

11. Click the City field in the list. Make sure that "If no exact match, then" is set to "do not copy" and the "Don't copy contents if empty" checkbox is checked (**Figure 6.64**).

In our example, selecting these options ensures that if there is an existing record with the same Zip code, the city and state that match it will be filled in automatically. If there isn't a record with that Zip code, nothing will be copied, so you can fill in the fields manually. Click OK, then OK again.

12. Repeat steps 8 through 11 if you have a second field to look up. In our example, we use the State field. Click Done when you're finished.

13. Go the layout where the data will be entered. Switch to Layout Mode.

14. Choose Layouts > Set Tab Order.

15. The Set Tab Order dialog box appears. If your layout doesn't have a tab order already, choose the Create new tab order radio button. Otherwise, select Edit tab order (**Figure 6.65**).

continues on next page

16. Click inside the arrows on the fields to change or create the tab order so that the number in the Zip field is lower than the numbers in the City and State fields (**Figure 6.66**).

17. Changing the tab order prompts you to enter the Zip code before the city and state, so that the lookup can take place.

18. In the Set Tab Order dialog box, click OK.

✔ Tips

■ The Tab Order setting does not control the order if the user is using the mouse to move between fields. You can put a text reminder on the layout telling the user to go to the Zip field before City and State.

■ Instead of using the Zip code in the above example, you could use the same technique with a relationship based on the Company field. Then you could set lookups for Address, City, State and Zip to avoid even more repetitive input.

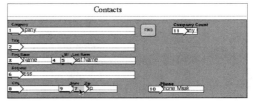

Figure 6.66 The tab order is set to bring you to the Zip Code field before City and State.

CREATING SIMPLE SCRIPTS

Databases are powerful things, but they sure can be tedious to set up and manipulate. Sometimes it seems as if you're using the same darned combination of mouse clicks and menu commands over and over. Why can't FileMaker learn how you work and do some of these functions for you? You may be surprised to discover that it can, if you're willing to take just a little time to train it by using scripts.

At its most basic level, a script is just a list of things you want FileMaker to do for you, written in exactly the order you want to have them done. It's like leaving a To Do list with an efficient helper, so that you can mentally "walk away" and return to find the tasks crossed off.

FileMaker scripts are patient, so if you need one to wait for more information before proceeding, you can build in a pause. They're also modular, so you can start with very simple lists and add more items to them as they occur to you. One script can be used together with other scripts, making a complex master script that efficiently automates many actions with one simple button. And once you've created a working script, it's foolproof. You'll never have to start over again because you chose the wrong drop-down menu, or forgot to change your page setup before printing.

We think scripting is addictive. Once you grow accustomed to planning them out, hundreds of different script combinations will occur to you. For instance, you can move records automatically between different files, click one button to sort and print files in a monthly report, and then export the result to Excel. If it can be done manually, chances are there's a script command to do it for you.

Planning a Simple Script

You never just launch into FileMaker and create databases and make fields "on the fly." If you did, you'd be sure to waste lots of time later correcting your mistakes, adding fields (and then the data for them) and adapting layouts. Creating a script is very much like creating a new database. If the end result is successful, it's because you carefully considered your goals and strategies first.

Begin by thinking about how you work. Ask yourself, "What things do I do in FileMaker that waste time, typing and mouse clicks because I always have to repeat them?" Make a list of these tasks. (If nothing occurs to you at the moment, open your database and start working!) For example, you might have, "Print out a list of accounts over 30 days past due."

You should temporarily skip any tasks that require you to choose between options at some point in the process (we'll get to those later). Of the tasks that remain, look for one that mostly involves several menu commands in sequence. Make a list of the main menu bar commands you choose when you do the task, in the order in which you do them.

When we look at the steps we take to get our overdue accounts statement, our list contains:

◆ *Find records*

◆ *Sort records*

◆ *Go to the overdue accounts layout*

◆ *Print the layout*

That's a good beginning, but always go back and look at the steps carefully to see if there are any you've missed. In this first list, we've forgotten that we need to set up the page for printing so the proper page size and orientation are used. Our revised list now reads:

◆ *Find records*

◆ *Sort records*

◆ *Go to the overdue accounts layout*

◆ *Set the printing options*

◆ *Print the layout*

There's one last step that you might not think about when you look at your process. Once you've finished printing, you don't usually need the printing layout on the screen. In fact, you probably want to return to whatever you were doing before you printed the overdue accounts statement. So the last step in the list should be:

◆ *Go back to where you started*

Once you've listed all your steps, look closely at the list for things you can group together. The nice thing about scripts is that you don't necessarily have to tackle them all at once, from start to finish. You can start with very small, short tasks and build up to more complex functions by adding new steps to the beginning, end or even the middle of a script.

Storing Settings Before Scripting

Looking at a list of steps you want to combine into a script, you'll probably notice that several steps depend on others. For example, if you want to print a report, you have to set up your printing options first. If you want to sort records, you have to find them first. The order in which you do things really does matter. This may seem pretty obvious when you look at it now, but it's actually easy to lose sight of this concept when you plan a script.

Settings like page size or sort order are easy to leave out, but you could get incorrect results if you've forgotten to consider them. Unless you tell it otherwise within the script steps, FileMaker will apply its most recently used settings, even if they're not appropriate for what you have in mind. Imagine how irritated you'd be to set a script in motion to print your 50-page accounts payable, only to find the data cut in two because the page setup specified portrait instead of landscape orientation.

To protect you from these frustrations, FileMaker allows you to store your settings when you create a script. Several script steps give you the option to Restore:

◆ **Go to Layout:** Restores the layout you were using when you created the script.

◆ **Perform Find:** Restores all the criteria for a find request, including any combination of omitted items.

◆ **Sort:** Restores the sort criteria for the records.

◆ **Import Records:** Restores the name of the file and its records, as well as any connections you've made between the imported and current files.

◆ **Export Records:** Restores the name of the file you're exporting to, the specific records you're exporting, as well as any export options you've set.

◆ **Page/Print Setup:** Restores page size, print percentage, number of copies and other printer-specific print settings.

In order to take full advantage of the Restore option, create all the settings you need just before creating the script. Don't assume that you know what these settings are. If you've done any work in FileMaker between the time you created your script pre-sets and when you sit down to make the script, create the pre-sets again.

To create pre-sets for a script:

1. Open your database and go to the layout you need to find your records.

   In our example, we create the pre-sets for accounts over 30 days, so we need our Sales Entry layout.

2. Choose View > Find Mode.

3. Enter the find criteria and click Find (**Figure 7.1**).

   In our example, we're searching for files with a sale date earlier than January 1, 2000.

continues on next page

Figure 7.1 If you want to use the Perform Find [Restore] step in your script, you must create a Find request before creating the script.

4. Choose Records > Sort (Ctrl+S/ Command-S).

5. When the Sort Records dialog box appears, double-click the fields in the left scrolling list to move them to the right Sort order box, then click Sort (**Figure 7.2**).

In our example, we sort by last name to get an alphabetical listing of the overdue accounts.

6. Click the Layout drop-down menu in the toolbar and switch to the layout you'll use to print the report (**Figure 7.3**).

7. Choose File > Print Setup (Page Setup on Macintosh). Set the print options needed for the script. Click OK (**Figure 7.4**).

Figure 7.2 The Sort order in use when you create a script will be used when the Sort [Restore] step is included.

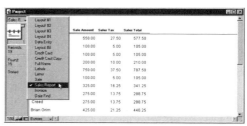

Figure 7.3 The Go to Layout step will use whatever layout you were in just before you created the script.

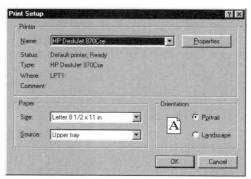

Figure 7.4 Print Setup options for Windows and Macintosh.

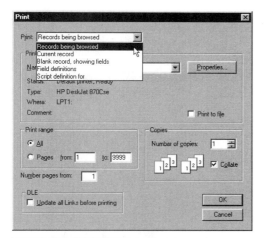

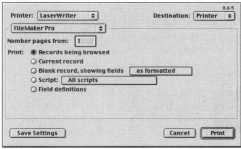

Figure 7.5 Windows and Macintosh Print dialog boxes.

8. Choose File > Print.

9. In the Print dialog box, click the Print drop-down list and choose "Records being browsed" (**Figure 7.5**). Click OK.

At this point, the basic pre-sets for the script you've planned are complete.

✔ Tip

■ FileMaker doesn't retain a previous sort order after a search. Anytime you execute the Find command, you must re-sort the database. Always remember to include the Sort command after a Find command in a script.

Using ScriptMaker

ScriptMaker is a module inside FileMaker for assembling scripts. Anyone who has ever had to do scripting for other purposes (like creating a roll-over with Javascript) will appreciate the simplicity and clarity of the two ScriptMaker dialog boxes:

Define Scripts (**Figure 7.6**) manages existing scripts. If you check the box next to a script, it will appear as an option in the Scripts menu. Otherwise, only the ScriptMaker module will appear in the Scripts menu (**Figure 7.7**). This feature lets you run an existing script at any time.

Script Definition (**Figure 7.8**) provides a working space for editing and creating new scripts.

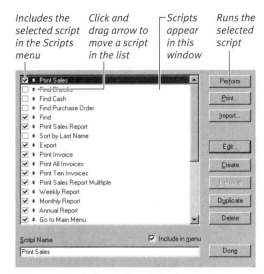

Includes the selected script in the Scripts menu — *Click and drag arrow to move a script in the list* — *Scripts appear in this window* — *Runs the selected script*

Figure 7.6 The Define Scripts dialog box is where you manage scripts you've already created.

Figure 7.7 In the first menu, we chose to have the script appear as a menu option. In the second menu, we didn't.

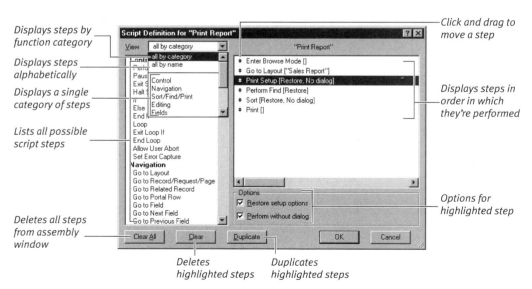

Displays steps by function category

Displays steps alphabetically

Displays a single category of steps

Lists all possible script steps

Deletes all steps from assembly window

Click and drag to move a step

Displays steps in order in which they're performed

Options for highlighted step

Deletes highlighted steps

Duplicates highlighted steps

Figure 7.8 The Script Definition dialog box is where you build or edit scripts. The six-step script in this picture is FileMaker's default script.

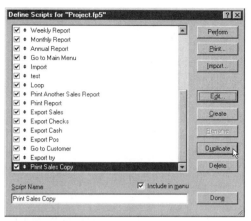

Figure 7.9 A duplicated script appears at the end of the Define Scripts window list.

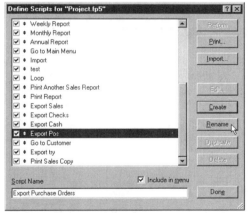

Figure 7.10 You can't choose Rename until you've edited the name of a script.

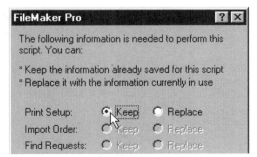

Figure 7.11 If you edit a script with restored settings, you can choose whether to keep the original settings or change them to the current settings.

To duplicate a script:

1. Choose Scripts > ScriptMaker.

2. In the Define Scripts list of scripts, highlight the script name you want to duplicate.

3. Click Duplicate. The script copy will appear at the end of the listing (**Figure 7.9**).

If you wish to adapt an existing script, the best strategy is to duplicate the script, then rename it and edit in the change.

To rename a script:

1. Choose Scripts > ScriptMaker.

2. In the Define Scripts list of scripts, highlight the script name you want to rename.

3. Type the new name in the Script Name box to make the Rename button active, then click Rename (**Figure 7.10**).

To delete a script:

1. Choose Scripts > ScriptMaker.

2. In the Define Scripts list of scripts, highlight the script name you want to delete.

3. Click Delete. When the warning dialog box appears, click Delete again.

To edit a script:

1. Choose Scripts > ScriptMaker.

2. In the Define Scripts list of scripts, highlight the script name you want to edit.

3. When the Script Definition dialog box appears, make whatever script changes you need, then click OK.

If you are modifying a script that has restored settings (like Find or Sort), a dialog box will appear that gives you the option of keeping or replacing each pre-set (**Figure 7.11**). In our example, only our Print Setup information has changed.

continues on next page

4. If you have changed any of the settings and want to use the new ones, click the Replace radio button for those settings. Otherwise, click the Keep radio button.

5. When you've finished, click OK.

✔ Tips

■ You can run any of the first ten scripts listed in the menu by holding the Ctrl (Windows)/Command (Macintosh) key and typing a number from 1 to 0 (**Figure 7.12**). You can rearrange the list to put different scripts in the top ten by clicking on the double arrow before the script name and dragging up or down (**Figure 7.13**).

■ If you rename a script, ScriptMaker updates the script name in every other script that refers to it so all your other scripts continue to work properly.

Figure 7.12
You can run the first ten scripts in the Script menu by pressing Ctrl/Command and a number key.

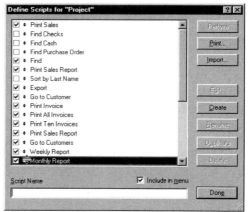

Figure 7.13 You can change the order of the scripts by clicking on the double arrows and dragging.

Understanding the Default Script

Every script step consists of two parts—the step name, which is a description of what it does, and the step options inside brackets. If the brackets are empty, the step doesn't have any options selected. If there are no brackets, the step has no options available.

If a step has options, their settings can be changed. Highlighting the step in the assembly window on the right displays its options below. ScriptMaker's default script automates printing (by far the most frequently used sequence of commands). You can add to, delete or change these steps as you experiment with scripting.

Here's what each step of the default script does:

◆ **Enter Browse Mode**

If you're in Find or Preview Mode when you run the script, FileMaker will switch to Browse Mode.

If you check the Pause box in the Options section, the script will wait in Browse Mode for you to enter data before moving on.

◆ **Go to Layout ["Layout Name"]**

Switches to the layout in use when the script was created.

Since the layout name is in brackets, it can be changed in Options to any other layout in the database (**Figure 7.14**).

If you check the Refresh Window box in Options, FileMaker will update the layout display for each change. Most of the time this just slows the script down, although it can sometimes be useful if you want to check how a script runs.

◆ **Print Setup (Windows)/
Page Setup (Mac)
[Restore, No dialog]**

Sets up the printer options for printing. The settings in brackets do two things:

Restore: Restores the print settings in use when the script was created. If you uncheck this box, whatever settings are currently in effect will be used instead of the ones you pre-set.

No dialog: FileMaker won't display the Print/Page Setup dialog box when the script runs. If you uncheck this box, the dialog box will appear so you can make changes.

sidebar continues on next page

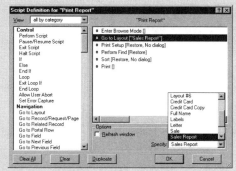

Figure 7.14 The layout name is an option that can be changed in the Specify drop-down box.

Understanding the Default Script *(continued)*

◆ **Show All Records**

Finds all of the records in the database.

or

Perform Find [Restore] (Figure 7.15)

Enters Find Mode and lets you change the criteria to either find all the records in the database, or just some of them.

One of these two steps appears in your default script depending on whether or not you've just done a search. If there is a Find setting in place, you'll see Perform Find. If there's no Find setting, you'll see Show All Records.

The Restore setting in brackets after Perform Find restores the Find criteria in use when you created the script.

◆ **Sort [Restore, No dialog]**

Sorts the records using the Sort criteria you defined when you created the script.

Like the options in Step 3, the bracketed options do two things:

Restore: Restores the sort criteria in effect when the script is created.

No dialog: The sort step will be carried out without displaying the sort dialog box.

◆ **Print**

Prints the records using the settings defined in the previous steps.

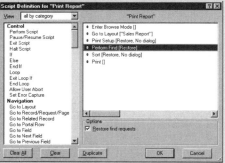

Figure 7.15 Show All Records makes all the records in your database available for printing. Perform Find with the Restore option restores the Find criteria in effect when you created the script.

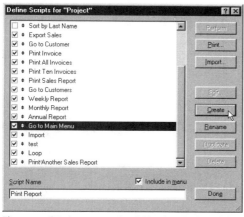

Figure 7.16 Script names should be descriptive of the script's function.

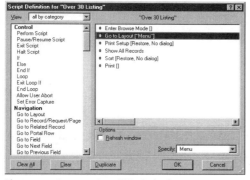

Figure 7.17 A new script will include these steps automatically.

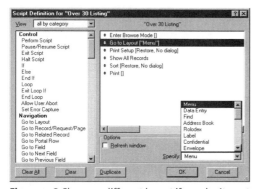

Figure 7.18 Choose a different layout if you don't want to use the current one.

Creating a Basic Script

When you create a script, FileMaker starts you out with a default set of steps (see the sidebar "Understanding the Default Script," page 125). You can use these steps as a basis for your script, or you can click the Clear All button in the Script Definition dialog box to delete all of the steps and add your own.

Using the default script as a starting point, we'll create a script that finds records, sorts them and prints a report from a specified layout. In creating this script, we have already followed the steps in "To create pre-sets for a script" on page 119.

To adapt the default script:

1. Choose Scripts > ScriptMaker.

2. When the Define Scripts dialog box appears, type a descriptive name for the script and click Create (**Figure 7.16**).

3. The default script steps will appear in the Script Definition dialog box. Click on Go to Layout to highlight it (**Figure 7.17**).

4. In the Options section, click the Specify drop-down list to choose the layout you want to use for the script (**Figure 7.18**).

5. Select the last step in the script. Doing this tells FileMaker where to add the next step. Otherwise, any new step will be inserted right after whatever step is high-lighted in the script assembly window.

continues on next page

6. In the step listing in the left column, double-click Go To Layout in the Navigation category to add this step to the end of the default script (**Figure 7.19**). Leave its Option set to original layout.

This step will return you to the layout you were in before you ran the script.

7. Click OK to save the script and return to the Define Scripts dialog box. Click Done.

✔ Tip

■ If you want a script to let you know that a particular step is complete (or that the script is finished), you can add a beep to it at the appropriate place in the script. The Beep step can be found in the Miscellaneous category of steps. It uses whatever sound file has been selected as the operating system's Alert sound (**Figure 7.20**).

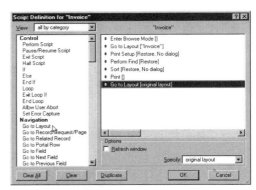

Figure 7.19 Double-click on a script step to add it to the script.

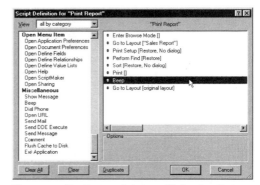

Figure 7.20 The Beep script step will play the Alert sound.

Figure 7.21 To use the restore option, you must do a search before creating the script.

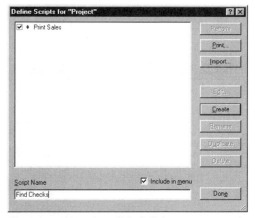

Figure 7.22 This script will find all the payments made by check.

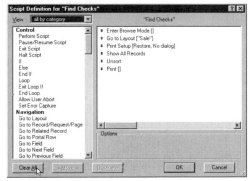

Figure 7.23 Clear All deletes all steps in the assembly window.

Creating Sub-scripts

You don't have to use the default script as your starting point for a script unless it contains most of the actions you need. You can create small sub-scripts that do one or two specialized tasks, then combine them with a more generic larger script to execute a variety of actions. These scripts may only contain one step apiece, but they allow you to retain a variety of settings without having to re-search or re-sort each time you want to create a variation on one script idea. For example, if you frequently have to sort your files by Last Name, you can pre-set your database with this sort, then create a sub-script that only has a Sort step in the script. Then you can add this sub-script to any other script—for updating accounts payable or analyzing account payment patterns—as you need it. We use this strategy to create a search script for payments by check.

To create a sub-script to find records:

1. Go to Find Mode. Go to the layout that contains the fields you need for your search. Input your criteria on the layout and click Find in the status area. In our case, we go to the Sales layout and search for all sales that were paid by Check (**Figure 7.21**).

2. Choose Scripts > ScriptMaker.

3. When the Define Scripts dialog box appears, type Find Checks in Script Name and click Create (**Figure 7.22**).

4. The Script Definition dialog box will appear with the default script in the assembly window on the right. Click Clear All to delete the default steps (**Figure 7.23**).

continues on next page

CREATING SUB-SCRIPTS

5. Scroll down to the Sort/Find/Print category in the left window and double-click Perform Find. Leave "Restore find requests" checked in Options to maintain the find criteria (**Figure 7.24**). Click OK.

6. Click Done to finish. You now have a script that will just find all of the records that were paid by check.

7. To create scripts for other types of payment, follow these steps but substitute other payment types. In our example, we created a total of four small scripts sorted for Cash, Purchase Orders and Credit Cards as well as Check (**Figure 7.25**).

To create a sub-script to sort records:

1. Choose Records > Sort.

2. Sort the records by the criterion that you want. For this example, we'll use Last Name.

3. Choose Scripts > ScriptMaker.

4. When the Define Scripts dialog box appears, type Sort by Last Name in Script Name and click Create.

5. The Script Definition dialog box will appear with the default script in the assembly window on the right. Click Clear All to delete the default steps.

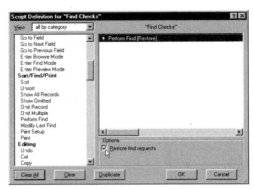

Figure 7.24 This script will restore the current find request.

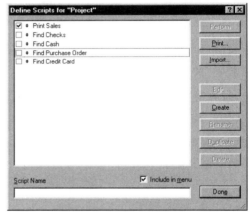

Figure 7.25 A separate script is required for each find request.

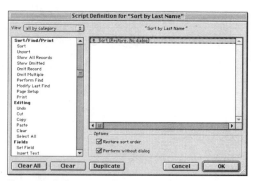

Figure 7.26 The sort script restores the sort order, so it doesn't require the dialog box.

This is the Payment field, showing that the search criterion was "check."

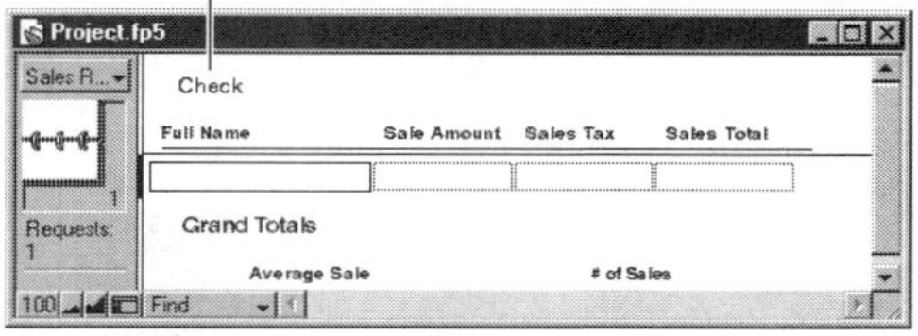

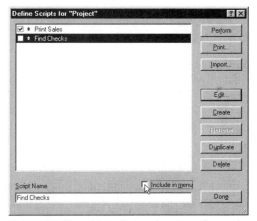

Figure 7.27 Records > Modify Find Request brings up the layout used for the original search with its search criteria indicated.

Figure 7.28 Since this script is only going to be used as a sub-script, it does not need to appear in the script menu.

6. Scroll down to the Sort/Find/Print category in the left window. Double-click Sort to move it to the assembly window. Leave both option boxes checked (**Figure 7.26**). This creates a small sub-script that will sort data by the Last Name field.

✔ Tips

- Sometimes you create subscripts and forget what settings you used for them, or you inherit scripts from other people who have worked on your database. To discover what search settings or sort settings are restored with a script, you must actually run the script first. Once the script is finished, go to Browse mode, then choose Records > Modify Last Find to see what search criteria are entered into the layout (**Figure 7.27**). To see the sort criteria, choose Records > Sort instead. To avoid having to backtrack, see "Adding Comments to a Script" on page 139.

- Sub-scripts can take up precious room in the Script menu listing. If you don't expect to use any of the sub-scripts by themselves, uncheck the "Include in menu" box next to their names in the Define Scripts dialog box (**Figure 7.28**).

131

Combining Sub-scripts

In "To create a sub-script to find records," we created several sub-scripts. Because they're small and modular, we can swap them in and out to create customized master scripts that do essentially the same things for a wide variety of different criteria. For this example we'll create a script that combines a Find sub-script and a Sort sub-script, and then prints the result.

To create a master script:

1. Go to the layout you want to use for your report. Choose File > Print Setup (Windows)/Page Setup (Mac).

2. Set the options for printing this report (**Figure 7.29**).

3. Choose Scripts > ScriptMaker.

4. When the Define Scripts dialog box appears, type `Print Sales Report` in the Script Name box and click Create.

5. The Script Definition dialog box will appear with the default script in the assembly window on the right. Click Clear All to delete the default steps.

6. In the step listing on the left, scroll down to the Navigation section and double-click Go to Layout.

7. In the Options section, choose your report layout from the Specify drop-down list (**Figure 7.30**). In our example, we use Sales Report.

8. Double-click Print Setup/Page Setup in the Sort/Find/Print section. Leave both options boxes checked (**Figure 7.31**).

9. In the step listing on the left, double-click Perform Script in the Control section to add it to the assembly window.

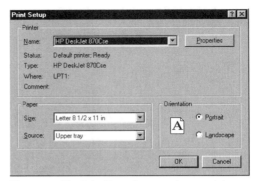

Figure 7.29 The Print/Page Setup options must be set before the script is created.

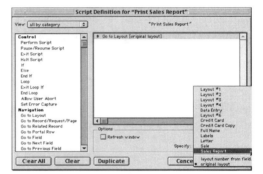

Figure 7.30 Specify a layout in the Go to Layout script step.

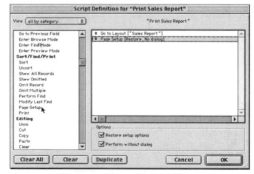

Figure 7.31 Restore will use the Print/Page Setup options in use when the script was created.

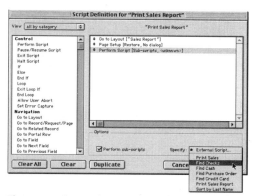

Figure 7.32 Choose the script to perform from the list in the Specify drop-down list.

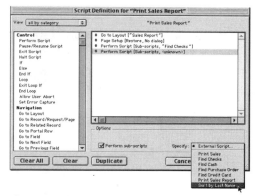

Figure 7.33 The Sort script must be run after the Find.

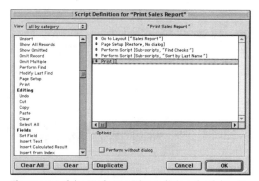

Figure 7.34 If the Perform without dialog check box is unchecked, the report will print to the current printer after prompting the user.

10. In the Options section, choose Find Checks from the Specify drop-down list (**Figure 7.32**).

11. Double-click Perform Script again.

12. In the Options section, choose Sort by Last Name (**Figure 7.33**).

13. In the step listing on the left, scroll to the Sort/Find/Print section and double-click Print. You can choose to have the Print dialog box display by unchecking the Perform without dialog box (**Figure 7.34**).

14. Click OK to add the script to the Define Scripts listing, then click Done.

Retaining Multiple Settings in a Script

Although you can simply edit the Options in a master script to change the sub-scripts you perform, it's more sensible to combine many similar actions into one script that automatically does them all at once. For example, in "To create a sub-script to find records," we created four separate sub-scripts that broke out sales by different types of payment. Chances are that we'd like to print all four reports at once. Since FileMaker can't handle more than one set of restore options per script, you can't simply search for one criterion, add a Perform Find step, then repeat. Instead, ScriptMaker uses sub-scripts to keep all the settings separate from each other, and Perform Script to call them up when you need them.

In this example, we make a copy of the script we created in "To create a master script." By duplicating and editing the original script steps, we make a new script which finds, sorts and prints several different reports. Although we create four report variations in our sample script, there's no limit to how many variations you can create in one script.

To retain multiple finds and sorts in scripts:

1. Choose Scripts > ScriptMaker.

2. When the Define Scripts dialog box appears, highlight the script name you want to use as a template in the script window and click Duplicate. In our example, we chose Print Sales Report (**Figure 7.35**).

3. Change the script name, then click Rename. Click Edit.

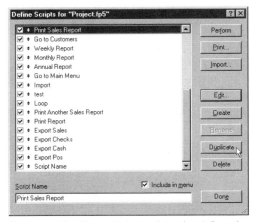

Figure 7.35 To edit an existing script, select it from the Define Scripts scrolling list, then duplicate and rename it.

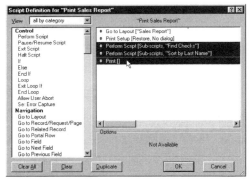

Figure 7.36 You can duplicate multiple steps in a script by shift-clicking to select them, and then using the Duplicate button.

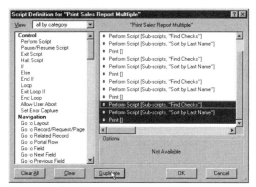

Figure 7.37 Duplicated script steps will appear at the end of the current list.

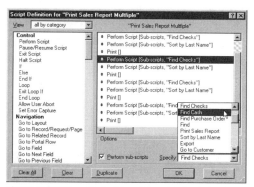

Figure 7.38 After duplicating steps, you just change the specification for each variation in Options.

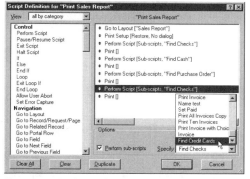

Figure 7.39 Replace sub-scripts by using Specify.

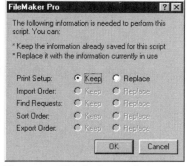

Figure 7.40 Click the Keep radio button to retain the same settings for the script.

4. When the Script Definition dialog box appears, click on the Perform Script [Sub-scripts, "Find Checks"] in the assembly window on the right. Hold down the Shift key and click on the last step (Print) (**Figure 7.36**).

This step selects the three steps in the script that we will want to duplicate for all of our reports.

5. Click the Duplicate button as many times as you have report variations. All the highlighted steps will be reproduced multiple times at the end of the list (**Figure 7.37**).

6. Click to highlight the first duplicated Perform Script [Sub-scripts, "Find Checks"] step. Choose "Find Cash" from the Specify list (**Figure 7.38**).

7. Click to highlight the next duplicated Perform Script [Sub-scripts, "Find Checks"] step. Choose "Find Purchase Orders" from the Specify list.

8. Click to highlight the last duplicated Perform Script [Sub-scripts, "Find Checks"] step. Choose "Find Credit Cards" from the Specify list (**Figure 7.39**).

9. Click OK to finish.

10. A dialog box will appear asking if you want to Keep or Replace the Page Setup information (**Figure 7.40**). Click the Keep radio button and then click OK.

11. Click Done. When you run it, the new script will print four reports, each with a different set of records, but all sorted by Last Name.

continues on next page

✔ Tips

■ You can select multiple non-contiguous steps in a script by using the Ctrl/Command key instead of Shift.

■ Copying multiple steps in a script and editing them makes it easy to combine scripts, but it also makes for scripts that are long and hard to read. In the examples above, all our scripts are individually sorted by last name. Your scripts will be cleaner and more professional if you combine the find and the sort steps together into one script, and eliminate the duplicated sort steps entirely from the master script (**Figure 7.41**). Your master script for printing reports will then be shorter and much easier to understand (**Figure 7.42**). Remember that the scripts must run in the right order, with the sort command coming after the find step.

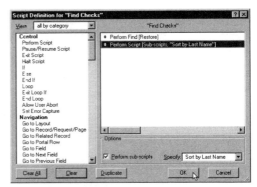

Figure 7.41 The sort command step must come after the find when you combine scripts.

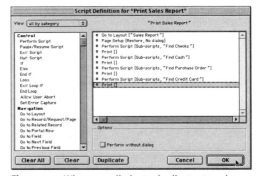

Figure 7.42 When you eliminate duplicate steps by incorporating them in sub-scripts, the master script is much easier to understand.

RETAINING MULTIPLE SETTINGS IN A SCRIPT

Figure 7.43 Choose a file format and specify a name for the export file.

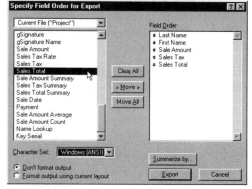

Figure 7.44 Choose the fields to be included in the export.

Using Sub-scripts for Multiple Export Settings

In Chapter 5, we showed you how to export data to a spreadsheet or accounting program. You can use the sub-script strategy in "To create a sub-script to find records" to create sub-scripts for different export settings. In this example, we create the sub-script that holds one export pre-set.

To create sub-scripts for multiple export settings:

1. Choose File > Export Records.

2. When the Export Records to File dialog box appears, type a name for the export file, choose a file format from the drop-down list and click Save (**Figure 7.43**).

   The name you choose in this step isn't important, because you can choose a different one in the script itself. You must name the file something, however, or FileMaker won't let you proceed!

3. When the Specify Field Order for Export dialog box appears, double-click the fields in the left window that you want to export to the new file (**Figure 7.44**).

4. Click Export to create the file on your disk. You've now created the pre-sets you'll need for your export script.

5. Choose Scripts > ScriptMaker.

6. When the Define Scripts dialog box appears, type a name in the Script Name box and click Create.

7. The Script Definition dialog box will appear with the default script in the assembly window on the right. Click Clear All to delete the default steps.

continues on next page

8. In the step listing on the left, scroll down to the Records category and double-click Export Records (**Figure 7.45**). Leave "Restore export order" checked to retain the settings you created in steps 2 and 3.

9. In Options, check the Specify box to choose a file name that will be used for the export file (**Figure 7.46a**).

10. When the Export Records to File dialog box appears, specify a file name for your export file. Click Save.

    If you don't specify a file name, you'll be prompted for one when the script runs, even if "Perform without dialog" is checked.

11. The script step will display the name and file type of the export file. Click OK to finish.

    You can repeat these steps to create new exports and their associated scripts.

✔ Tips

■ You can change the file name you specify for your export script at any time by returning to ScriptMaker and editing the script. First, highlight Export Records in the assembly window. In Options, click File (Windows)/Specify File (Mac) (**Figure 7.46b**). Doing this brings up the Export Records to File dialog box again, allowing you to select a new file name.

■ Once you've created several export sub-scripts, you can combine them into a master script to create and export different sets of data. For example, at the end of a quarter you might need to move your account sales data both to an accounting program and an Excel spreadsheet. A master script allows you to export the same data in both formats at the same time. To do this, follow the steps in "To retain multiple finds and sorts in scripts" to create a script that uses a series of Perform Script steps (**Figure 7.47**).

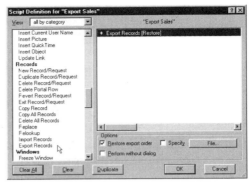

Figure 7.45 Check Restore export order to use the same fields in the same order as the last export.

Figure 7.46a If you check Specify, you can set a file name that will be used every time the export script runs.

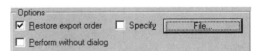

Figure 7.46b Clicking File lets you choose a different file name for your export file.

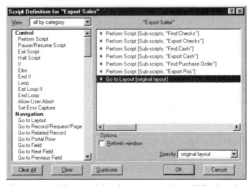

Figure 7.47 The combined master script will find and then export each set of records separately.

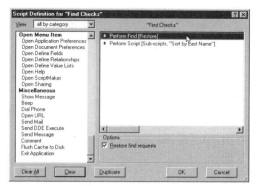

Figure 7.48 Select steps that will need explanations later.

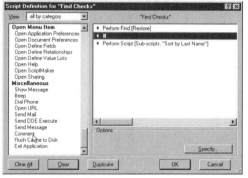

Figure 7.49 Choosing the Comment step adds a new line beneath the step you want to annotate.

Adding Comments to a Script

One of FileMaker's serious scripting weaknesses is that it doesn't provide an automatic way to see the settings it stores with the script. If you create a script and then forget its criteria, or have to troubleshoot someone else's scripting, you have to run the script first to restore the settings. This is particularly irritating if the script includes printing a very long report or series of records. Either you temporarily clear the print step (and then have to remember to put it back!) or you waste a stack of paper.

Even worse, if all of the fields that were used for the search don't appear on the current layout, you won't see an accurate picture of the settings, nor will you have any clue that this is the case.

"There must be a better way," you're thinking. And there is, although it does require additional work on your part. You can insert comments in a script as a reminder of what the steps do. In fact, you can add any information as a comment, not just find and sort criteria. For this example, we add comments to a sub-script.

To add comments to a script:

1. Choose Scripts > ScriptMaker.

2. In the Define Scripts list of scripts, highlight the script name you want to annotate and click Edit.

3. When the Script Definition dialog box appears, select the step you want to explain in the assembly window (**Figure 7.48**).

4. Scroll down to Miscellaneous in the step list. Double-click on Comment (**Figure 7.49**). A new line beginning with a # symbol is inserted after the step.

continues on next page

5. Click Specify to open the Specify input window.

6. Type the text of your comment Although you can type as much as you want, keeping the comment short and sweet is best so it will fit on one line in the script assembly window (**Figure 7.50**). When you're finished click OK.

7. The comment will appear in the script steps list (**Figure 7.51**). Click OK.

8. A dialog box will appear asking if you want to Keep or Replace the settings. Click the Keep radio button and then click OK.

✔ Tips

■ If you create a comment that's too long to fit in the script steps listing, it will be cut off in the assembly window because ScriptMaker doesn't wrap long sentences to the next line. Double-click on the comment to read all of it.

■ The # symbol that begins a comment line in ScriptMaker is a visual cue to let programmers and scripters know that the rest of the line that follows isn't a step in the script. It's used in almost every scripting and programming language, not just for FileMaker. Comments aren't considered steps because they don't perform any actions.

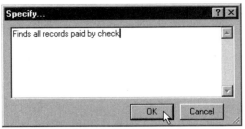

Figure 7.50 Type your comment in the Specify dialog box.

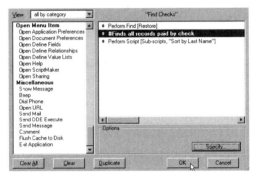

Figure 7.51 Your typed comment is inserted after the # sign.

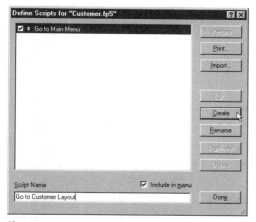

Figure 7.52 Use a script name that describes what the script will do.

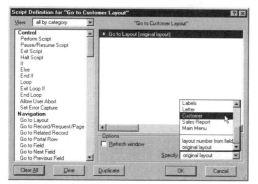

Figure 7.53 Create the script that will be called by the external script.

Using External Scripts

In "Combining sub-scripts" we ran scripts from inside a master script. However, all of the sub-scripts we used were in the same file as the master script. Scripting also allows you to run scripts in other files. Doing this allows you to access data from a second file while working in the first database. Using a script to switch to another file is much simpler than selecting the file from the window menu, then choosing a layout. If the second file is not already open, the script will open it and then run the external script.

In this example, we create a master script that switches from the Project file (where sales data is maintained) to the Customer layout in the Customer file (where customer data is kept). You might use this script to transfer contact information from a new customer's invoice in the sales file, and add it to your customer database.

To run a script in another file:

1. Go to the file that will be called by the external script. In our example, we use the Customer database.

2. Choose Scripts > ScriptMaker.

3. When the Define Scripts dialog box appears, type a name for the script and click Create (**Figure 7.52**).

4. When the Script Definition dialog box appears, click Clear All to delete the default script.

5. In the step listing on the left, double-click Go to Layout in the Navigation section to add it to the script assembly window.

6. In the Options section, choose your report layout from the Specify drop-down list (**Figure 7.53**). In this example, we choose Customer. Click OK, then Done.

continues on next page

USING EXTERNAL SCRIPTS

When this script runs, it will open the Customer database if it is not already open and then switch to the Customer layout.

7. Open the file in which you will create the script that calls the external script. In our example, we use Project.

8. Choose Scripts > ScriptMaker.

9. When the Define Scripts dialog box appears, type the script name and click Create (**Figure 7.54**).

10. When the Script Definition dialog box appears, click Clear All to delete the default script.

11. In the step listing on the left, double-click Perform Script in the Control section.

12. In Options, choose External Script in the Specify drop-down list (**Figure 7.55**).

13. When the Specify External Script dialog box appears, click Change File (**Figure 7.56**).

14. In the Open File dialog box, navigate to the FileMaker database you used in steps 1-10 above. Double-click to select it.

15. In the Specify External Script, choose the script that you want to run from the drop-down menu (**Figure 7.57**). Click OK.

   The external script will display the name of the external file that you chose. It won't show you the script name (**Figure 7.58**).

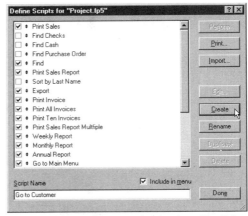

Figure 7.54 Create the external script that will call the layout script in the other database.

Figure 7.55 Choose External Script instead of one of the current file's scripts listed below it.

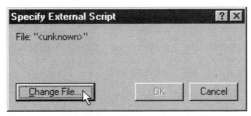

Figure 7.56 Click Change File to replace the File "<unknown>" setting with the name of the other file.

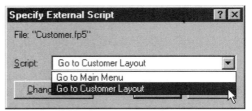

Figure 7.57 The pop-up will list all of the scripts in the external file.

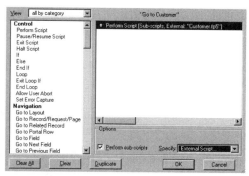

Figure 7.58 Only the name of the external file is visible in the script step, not the name of the script.

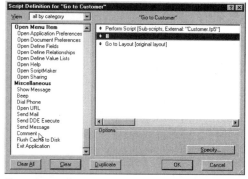

Figure 7.59 Write a comment with the name of the script in the external file.

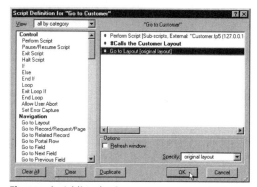

Figure 7.60 Adding the Go to Layout step to the end of a script returns you to the database and layout from which you ran the script.

16. To prevent you from forgetting which external script you are using, create a comment for this step. From the step listing in the Miscellaneous section, double-click to select Comment. A new line beginning with a # symbol is inserted after the step (**Figure 7.59**).

17. Click Specify to open the Specify input window.

18. Type the text of your comment and click OK to add it to the script assembly window. Click OK, then Done.

When this script is run, it opens the Customer layout in the Customer database, where you can edit or add data.

✔ Tip

■ When the last command in a script performs another script, the script sequence will end when the second script finishes. As a result, you'll end up in the layout and database where the external script ran, not in the original layout and database where you ran the master script. A common technique to return you to the other database is to use the Go to Layout [original layout] as the last step in a script (**Figure 7.60**). This technique will work even if the sub-script was in another file.

USING EXTERNAL SCRIPTS

Working with Conditional Script Steps

Simple scripting is basically a time- and finger-saver. It automates menu items, batch-processes straightforward procedures like sorting and printing, and with the use of comments, helps you keep track of your own procedures. But if you never reach beyond a step-by-step record of your actions, you miss out on some of the best reasons to script.

Every time you work with FileMaker, you have to make choices based on the task and what you want to accomplish. When you check an account listing against a database of paid invoices, you act one way when you find a paid invoice (pay bills) and another when you discover that the account is still outstanding (send out past due statements). Wouldn't it be nice if you didn't have to spend the time matching up accounts and actions? By adding conditional steps to a script, you can kiss such chores goodbye. Conditional steps allow you to create "smart" scripts that make your decisions by examining options and following the guidelines you provide.

About Conditional Steps

Look closely at a simple, menu-driven script step. It's just a series of terse commands. "Go to this layout," "Find these records" or "Sort this file." The script has no contingency plan. Add a conditional step, and the script can ask the question "Under what *condition* should I perform this command?" More to the point, it can answer the question by examining the options you've provided.

What makes a step conditional? That word of possibilities: *if*. In ScriptMaker, If is always followed by a *condition*. Conditions are very much what you might think they are: the situation under which the script can act. "If the account is based in Boston," "If the part is listed in inventory" and "If it's after March 31" are all examples of conditional statements. If the phrase following the If is true (it's a Boston account, the part is in inventory) the script will execute any commands that follow the If step. When the answer is no, the script may execute a different command or do nothing, depending on how you've structured the rest of the If command.

If you don't add to the If, the script will end without doing anything. You can, however, add an Else step inside the If. FileMaker will do whatever follows the Else step if the answer to the If is negative.

To figure out whether you need a simple If or an If combined with Else, write down what you'd like to have happen. For example, if you want a script to print a statement *if* there's a balance due in the account, you'd say:

```
If there's a balance due,
Print a statement.
```

Since there isn't anything you want to do as an alternative to printing, you need a simple If step.

On the other hand, if you want a script to mark the Paid field with a Y or N depending on whether or not there's a balance due in the account, you'd say:

```
If there's a balance due
Enter Y.
If there's not a balance due
Enter N.
```

In this case, you have two different actions you want to take place when the script runs. Because of that, your If command will need an Else step inside it.

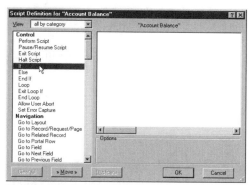

Figure 8.1 Double-click If to add it to the assembly window.

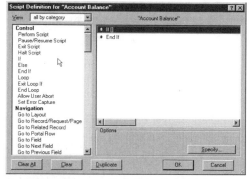

Figure 8.2 When you add an If step to a script, the End If is added automatically.

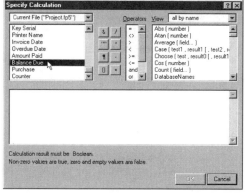

Figure 8.3 Choose the field you want the script to test in the If statement.

Using the If Command

Once you've figured out what kind of conditional step you need, you create the script in ScriptMaker. The syntax for a simple If statement to print a statement isn't much more complex than plain English.

To use the If command step:

1. Choose Scripts > ScriptMaker.

2. When the Define Scripts dialog box appears, type a name for the script (in this case Account Balance) and click Create.

3. The Script Definition dialog box will appear with the default script in the assembly window on the right. Click Clear All to delete the default steps.

4. From the Control category in the left window, double-click If (**Figure 8.1**).

   When you add If to a script, you will see two lines in the script steps: If and End If (**Figure 8.2**). End If is added by default every time you choose If to mark the place in the script where the If steps end. Everything you want in your If statement must be placed between If and End If.

5. In the Options section, click Specify to bring up the Specify Calculation dialog box. The If step uses the same formula builder you use to create a Calculation Field (see Chapter 4).

6. In the field list on the left, scroll to find your field (we're using Balance Due). Double-click to add it to the formula box (**Figure 8.3**).

7. Choose the greater than (>) symbol from the Operators scrolling list by double-clicking it.

continues on next page

8. Type a zero (0), then click OK (**Figure 8.4**).

The Script Definition dialog box now displays the highlighted If statement with its condition (**Figure 8.5**).

9. From the step list on the left, double-click the action you want performed. In this example, we chose Perform Script, because we want to run an existing print statement script we created (**Figure 8.6**). The new step is added below the If step. It's also indented from the left to show that it's inside the If step. This line is just a standard script command. (For more information about Perform Script, see Chapter 7.) Any script steps can be placed inside an If step—even another If step.

10. From Options, choose the script you want performed if there's a balance due (**Figure 8.7**). Since you don't have anything else you want the script to do if there's no balance due, the If statement is finished.

11. Click OK, then Done to close ScriptMaker.

✔ Tip

■ You can just type the condition in the formula box for a statement as simple as "Balance Due > 0". However, when you start creating more complicated scripts, or if your fields have somewhat long names, it's better to stick to selecting field names and operators, as well as functions, from the scrolling lists. Computer programs aren't very good at intuiting what you want. You must have a field that exactly matches what's in the conditional statement so that FileMaker can check its value. One of the hardest and most time-draining aspects of scripts is that they frequently won't work right simply because you didn't catch a typing error.

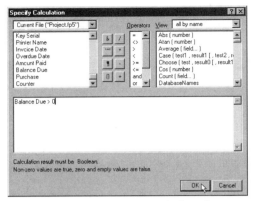

Figure 8.4 Type a zero manually in the formula builder.

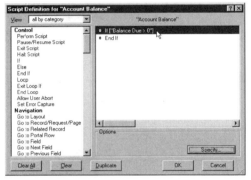

Figure 8.5 Your conditional statement is added automatically to the If statement brackets.

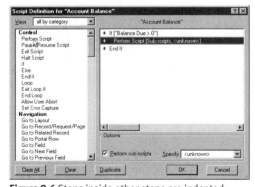

Figure 8.6 Steps inside other steps are indented.

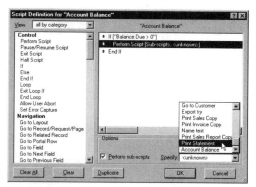

Figure 8.7 This step runs the sub-script "Print Statement."

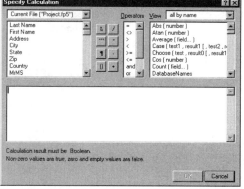

Figure 8.8 When you choose Specify, ScriptMaker brings up the Specify Calculation dialog box.

Using If with Else

Sometimes you want the script to do something when the answer to the If condition isn't "yes." You use an Else step within an If when you want the script to choose a different action when the If statement isn't true. Else steps are only executed if the condition is not True. Otherwise, they're ignored.

This script uses If and Else to move through the records of a database, changing data in the Paid field for each record until it reaches the last one.

To use If and Else to modify data:

1. Choose Scripts > ScriptMaker.

2. When the Define Scripts dialog box appears, type a name for the script (in this case Set Paid) and click Create.

3. The Script Definition window appears with the default script in the assembly window on the right. Click Clear All to delete the default steps.

4. From the Control category in the left window, double-click If.

5. In the Options section, click Specify to bring up the Specify Calculation dialog box (**Figure 8.8**).

6. In the field list on the left, scroll to find your field (we're using Balance Due). Double-click to add it to the formula box.

7. Choose the greater than (>) symbol from the Operators scrolling list by double-clicking it.

8. Type a zero (0), then click OK. The Script Definition dialog box now displays the highlighted If statement with its condition.

continues on next page

9. In the step list on the left, double-click the action you want performed. In this example, we chose Set Field from the Fields section (**Figure 8.9**). It replaces the contents of a field with whatever you choose.

10. In Options, click the Field (Windows)/ Specify Field (Mac) button (**Figure 8.10**).

11. When the Specify Field dialog box appears (**Figure 8.11**), choose the field name (in our example, we choose Paid). If you don't yet have the field you need, click Define Fields to create it. Click OK to close the box and return to the Script Definition window.

12. In Options, click the Specify button.

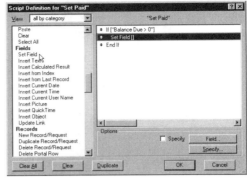

Figure 8.9 Choose Set Field to insert new information into an existing field.

The Specify check box *(for choosing a field)* ⌐

The Field (Windows)/ *Specify Field (Mac) button* *(for choosing a field)* ⌐

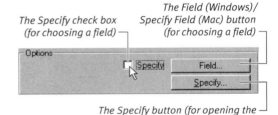

The Specify button (for opening the ⌐ *Specify Calculation dialog box)*

Figure 8.10 The Specify check box allows you to specify the field you want to change.

Figure 8.11 Choose or create the field you want in the Specify Field dialog box.

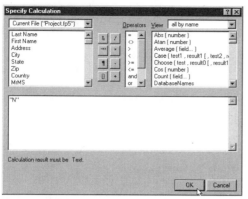

Figure 8.12 If there's a balance, Set Field marks the Paid field with an N for not paid.

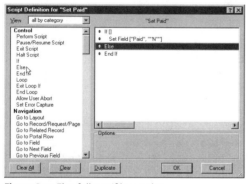

Figure 8.13 Else follows If in a script.

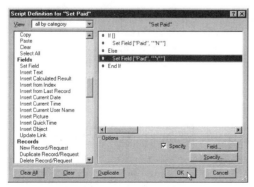

Figure 8.14 The finished If/Else script.

13. When the Specify Calculation window appears, click the quotes operator button (""), then type an **N** between the quotes. Click OK to close the dialog box (**Figure 8.12**).

At this point, your script checks to see if the balance in the account is more than zero. If it is, the script marks the Paid field with an N for not paid.

14. In the step list, double-click Else to add it to the assembly window (**Figure 8.13**).

15. Repeat Steps 9-12 above.

16. When the Specify Calculation window appears, click the quotes operator button (""), then type a **Y** between the quotes. Click OK to close the dialog box (**Figure 8.14**).

Now your script marks the Paid field with a Y for paid if there was no balance due.

17. Click OK, then Done to close ScriptMaker.

USING IF WITH ELSE

Commonly Used Status Functions

Although there are dozens of status functions in the function list, some of them are much more useful than others. These are some of our favorites, and are used frequently in scripts we create.

Date & Time

Status (CurrentDate)
The current date according to your computer.

Status (CurrentTime)
The current time according to your computer.

Script

Status (CurrentError)
The error code for the most recent error.

Status (CurrentMessageChoice)
A number which stands for one of three possible buttons a user can choose from an alert message. All three can be changed using the Show Message step in a script.

1= 1st Button (Default)
2= 2nd Button
3= 3rd Button

Status (CurrentScriptName)
The name of the script that's currently running.

Field & Layout

Status (CurrentFieldName)
The name of the active field.

Status (CurrentLayoutName)
The name of the current layout.

Status (CurrentPortalRow)
The number of the current portal row. If no portal is selected, this number will be 0 (zero).

Status (CurrentRepetitionNumber)
The number of the current repetition in a repeating field.

Database

Status (CurrentFileName)
The name of the current file.

Status (CurrentFoundCount)
The number of records in the current found set.

Status (CurrentRecordCount)
The number of records in the database.

Status (CurrentMode)
0= Browse Mode
1= Find Mode
2= Preview Mode
3= Printing in progress

Status (CurrentSortStatus)
0 = Unsorted
1= Sorted
2= Partially sorted

Multi-User

Status (CurrentMultiUserStatus)
0= single user
1= multi-user
2= multi-user from a guest computer or server.

Status (CurrentGroups)
The group (or groups) that the current user is a member of, based on the current password.

Status (CurrentUserName)
The name of the current FileMaker Pro user.

System Settings

Status (CurrentSystemVersion)
The version of the current operating system.

Status (CurrentPlatform)
1 = Macintosh
2 = Windows 95 or 98
-2 = Windows NT

The most recent version of FileMaker was released before Windows 2000.

Status (CurrentPrinterName)
The name of the current printer, printer type and network zone (Mac)/Port Name (Windows).

About Status Functions

Status functions are a special group of formulas that capture what's going on while you're working. They can peek at FileMaker's current settings and preferences, such as what mode it's in, what file is currently open or what layout is active. Status functions can also check out information about your computer, like what version of the OS you're running, what user is currently logged in or what the computer sees as the current date.

Being able to extract this type of data may initially seem pointless—or too advanced. Not so. For example, imagine that you wanted to write a script that would set different preferences or allow different levels of access to data depending on who is using the computer. Or you want to insert the current date into an invoice or statement layout. Only a status function can pry this information out of the computer and make it available to the script.

There's a generic status function in the Specify Calculation dialog box, but it's much more useful to use the specific function you need.

To see the available status functions:

1. Choose File > Define Fields.

2. When the Define Fields dialog box appears, input a field name and choose Calculation as the type. Click Create. Since this is just a test, you can use any field name.

3. When the Specify Calculation box dialog box appears, click the View drop-down menu, scroll down and select Status Functions. The list of specific status functions will take the place of all the generic functions.

Applying Status Functions

If you're having problems visualizing how these status functions might be used, here are some practical suggestions to start your imagination working:

Date and Time
Use date and time functions in scripts to time stamp changes and additions.

Current Message Choice
Make a user's choice the condition for an If/Else statement.

CurrentLayoutName
CurrentMode
CurrentUserName
Good for scripting custom navigation within a database. You can really fine-tune what each user sees and where they go in the database with these tools. CustomUserName is also great for identifying which user is using which of your scripts.

CurrentFoundCount
Use this function to determine whether or not a scripted Find had the desired results. If you use it in combination with Set Error Capture [On] it will enable a script to return a custom result for a scripted Find.

CurrentSystemVersion
CurrentPlatform
These can be invaluable if you have to adjust your scripts for older operating systems, for fine-tuning printing issues between Macs and Windows, or for keeping specialized FileMaker plug-ins straight on the different platforms.

Using Status Functions with If Steps

Combining a status function with a conditional step, we can create a script that automatically adds the current date to an invoice, calculates the net 30 date when it will become overdue, then prints the invoice. Before you create the script, remember to set the Print/Page Setup options for the invoice.

To date and print an invoice using status functions:

1. Choose Scripts > ScriptMaker.

2. When the Define Scripts dialog box appears (**Figure 8.15**), type a name for the script (in this case `Print Invoice`) and click Create.

3. The Script Definition dialog box will appear with the default script in the assembly window on the right. Click Clear All to delete the default steps.

4. From the Control category in the left window, double-click If.

5. In the Options section, click Specify to bring up the Specify Calculation dialog box. In the function list on the right, double-click the IsEmpty function (**Figure 8.16**).

   IsEmpty checks whatever field you put in the parentheses to see if there is data in it.

6. From the field list on the left, double-click Invoice Date. Click OK to close Specify Calculation.

   This section of the script checks the Invoice Data field to see if you have already entered anything in it (**Figure 8.17**).

7. In the Script Definition dialog box, scroll down to the Field category in the left window and double-click Set Field.

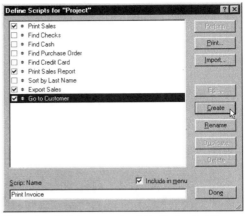

Figure 8.15 Script names should indicate what the script will do.

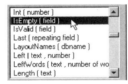

Figure 8.16
IsEmpty checks for data in a field.

Figure 8.17 IsEmpty checks to see if the record has an Invoice Date.

Figure 8.18 The fields in IsEmpty and the Set Field step must match.

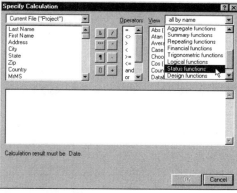

Figure 8.19 The View drop-down list lets you choose functions by category.

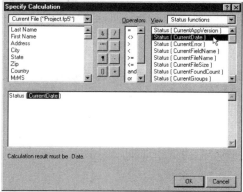

Figure 8.20 The Status(CurrentDate) function returns the computer's current date.

8. In Options, click the Specify check box.

9. When the Specify Field dialog box appears, choose the same field name you used in the If step. Click OK (**Figure 8.18**).

10. In Options, click the Field (Windows)/Specify Field (Mac) button.

11. When the Specify Calculation window appears, click the View drop-down menu and scroll down to choose Status Functions (**Figure 8.19**).

12. From the list of Status functions, double-click on Status(CurrentDate) (**Figure 8.20**). Click OK.

This portion of the script will check the computer's settings and enter the current date in the Invoice Date field.

13. The Set Field step in the script assembly window should be highlighted. Click the Duplicate button. A copy of the step appears below the original (**Figure 8.21**).

continues on next page

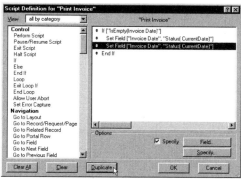

Figure 8.21 Since this step is almost the same as the previous, duplicating it is easier than creating it.

USING STATUS FUNCTIONS WITH IF STEPS

14. We need to edit this step so that it will check the status of a different field. In Options, click the Field button (**Figure 8.22**).

15. When the Specify Field dialog box appears, choose the field name (in our example, we choose Overdue Date). Click OK (**Figure 8.23**).

The second Set Field step now looks at a different field.

16. In Options, click the Specify button.

17. When the Specify Calculation window appears, click inside the formula box just after Status(CurrentDate) and type +30 (**Figure 8.24**). Click OK.

This script line (**Figure 8.25**) checks the status of the current date, adds thirty days to it, and inserts that date into the Overdue Date field.

18. In the script assembly window, click to select the End If step.

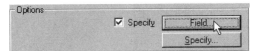

Figure 8.22 Click the Field button to edit a field you've previously specified.

Figure 8.23 The duplicated step needs to have a new field chosen.

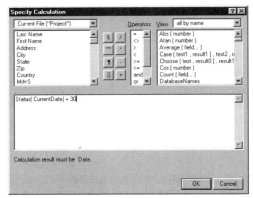

Figure 8.24 The Overdue Date field is set to thirty days after the Current Date.

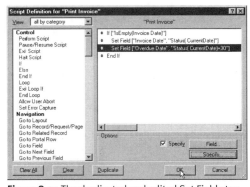

Figure 8.25 The duplicated and edited Set Field step.

USING STATUS FUNCTIONS WITH IF STEPS

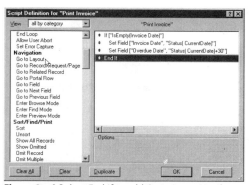

Figure 8.26 Select End If to add Go to Layout to the end of the script.

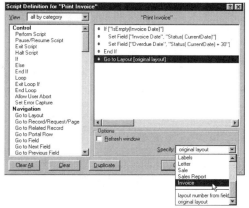

Figure 8.27 The script switches to the Invoice layout before printing.

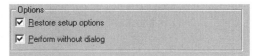

Figure 8.28 The Restore option will ensure that the invoice prints using the correct Page/Print Setup.

19. Scroll down to the Navigation category in the left window and double-click Go to Layout (**Figure 8.26**).

20. In the Options section, choose Invoice from the Specify drop-down list (**Figure 8.27**).

This step switches the mode from its current status to Layout, and chooses the Invoice layout.

21. Scroll down to the Sort/Find/Print category in the left window and double-click Print (Windows)/Page (Mac) Setup.

Leave the options checked (**Figure 8.28**).

22. In the left step window, double-click on Print.

continues on next page

USING STATUS FUNCTIONS WITH IF STEPS

23. In the left step window in the Navigation section, double-click on Go to Layout. Leave Specify set to "original layout" (**Figure 8.29**).

This last part of the script returns you to the original layout.

24. Click OK, then Done.

✔ Tip

■ There's a step called Insert Current Date that some people use instead of Set Field and Status(CurrentDate) (**Figure 8.30**). But Insert Current Date requires that the field where the date is entered be on the current layout. Set Field is a better choice because it works even if the field is not on the layout. Good script design makes the fewest assumptions about the database's current state.

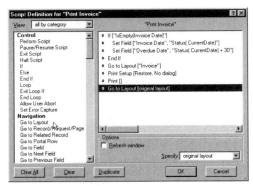

Figure 8.29 The last step in this script will return you to the layout where the script started.

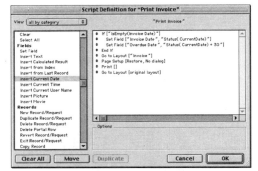

Figure 8.30 Insert Current Date is an alternative to Set Field with a status function.

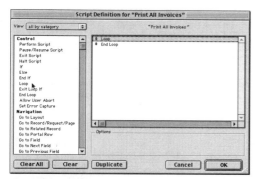

Figure 8.31 When you choose the Loop step, End Loop will be added automatically.

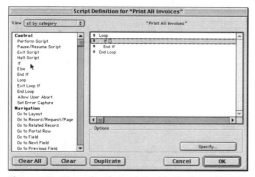

Figure 8.32 Since the If step is inside the loop, it will be executed for each loop.

Using Loop in a Script

If the whole purpose of scripting is to automate repetitious actions, the Loop step is probably the ultimate scripting command. Any steps you *nest* (create inside) in a Loop will continue until the loop runs out of records or you tell it to stop.

The script in "To date and print an invoice using status functions" prints invoices one record at a time. That's nice, but you still have to sit at your computer and run each record individually. Place the Print Invoice script inside a loop that prints automatically whenever it finds a balance in an account, and you can completely automate your invoicing process.

To use Loop to print invoices:

1. Choose Scripts > ScriptMaker.

2. When the Define Scripts dialog box appears, type a name for the script (in this case, Print All Invoices) and click Create.

3. The Script Definition dialog box will appear with the default script in the assembly window on the right. Click Clear All.

4. In the step window on the left, double-click Loop (**Figure 8.31**).

   As with If and End If, FileMaker automatically inserts both Loop and End Loop in the script assembly window.

5. In the left window, double-click If (**Figure 8.32**).

   Notice that If and End If are indented under the Loop step to indicate that they're running inside the Loop step.

6. In the Options section, click Specify.

continues on next page

7. When the Specify Calculation window appears, choose Balance Due from the field list on the left.

8. Click the > (greater than) operator button and type a zero (**Figure 8.33**). Click OK.

So far, this script looks to see if the Balance Due field has any data in it.

9. In the left window, double-click Perform Script.

Perform Script is indented one more level than the If statement, and two indents below Loop (**Figure 8.34**).

This structure is a visual clue to help you keep track of complicated nested scripts.

10. In the Options section, choose Print Invoice in the Specify drop-down list (**Figure 8.35**).

If there's a balance in the first record, FileMaker will follow the steps in the "Print Invoice" script.

11. To make sure that the next script steps are inserted after the If statement, click to select End If in the script assembly window.

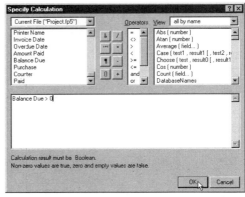

Figure 8.33 The Print Invoice script will only run if there is a balance greater than zero.

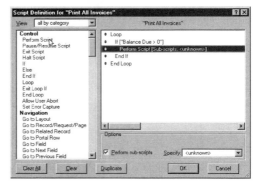

Figure 8.34 The Perform Script step is contained by both the Loop and the If steps.

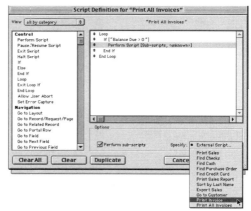

Figure 8.35 Rather than recreate the steps in the Print Invoice script, you can run it as a sub-script.

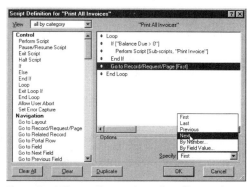

Figure 8.36 Choose Next so the script will go to the next record.

12. Scroll down to the Navigation category in the left window and double-click Go to Record/Request/Page.

13. In the Options section, click the "Exit after last" check box and choose Next in the Specify drop-down list (**Figure 8.36**). These options tell the script to go to the next record in the database until it comes to the last one.

14. Click OK, then Done.

✔ Tip

■ When creating a looping script with printing steps, remember to leave No Dialog chosen as the option in the Print command. Otherwise, the script will pause and ask you to click OK every time!

Using Counters to Control Loops

Just as the If step is made more flexible and dynamic by the addition of Else, so is looping improved by the Exit Loop If step. If you don't want a loop to continue through every record in your database (and lots of times you really don't!), Exit Loop If provides a way to target your loop to a specific number or group of records.

There are many ways to define your exit point, but one of the most elegant methods is with a counter. Counters do precisely that: You can set them to start at zero, or any other number you need. When it comes to loops, counters are particularly useful in keeping track of how many times a loop has run, allowing you to stop it after as few or as many iterations as you need. For example, in this script we use a counter with the Exit Loop If to print only ten invoices at a time.

To use a loop to print multiple invoices:

1. Choose Scripts > ScriptMaker.

2. When the Define Scripts dialog box appears, type a name for the script (in this case, Print Ten Invoices) and click Create.

3. The Script Definition dialog box will appear with the default script in the assembly window on the right. Click Clear All to delete the default steps.

4. In the Script Definition dialog box, scroll down to the Fields category in the left window and double-click Set Field.

5. In Options, click the Field (Windows)/ Specify Field (Mac) button.

6. When the Specify Field dialog box appears, click Define Fields (**Figure 8.37**).

Figure 8.37 You can define new fields when creating scripts.

Figure 8.38 Counter is a Global field with a Number data type.

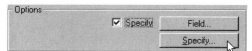

Figure 8.39 Choose Specify to access the Specify Calculation dialog box.

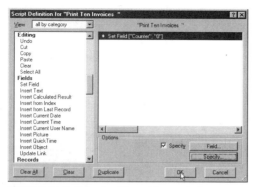

Figure 8.40 Counter must be set to zero before running the script.

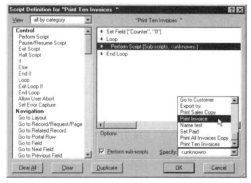

Figure 8.41 The sub-script Print Invoice will be executed in each loop.

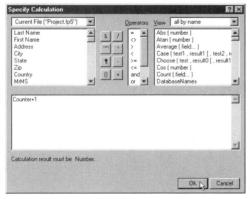

Figure 8.42 Counter is increased by 1 after each invoice is printed.

7. When the Define Fields dialog box appears, type Counter for the field name and choose Global as the Type. Click Create.

8. In the Options dialog box, choose Number from the Data type pop-up menu (**Figure 8.38**).

9. Click OK and then done.

10. Choose Counter from the list of fields in the Specify Fields dialog box, then click OK.

11. In Options, click the Specify button (**Figure 8.39**).

12. When the Specify Calculation window appears, type a zero (0) and click OK. You have a global counter field which will start counting from zero in each record it finds (**Figure 8.40**). In the left window, double-click Loop.

13. In the left window, double-click Perform Script.

14. In the Options section, choose Print Invoice from the Specify drop-down menu (**Figure 8.41**).

15. Scroll down to the Fields category in the left window and double-click on Set Field.

16. In Options, click the Field (Windows)/Specify Field (Mac) button. When the Specify Field dialog box appears, choose Counter. Click OK.

17. In Options, click the Specify button.

18. When the Specify Calculation window appears, scroll to Counter in the field list on the left and double-click to select it. Type +1 to the right of the field name. Click OK (**Figure 8.42**).

The script will go to the Counter field and add one to whatever number is in the field.

continues on next page

USING COUNTERS TO CONTROL LOOPS

19. In the left window, double-click Exit Loop If (**Figure 8.43**).

20. In the Options section, click Specify.

21. In the Specify Calculation dialog, scroll to Counter in the field list on the left and double-click to select it. Click > in the Operators list and type 10 (**Figure 8.44**). Click OK.

22. Click OK, then Done. The script will start by setting Counter to 0, print an invoice, add 1 to Counter and exit the loop (and script) after the tenth invoice.

✔ Tip

■ When a user makes an entry in a global field (or a script the user is running does) in a multi-user database, that value only appears in that user's database. Other users do not see the value and can use other values in the same field.

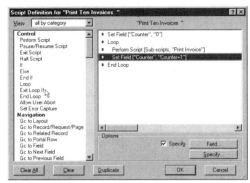

Figure 8.43 Choose Exit Loop If while the Set Field step is selected.

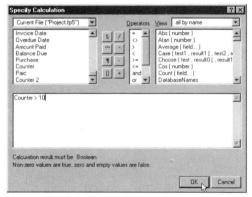

Figure 8.44 The Exit Loop tests to see if Counter has reached 10. If it has, the loop is exited.

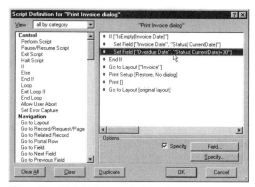

Figure 8.45 Select the step before the one you want to insert.

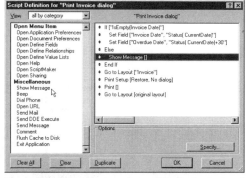

Figure 8.46 Show Message is used to display text and get input from the user.

Controlling Scripts with User Input

You can use the Show Message script step to prompt a user entry to control a script. The Message text will display text in a dialog box.

Using the Print Invoice script, we can add a step that checks whether there is an Invoice Date and, if there is, asks you if you want to print the invoice anyway. This will prevent unintentional duplicate invoices. You can include If steps within other If steps (*nested Ifs*). Just as steps in an If are run only when the preceding If is true, a nested If is evaluated only when the first If is true.

If the user chooses the Print button, the script will execute the rest of the steps. If the user chooses Don't Print, the script will stop.

To control scripts with user input:

1. Choose Scripts > ScriptMaker.

2. In the Define Scripts dialog box, click the script you want to add user controls to. In our case, it's the Print Invoice script. Give it a slightly different name and click Create (which makes a new script), then click Edit.

   Keeping your original script intact can be very useful if you make a mistake when you edit it.

3. When the Script Definition dialog box appears, click the second Set Field step in the assembly window (**Figure 8.45**).

4. In the step window on the left, double-click Else.

5. Scroll down to the Miscellaneous category in the left window and double-click Show Message (**Figure 8.46**).

6. In the Options section, click Specify.

continues on next page

7. The Specify Message dialog box opens (**Figure 8.47**).

This dialog box will generate a customized message and buttons in your operating system's standard format. The dialog box can have up to three labeled buttons.

8. In Message Text, type This record looks like it's already been invoiced. Do you want to print another copy?

9. In Button Captions, type Print in the First (default) box and type Don't Print in the Second box (**Figure 8.48**). Click OK.

When you run the script, these choices will generate your custom message **Figure 8.49**).

10. In the step list on the left, double-click If.

11. In the Options section, click Specify.

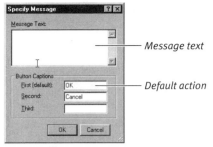

Message text

Default action

Figure 8.47 You can enter text to create a customized message and set of buttons. OK and Cancel are the default choices, but you can replace them with custom text.

Figure 8.48 Designate your message choices in the Specify Message dialog box.

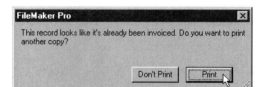

Figure 8.49 This custom dialog box will display when you run the script.

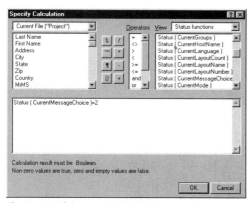

Figure 8.50 If the user clicks the second button, Status(CurrentMessageChoice) will equal 2.

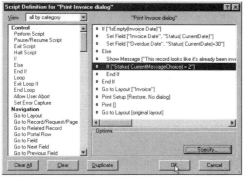

Figure 8.51 The "2" in this step refers to the second button choice in the dialog box.

12. When the Specify Calculation box dialog box appears, click the View drop-down menu and scroll down to Status Functions. Click to select it and display the detailed status functions list. Double-click on Status(CurrentMessageChoice). Click to the right of it in the formula box and type =2 (**Figure 8.50**). Click OK.

    This If step looks at which button you clicked. If you chose the second (don't print) button, it ends the script without printing anything (**Figure 8.51**).

13. Click OK, then OK again to keep your print settings. Click Done to finish.

    When you run this script, FileMaker will look for an Invoice Date and print an invoice if it doesn't find one. If there is an Invoice Date, the alert dialog will ask if you want to print a second one.

✔ Tips

- Although they're terribly addictive, try to avoid the temptation of too many nested If statements. They become next to impossible to follow in the script editor, guaranteeing lots of wasted time if you have to troubleshoot them.

- The first button in a Show Message custom dialog box is always the default choice. If you press Enter instead of clicking a button when the message box is displayed, the Status(CurrentMessageChoice) will react as if you chose the default button. Protect your users from unpleasant accidents by choosing the least destructive option as the default choice.

Customizing Documents with If Steps

One of the things small businesses and free agents regularly do is generate repetitive documents. Whether it be contracts, form letters or promotions, you build a "customized" document by combining relevant paragraphs of boilerplate text and specific names and addresses from a database. You end up keeping several versions of the same basic stuff around, and then you have to manually edit each one to customize it for a specific mailing or legal document.

Although you might automatically reach for a word processing program for these kinds of projects, think again. You can crank up FileMaker's scripting muscle to generate your documents with far less pain. It's true that the set-up involves several separate tasks and will take a little time, but if you deal frequently with contracts (or any other text-based form with several modular variations), you'll find the result worth the effort.

The document script has some prerequisites before it will work its magic. First, you need several global fields to hold the boilerplate text paragraphs and modular choices. The text itself can be typed directly into the fields, or cut-and-pasted from any existing text document. Second, you need to create two layouts: one to hold your mix-and-match templates, and another formatted as a finished document. We'll create the fields and layouts before creating the script to put it all together.

To build the formatted document efficiently, see "To create a label field" on page 57 of Chapter 4. We will use this calculated field to include a complete name and address field on the document the script creates.

Once you have your building blocks, you can design a script that constructs a document by combining the boilerplate text with the choices you make from the template elements.

To create modular text fields:

1. Choose File > Define Fields.

2. When the Define Fields dialog box appears, type Paragraph 1 in the Field Name box, choose Global as the field type and click Create (**Figure 8.52**).

3. In the Options dialog box, choose Text as the data type and click OK (**Figure 8.53**). This creates a field to hold one paragraph of modular text.

Figure 8.52 Paragraph 1 is a Global field that will contain the text of the first boilerplate paragraph.

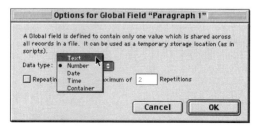

Figure 8.53 This Global field will contain text.

Figure 8.54 Increase the name of each paragraph by one as you add them.

Figure 8.55 There should be as many Include Paragraph fields as there are Paragraph fields.

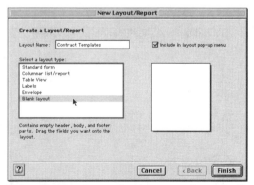

Figure 8.56 Use the template layout to select and edit the contents of the Paragraph fields.

4. Repeat Steps 2 and 3 for as many additional modular paragraphs as you need.

In our example, we create a total of four global fields, named Paragraph 1 through 4 (**Figure 8.54**).

5. In the Define Fields dialog box, type Include Paragraph 1 in the Field Name box, choose Text as the field type and click Create. This creates a field to use as a check box for choosing Paragraph 1.

6. Repeat step 5 to create as many check box fields as you just created fields for the modular paragraphs.

In our example, we create a total of four text fields, named Include Paragraph 1 through 4 (**Figure 8.55**).

7. We need one field to contain the compiled text that the script creates. Type the document's name in the Field Name box, choose Text for the field type and click Create. Click Done to close the Define Fields box.

In our example, we're building a contract, so our field name for the compiled text is Contract.

To create a template layout:

1. Choose View > Layout Mode (Ctrl+L/ Command-L).

2. Choose Layouts > New Layout (Ctrl+N/ Command-N).

3. In the New Layout dialog box, type a name for the layout in the Layout Name box and select Blank layout for the layout type (**Figure 8.56**). In our example, we use the name Contract Templates. Click Finish.

4. In the blank layout, drag the Header and Footer tabs up so they disappear, then drag the Body tab down to fill the window.

continues on next page

5. Drag the Field tool onto the layout to bring up the Specify Field dialog box. Double-click Include Paragraph 1 in the field name list.

6. Click the Include Paragraph 1 field on the layout.

7. Choose Format > Field Format (Ctrl/Command-Shift-M) to access the Field Format dialog box.

8. In the Style section, select the second radio button and choose Check boxes from the drop-down menu (**Figure 8.57**).

9. In the "using value list" portion of the same radio button, choose Define Value Lists (**Figure 8.58**).

10. When the Define Value Lists dialog box appears, click New.

11. In the Edit Value List dialog box, type Y as the Value List Name, and type Y in the Use custom values box (**Figure 8.59**). Click OK.

    The single value in the Value List will display on the layout as one check box.

12. Click Done in the Define Value Lists dialog box, then click OK.

13. On the layout, resize the Include Paragraph 1 field so that only the check box is visible (**Figure 8.60**).

    The check box field you've just created will allow you to include the first paragraph of text when the script runs.

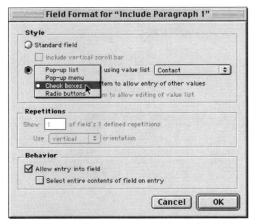

Figure 8.57 Use Check boxes to tell the script which paragraphs to include.

Figure 8.58 You'll need to define a Value List for the check boxes.

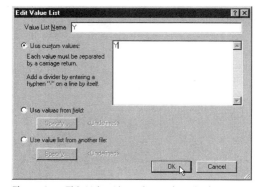

Figure 8.59 This Value List only needs a single value, "Y".

Figure 8.60 You only need to see the check box for this field.

Figure 8.61 Edit the Paragraph fields on this layout.

14. Drag the Field tool onto the layout to bring up the Specify Field dialog box. Double-click Paragraph 1 in the field name list (**Figure 8.61**).

15. Resize this field to fit the paragraph, then arrange the label, check box field and the Paragraph 1 field as you'd like on the page (**Figure 8.62**).

16. Repeat steps 6 through 15 for as many paragraph fields as you created (or see the tip below) (**Figure 8.63**).

17. Choose View > Browse Mode.

18. Enter the text for each paragraph of the document in the respective Paragraph fields. You can type this text in, or paste it in from an existing text document.

We now have a group of modular paragraphs that we can mix and match to create a customized document when we run our script.

continues on next page

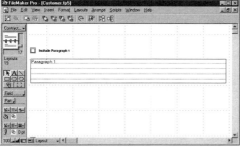

Figure 8.62 Make the field large enough for the paragraph text.

Figure 8.63 Add all of the Paragraph and Include fields to the layout.

CUSTOMIZING DOCUMENTS WITH IF STEPS

✔ Tips

- Although you *can* create the check boxes and paragraph fields separately, frankly that's pretty tedious. It's faster to Shift-click the Include Paragraph 1 field, its label and the Paragraph 1 field to select them all, then hold down Ctrl+Alt (Windows)/Command-Option (Mac) as you drag the mouse (**Figure 8.64**). Arrange the duplicated layout items below the first group on the layout. Double-click each layout item and select the next field name in the Specify Field dialog box to match the next paragraph (**Figure 8.65**). Remember to edit the paragraph numbers on the labels as well.

- If you're creating a boilerplate document that people other than yourself might use, it's a good idea to add some instructions to the template layout (**Figure 8.66**).

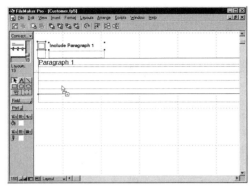

Figure 8.64 Ctrl/Option dragging a field retains the size and formatting in the copied field.

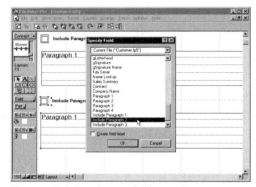

Figure 8.65 Select the next field name in sequence.

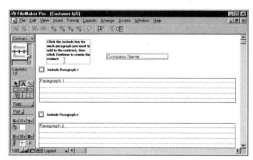

Figure 8.66 Add text to explain how to use the layout.

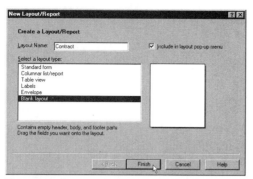

Figure 8.67 The compiled layout will contain the assembled text.

Figure 8.68 Don't add field labels, since this layout will be printed.

To create a layout for the compiled document:

1. Choose View > Layout Mode.

2. Choose Layouts > New Layout Ctrl+N/Command-N).

3. In the New Layout dialog box, type a name in the Layout Name box and select Blank layout for the layout type. Click Finish (**Figure 8.67**).

4. In the blank layout, drag the Header and Footer tabs up so they disappear, then drag the Body tab down to fill the window.

5. Drag the Field tool onto the layout. In the Specify Field dialog box, uncheck the Create Field Label check box and double-click Label (**Figure 8.68**).

6. Ctrl+Alt (Windows)/Command-Option (Mac) drag the Label field to the layout to duplicate it. In the Specify Field dialog box, choose the field you created to hold your compiled document (**Figure 8.69**).

continues on next page

Figure 8.69 Double-click to specify another field.

CUSTOMIZING DOCUMENTS WITH IF STEPS

7. Resize the fields to fit their text (**Figure 8.70**).

8. Click the Text tool and add any additional text that you want to appear on the document when it's printed (**Figure 8.71**).

To create a modular document script:

1. Choose Scripts > ScriptMaker.

2. Type a script name in the Script Name box and click Create.

We use Create Contract, because that's what we're doing in our example.

3. The Script Definition dialog box will appear with the default script in the assembly window on the right. Click Clear All to delete the default steps.

4. In the step listing on the left, scroll down to the Navigation section and double-click Enter Browse Mode.

5. In the Navigation section of the step listing, double-click Go to Layout. In Options, choose your template layout from the drop-down list (**Figure 8.72**).

When the script runs, this step will bring you to the layout we created in "To create a template layout" on page 169.

6. In the step listing, double-click Pause/Resume Script.

This step halts the script, allowing you to choose which paragraphs to include.

7. In the Field section of the step listing, double-click Set Field. In Options, click the Field (Windows)/Specify Field (Mac) button and choose the compiled text field (in our example, Contract) from the Specify Field dialog box by double-clicking it.

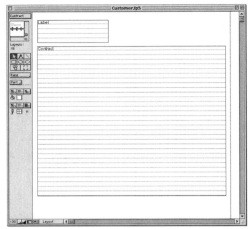

Figure 8.70 The fields need to be large enough for all of the text.

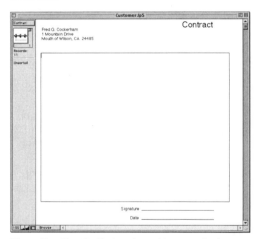

Figure 8.71 Use the Text tool to add text to the layout.

Figure 8.72 The script will bring you to the template layout.

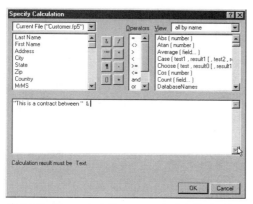

Figure 8.73 In a calculation, you put printable text in quotes.

Figure 8.74 The Introductory text will include the full name of the customer.

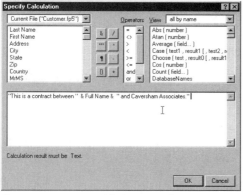

Figure 8.75 Enter *and* with the name of your company in quotes.

8. If you want to include the name of a person from a database within the text, click the Specify button to bring up the Specify Calculation dialog box.

In our example, we're creating a contract, so we'll create a calculation to insert a name in the right place in the contract text.

9. Click the quotes operator. Inside the quotes, type your opening text (in our case, we use "This is a contract between") followed by a space at the end of the phrase. Click to the right outside the quotes and then click the ampersand (&) operator button (**Figure 8.73**).

10. In the field list on the left, double-click the Full Name field. Click the ampersand button again (**Figure 8.74**).

The Full Name field is a calculation field that combines the First Name, Last Name and Middle Initial fields into one. See Chapter 4 for more on calculation fields.

11. Click the quotes operator button and type *and* between the quotes. (There's a space before and after the and)

After the space, we've typed the name of the company followed by a period to complete the typical contract phrase (**Figure 8.75**).

continues on next page

CUSTOMIZING DOCUMENTS WITH IF STEPS

12. Go to the right of the quotes, click the ampersand button and the quotes button. Click the paragraph button (**Figure 8.76**). Click OK to return to the Script Definition window.

This complex-looking field is just a text line that inserts a name from the database in the right place in a sentence.

13. In the step listing on the left, double-click If, then in Options, click Specify.

14. In the Specify Calculation dialog box, double-click the Include Paragraph 1 field.

15. Type =Y and click OK (**Figure 8.77**).

16. Double-click Set Field.

17. In Options, click the Field (Windows)/ Specify Field (Mac) button to bring up the Specify Field dialog box, then double-click Contract in the list.

18. In Options, click the Specify button to bring up the Specify Calculation dialog box. Double-click Contract in the field list on the left.

19. Click the ampersand button, then double-click the Paragraph 1 field (**Figure 8.78**).

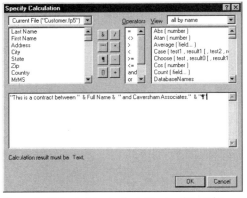

Figure 8.76 The finished calculation combines the text entered with the contents of the Full Name field to create the opening paragraph of a contract.

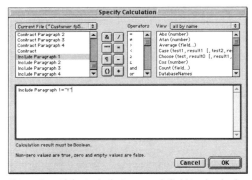

Figure 8.77 If the Include Paragraph field is checked, the contents of the field is actually "Y".

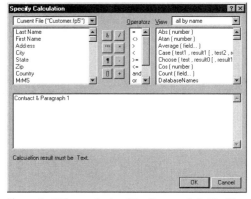

Figure 8.78 The contents of the Paragraph field will be added to the field holding the compiled text.

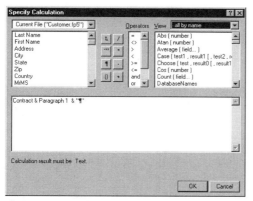

Figure 8.79 You add a paragraph marker to space down to the next paragraph.

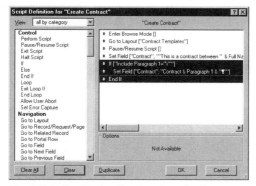

Figure 8.80 Duplicating the steps is easier than adding them manually.

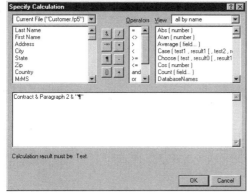

Figure 8.81 Change the number to indicate the second paragraph.

20. Click the ampersand button, then the quotes button. Click between the quotes and then click the paragraph button (**Figure 8.79**). Click OK to return to the Script Definition window.

This If step adds the first paragraph if you check it in the template layout.

21. In the script assembly window, click the If step, hold down the Shift key and click End If. Click the Duplicate button (**Figure 8.80**).

22. Double-click on the duplicate If step. When the Specify Calculation dialog box appears, change the 1 to 2, then click OK.

23. Click on the duplicate Set Field step. In Options, click Specify. When the Specify Calculation dialog box appears, change the 1 to 2, then click OK (**Figure 8.81**).

continues on next page

24. Repeat Steps 22 and 23 for as many additional paragraphs as you created. In our example, we do this for numbers 3 and 4 (**Figure 8.82**).

25. In the step listing on the left, double-click Go to Layout. In Options, choose the layout for the compiled document (in our case, Contract) in the Specify drop-down list. Click OK and then Done to finish.

When you run the script, it goes to the template layout and waits for you to make choices. It finishes by switching to the second layout, where it compiles your choices into a text document. You can make additional changes to the text before printing.

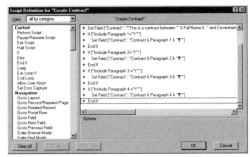

Figure 8.82 Add and modify a set of Ifs for each paragraph in the contract.

EXTENDING THE INTERFACE WITH SCRIPTS

Although you're pretty comfortable with FileMaker, you may not be the only person who uses your files. Other people may not be as savvy as you are, or may be such occasional users that they never memorize the FileMaker commands. You can make it easier for others to work with your files by creating a custom interface for them.

This may seem a little daunting. After all, real interface design is pretty challenging, since it involves both graphics and programming skills. But you don't have to have strong skills in either of these areas to create a mini-interface of common tasks in FileMaker. Scripts and buttons make it easy to create navigation bars, buttons and menus to insulate others from commands—and also protect your database from well-intentioned errors. Even if everyone who uses the database is a FileMaker whiz, they'll appreciate these shortcuts. Clicking a single button is always easier than accessing one (or more) menu commands.

Making a Find Layout with a Script

Because setting up a Find request takes time and typing, you'll frequently find yourself creating scripts that hold your typical search criteria. But you can't always predict what the criteria will be, although you might be able to predict the category. For example, every once in a while you may want to print out a record of your receivables. For those occasions you can create a generic date-search script with its own layout that generates a report when it's done. Once you have the script, you can run it from the menu bar, or from any layout that contains a script button you create.

To create a layout for searching:

1. If the script you are creating requires a Sort, perform the Sort. If this script will use a Print command, set the Print/Page Setup to the desired settings.

2. Choose View > Layout Mode (Ctrl+L/Command-L).

3. Choose Layouts > New Layout (Ctrl+N/ Command-N). In the New Layout dialog box, type a name for the layout. For this example, we'll use Date Find.

4. Choose Blank layout as the layout type and click Finish (**Figure 9.1**).

5. Drag the Header and Footer parts up until they disappear, since we only need the Body part.

6. Drag the Field tool onto the layout. From the Specify Field dialog box that appears, choose your date field. Here, we add Sale Date (**Figure 9.2**).

7. Using the Text tool, add directions on how to use the layout and arrange the text and field on the layout page (**Figure 9.3**).

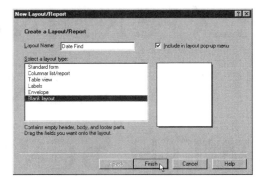

Figure 9.1 Since only one field will be used on this layout, choose the Blank layout.

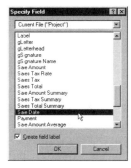

Figure 9.2 Choose the field for the Find criteria in the Specify Field dialog box.

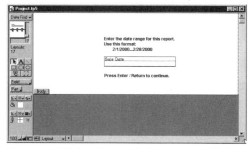

Figure 9.3 Add directions to the layout to explain how to use it.

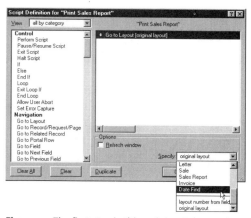

Figure 9.4 The first step in this script switches to the Date Find layout.

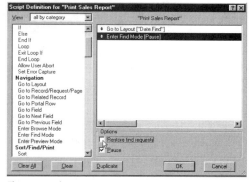

Figure 9.5 The script pauses to allow you to enter the Find criteria.

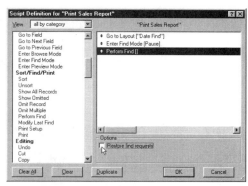

Figure 9.6 Since you'll enter new Find criteria each time, don't use the Restore option.

Next we'll create the script to do the Find request and print the result.

8. Choose Scripts > ScriptMaker. In the Define Scripts dialog box, type a name for the script. (We use Print Sales Report.) Click Create.

9. When the Script Definition dialog box appears, delete the default script in the assembly window by clicking Clear All.

10. From the step list on the left, double-click Go to Layout.

11. In Options, choose the layout you just created from the Specify drop-down list (**Figure 9.4**).

12. From the Navigation section in the step list on the left, double-click Enter Find Mode.

13. In Options, uncheck the Restore find requests box. Leave the Pause box checked (**Figure 9.5**).

Since you will choose different dates each time the script runs, we don't want to use the Restore option. The Pause option makes the script wait for your input before continuing.

14. From Sort/Find/Print in the step list on the left, double-click Perform Find. Uncheck the Restore find requests box (**Figure 9.6**).

continues on next page

15. If you want to use a Sort, double-click Sort in the list of steps and leave the Restore sort order box checked (**Figure 9.7**).

16. From the step list on the left, double-click Go to Layout.

17. In Options, choose the layout you want the found set to appear in from the Specify drop-down list (**Figure 9.8**).

18. From Sort/Find/Print in the step list on the left, double-click Print Setup (Page Setup on the Mac). Leave the Restore setup options and Perform without dialog boxes checked (**Figure 9.9**).

This step will set the Print/Page Setup options for the printing in the next step.

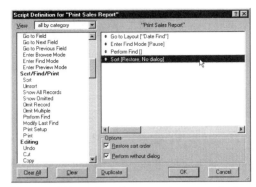

Figure 9.7 If the script will use a sort, you can check the Restore option.

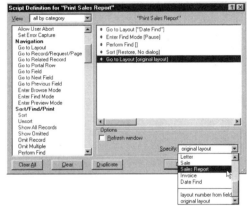

Figure 9.8 This script will switch to the Sales Report layout before printing.

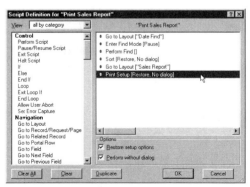

Figure 9.9 The Print/Page Setup with the Restore option will create the correct print settings.

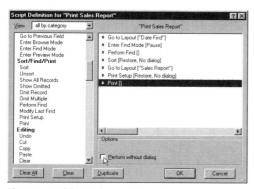

Figure 9.10 If the Perform without dialog box is checked, you won't be prompted before printing.

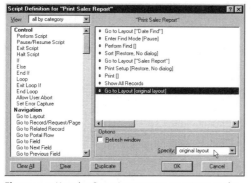

Figure 9.11 Use the Go to Layout step to return to the layout you were viewing when you ran the script.

19. From the step list on the left, double-click Print. If you want to see the Print dialog box, uncheck the Perform without dialog box (**Figure 9.10**).

20. From the step list on the left, double-click Show All Records.

This will reset the database to All Records after you've finished printing the found set.

21. From the step list on the left, double-click Go to Layout. Leave the options untouched (**Figure 9.11**).

This step will return you the layout from which the script was run.

22. Click OK, then Done.

Creating Script Buttons

Although you can run any script from the Script menu list, it's a better idea to use script buttons. Naturally, it's easier to click once than to click, drag and select. But script buttons are more than a lazy way to save a couple of seconds. For one thing, it's easy to forget which script belongs with a layout. And if other people use your database they could make a remarkable mess of it by running the wrong script at the wrong time.

To create a button for a script:

1. If you're not already there, enter Layout Mode and switch to the layout where you want to place the button.

2. Click the Button tool (**Figure 9.12**).

3. Dragging the cursor on the layout creates the button and brings up the Specify Button dialog box. From the list on the left, click Perform Script.

4. From Options, choose the script name from the Specify drop-down list and click OK (**Figure 9.13**).

5. The button will appear on the layout with the text cursor flashing (**Figure 9.14**). Type a descriptive label, then select the text and format it as desired.

6. Switch to Browse Mode and click the new button to test the script.

✔ Tips

- You're not limited to the default look of a FileMaker button. The tools used for creating graphics can also be used to change the thickness or color of the lines and the color or fill pattern of a button.

- If you use a graphic element to create a button (instead of the Button tool), click on the graphic and choose Format > Button to specify what the button does.

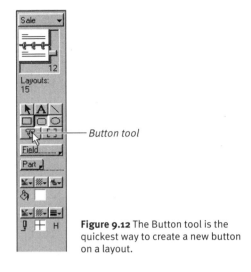

Figure 9.12 The Button tool is the quickest way to create a new button on a layout.

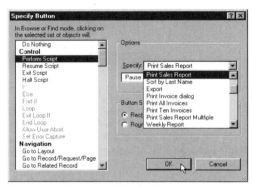

Figure 9.13 After you add the button to the layout, specify the action the button will perform.

Button in progress

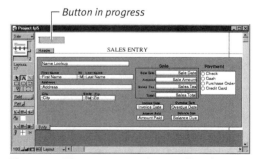

Figure 9.14 When you create a button, FileMaker automatically switches to the Text tool for input.

About Buttons

There are many ways to make buttons for your interface. The easiest is to just use the Button tool, which does a reasonable job of making simple text buttons with geometric shapes. You can also use pre-made art. Earlier versions of FileMaker included sample graphic buttons (**Figure 9.15**), but unfortunately FileMaker 5 doesn't. If you have an older version of FileMaker, you can still use these samples in the new version. In addition, you'll find contact information in Appendix A for pre-made button sets that you can download.

If you own a graphics program and are artistically inclined, you can design unique button icons. Intelligently designed graphical elements can enhance a button's usefulness. A printer icon is much more universally recognized than text that says "Print."

If you decide to make custom graphics for your FileMaker databases, follow the same guidelines you would if you were creating them for the Internet. Buttons that use many colors, are very big or complex take longer to display on the screen, and a lot longer to open on a networked multiuser database. Each time the user switches screens, the local computer needs to download the layout elements from the server and redraw them.

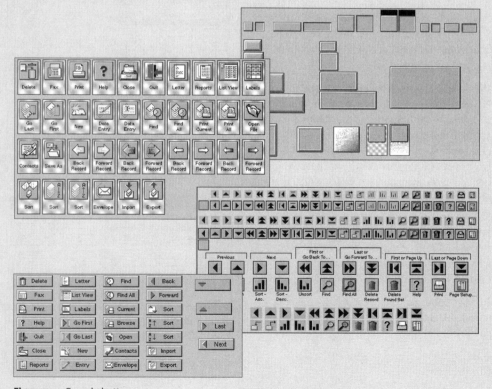

Figure 9.15 Sample buttons.

Deleting Records in a Related File

When you create records using a portal (See Chapter 6, About Portals), you may want to be able to delete specific records (portal rows) in the other file. For example, if a customer cancels an order, you'll need to remove the entry from the sales database. Rather than going to the related file and searching for the record to delete, you can create a button to delete the record without leaving the first file.

To delete records in a related file:

1. Go to the layout that contains the portal. Choose View > Layout Mode (Ctrl+L/Command-L).

2. Double-click the portal. When the Portal Setup dialog box appears, make sure that the "Allow deletion of portal records" box is checked (**Figure 9.16**). Click OK.

3. While in the portal, follow the steps in 'To create a button for a script" on page 184, but in the Specify Button dialog box, scroll down to the Records section and choose Delete Portal Row (**Figure 9.17**). Do not check Perform without dialog because you want to be able to cancel the choice if you've made a mistake.

    When you click the button a dialog box appears. If you click Delete, the portal row and its related record will be deleted from the other database. If you click Cancel, it won't be.

4. At the flashing cursor, type X (the universal icon for Delete). To add emphasis, make the X bold (**Figure 9.18**).

5. Choose View > Browse Mode (Ctrl+B/Command-B).

Figure 9.16
The portal must be set to allow deletion of rows.

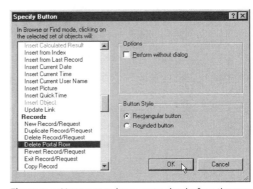

Figure 9.17 You want to have a warning before the row is deleted, so leave the Perform without dialog option unchecked.

Delete button

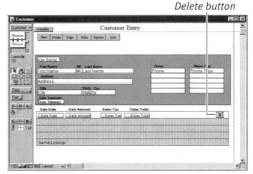

Figure 9.18 The bold X gives you a visual cue as to what the button does.

— Delete button

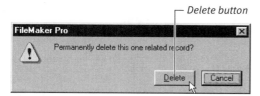

Figure 9.19 The row will not be deleted unless you confirm the choice.

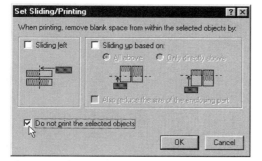

Figure 9.20 If a layout element is formatted with the "Do not print the selected objects" option on, it will appear in Browse Mode but not in Preview Mode or on printouts.

6. Test the button by clicking it in any row that you want to delete. The warning dialog box will appear to confirm the deletion (**Figure 9.19**).

✔ Tips

■ If the layout you put a button on is one you use for printing, the button will print out too. To hide the button when you print, switch to Layout Mode and select the button. Choose Format > Sliding/Printing. Click the "Do not print the selected objects" check box and then OK (**Figure 9.20**). The button will appear on the layout but won't appear on printouts.

■ Add a series of buttons to a layout, either grouped vertically along the left side (**Figure 9.21**) or horizontally along the top (**Figure 9.22**), to create a button bar. Put this group of buttons on the layout you use most to speed up access to other layouts and scripts. You can put a button on those other layouts that switches back to the main layout.

Figure 9.21 Buttons can be grouped vertically along the left side of the layout.

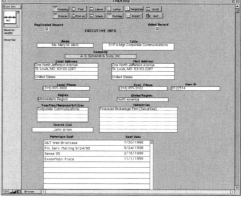

Figure 9.22 If the layout will not scroll, you can place the buttons in a row at the top of page.

Creating a Main Menu Layout

If you have a really large or complex database with several files and dozens of layouts, the simple task of navigating from one place to the next can become difficult. A button bar can help, but once your database gets really cumbersome, all the buttons you need will take up too much space on a layout—space you need for real work. When this happens, you can create a Main Menu layout that contains only buttons. The buttons will take you to the most important layouts (like Data Entry) or execute scripts that search or print reports. Each of the other layouts in the database need contain only one button that returns you to the Main Menu.

To create a Main Menu layout:

1. Choose View > Layout Mode (Ctrl+L/Command-L).

2. Choose Layouts > New Layout (Ctrl+N/Command-N).

3. In the New Layout dialog box, type a name for the layout. (We use Main Menu.) Choose Blank layout as the layout type (**Figure 9.23**). Click Finish.

4. Drag the Header and Footer parts up until they disappear, since we only need the Body part, then drag the Body tab down to make room for the buttons you're going to add.

5. Follow the steps in "To create a button for a script" on page 184 to add a button to the layout.

6. Select the new button. Holding down the Ctrl/Option key, drag to duplicate the button, changing the labels and scripts for each one (**Figure 9.24**). Repeat this step as many times as you need to create the total number of buttons for the layouts and scripts you use frequently.

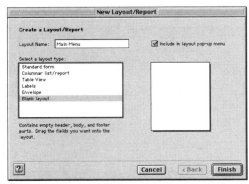

Figure 9.23 Since the Main Menu will only contain buttons, begin with a blank layout.

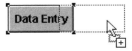

Figure 9.24 Ctrl/Option dragging allows you to create one button and then duplicate it, retaining its size and formatting.

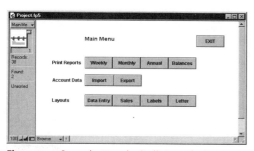

Figure 9.25 Group buttons logically to make it easy to use them later.

Figure 9.26 Choose the layout you want to go to when you click the button.

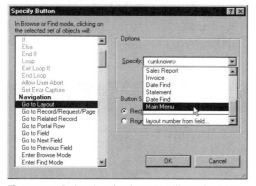

Figure 9.27 Scripts in other layouts will run the Go to Main Menu script.

7. Arrange the buttons on the page and add labels and headings. It's a good idea to group functions logically so you won't waste time later reading every button to find the one you want (**Figure 9.25**).

You now have a layout with buttons that link you around your database. All that's left is to create a script you can use to link your other layouts back to the Main Menu.

8. Choose Scripts > ScriptMaker. In the Define Scripts dialog box, type a name for the script. (We use Go to Main Menu.) Click Create.

9. When the Script Definition dialog box appears, delete the default script in the assembly window by clicking Clear All.

10. From the step list on the left, double-click Go to Layout.

11. In Options, choose Main Menu from the Specify drop-down list (**Figure 9.26**). Click OK, then Done.

12. On layouts in the same database file as the Main Menu, follow the steps in "To create a button for a script" on page 184 to add a button to the layout.

13. In the Specify Button dialog box, select Go to Layout from the list on the left and Main Menu from the Specify drop-down list in Options (**Figure 9.27**). Label the button Main Menu.

14. Repeat this step for as many layouts as you need to be linked to the Main Menu.

Linking to the Main Menu

If you create a Main Menu, you quickly discover its fatal weakness. You can almost instantaneously jump from the Main Menu to someplace else, but getting back is another story. To avoid confusion, you should also provide easy access back from the linking layouts, especially those in different databases than where the Main Menu itself is placed.

To link to Main Menu from layouts in different files:

1. Go to an external file that you want to link to from the Main Menu. Choose Scripts > ScriptMaker.

2. In the Define Scripts dialog box, type a name for the script. We use Go to Main Menu. Click Create.

3. When the Script Definition dialog box appears, delete the default script in the assembly window by clicking Clear All.

4. From the step list on the left, double-click Perform Script.

5. In the Specify drop-down list, choose External Script (**Figure 9.28**).

6. In the Specify External Script dialog box, click the Change File button (**Figure 9.29**).

7. When the Open File dialog box appears, navigate to the file with the Main Menu layout and double-click to select it.

8. In the Specify External Script dialog box, choose the Go to Main Menu script from the drop-down list of scripts in the external file (**Figure 9.30**). Click OK, OK again and then Done.

9. Follow the steps in "To create a button for a script" on page 184 to add a button to the layout in the external file. In the Specify Button dialog box, select Perform Script from the list on the left and choose the Go to Main Menu script (**Figure 9.31**).

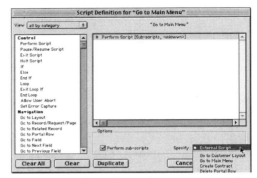

Figure 9.28 Set the Perform script step to run a script in another file.

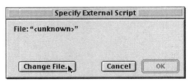

Figure 9.29 You must specify the file that contains the external script.

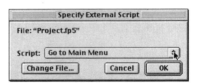

Figure 9.30 Specify the script to run in the other file.

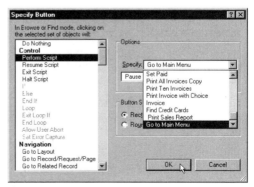

Figure 9.31 To switch to a particular layout in another file, you must perform a script.

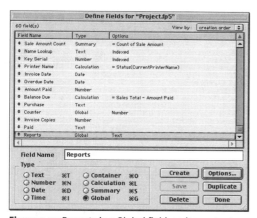

Figure 9.32 Reports is a Global field, so its contents are the same in every record.

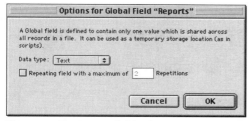

Figure 9.33 The Reports field will contain text.

Figure 9.34 Specify Reports when you add the field to the layout.

Running Scripts from Fields

Three or four buttons are efficient, but as you add more buttons your layout will look (and feel) cluttered and cramped. You'll be back where you started, having to negotiate too many chaotic choices. Although you could make a Main Menu page, not all databases lend themselves to this solution. If you have a database with many reports, for example, you might be better off creating one field with a drop-down list of choices.

Before you can create this script, you'll need a global field formatted as a drop-down list, and a list of scripts you want to use for the value list.

To make a formatted global field:

1. Choose File > Define Fields.

2. In the Define Fields dialog box, type a name for the field (we use Reports). Choose Global for the field type (**Figure 9.32**). Click Create.

3. When the Options dialog box appears, choose Text as the Data type, then Click OK (**Figure 9.33**). Click Done.

4. This field will automatically be added to your layout. Next we'll create a Value List of script names to display in the field.

5. Go to the layout where you want to place this button. Choose View > Layout Mode (Ctrl+L/Command-L).

6. Drag the field tool onto the layout. Choose Reports in the Specify Field (**Figure 9.34**). Click on the Reports field and choose Format > Field Format (Ctrl+Shift+M/Command-Shift-M).

continues on next page

RUNNING SCRIPTS FROM FIELDS

7. When the Field Format dialog box appears, click the Pop-up List radio button. From the value list drop-down list, choose Define Value Lists (**Figure 9.35**).

8. When the Define Value Lists dialog box appears, click New (**Figure 9.36**).

9. When the Edit Value List dialog box appears, give the value list the same name that you gave the global field. (We use Reports.)

10. Click inside the Use custom values box and type the names of the scripts that you want to choose from (**Figure 9.37**). Click OK. Click Done and then click OK to finish.

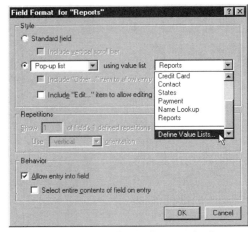

Figure 9.35 The Reports field will use a value list to display the choices.

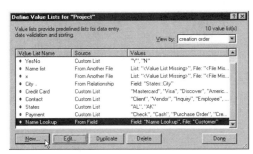

Figure 9.36 You'll create a new value list for the names of the scripts.

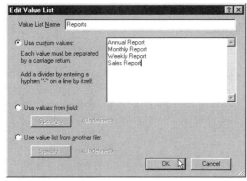

Figure 9.37 Enter the script names for the drop-down list.

Figure 9.38
Before it can do anything else, the script must be in the Reports field.

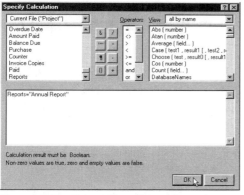

Figure 9.39 The If step will run the script you choose. Specify the first report in your value list by typing it within the formula quotes.

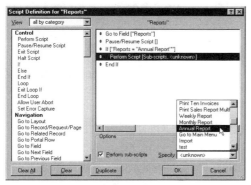

Figure 9.40 Specify which script will run when you choose the report.

You now have the global field placed on a layout, with all of the choices listed in a drop-down list. All you need now is the script to run these choices for you.

To make a script to run scripts:

1. Choose Scripts > ScriptMaker. In the Define Scripts dialog box, type a name for the script. (We use Choose Report.) Click Create.

2. When the Script Definition dialog box appears, delete the default script in the assembly window by clicking Clear All.

3. From the step list on the left, double-click Go to Field. In Options, click Specify.

4. When the Specify Field dialog box appears, select Reports (**Figure 9.38**). Click OK.

5. From the step list on the left, double-click Pause/Resume Script.

   This step makes the script wait while you select a report from the drop-down list.

6. From the step list on the left, double-click If. In Options, click Specify.

7. In the field list on the left in the Specify Calculation dialog box, double-click Reports.

8. Double-click the = operator, then click the quotes. Within the quotes, type the name of the first report you added to the value list in your global field (ours was Annual Report) (**Figure 9.39**). Click OK to close the dialog box.

9. From the step list on the left, double-click Perform Script.

10. In Options, choose the script that matches your first report from the Specify drop-down list (**Figure 9.40**).

continues on next page

RUNNING SCRIPTS FROM FIELDS

Our If step says that if you choose Annual Report from the drop-down list, the script called Annual Report will run.

11. In the assembly window, click the If step, hold down the Shift key and click End If. Click Duplicate to make a second copy of the entire If sequence (**Figure 9.41**).

12. Double-click the new If step to bring up the Specify Calculation dialog box.

13. Edit the report name in the formula box to match your second script (**Figure 9.42**). Click OK.

14. Click the new Perform Script step.

15. In the Specify drop-down list in Options, select the script that matches the report name you just typed (**Figure 9.43**).

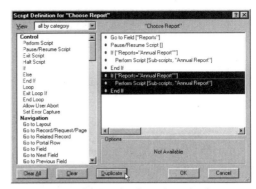

Figure 9.41 Duplicating the If step is easier than creating additional ones from scratch.

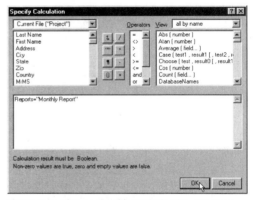

Figure 9.42 Change the If formula for the new steps.

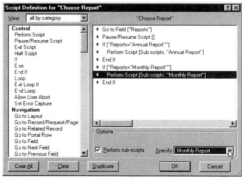

Figure 9.43 Edit each If and Perform Script step. Make sure they always match each other.

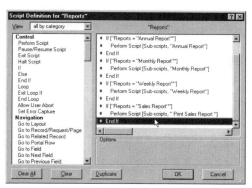

Figure 9.44 A new step is added after a highlighted step.

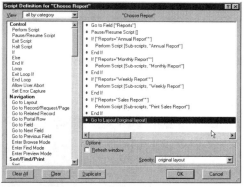

Figure 9.45 After the script is run, this step will return you to the layout you were originally in.

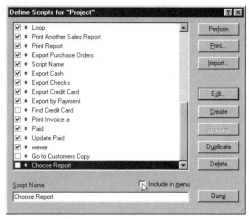

Figure 9.46 This script will only run when you click its button, so there's no point in having it appear in the script menu.

16. Repeat Steps 11–15 for as many reports as you want in the drop-down list.

17. Highlight the last End If step in the script assembly window (**Figure 9.44**). From the step list on the left, double-click Go to Layout. Leave original layout as the selected option (**Figure 9.45**).

18. Click OK. If Include in Menu is checked in the Define Scripts dialog box, uncheck it (**Figure 9.46**). Click Done to finish.

Now that we have a script, we need to connect it to the Reports field by making the field a button.

To make a field into a button that runs a script:

1. Click on the field you want to run the script (in our layout, it's the Reports field) and choose Format > Button.

2. In the left scrolling list, click Perform Script.

3. In Options, select the script you just created (for us, it's Choose Report) from the Specify drop-down list (**Figure 9.47**). Click OK.

4. Use the Text tool to add helpful instructions to the layout (**Figure 9.48**).

✔ Tip

■ To speed up the process of adding new fields to an existing layout, choose Edit > Preferences > Application. Select the Layout tab and check "Add newly defined fields to current layout" (**Figure 9.49**). Now you can go to the layout where you want a field, define the new field, and see it appear automatically on the layout. This is much more convenient than the manual method of defining each field, then returning to the layout, clicking on the Field tool and dragging it to define the field.

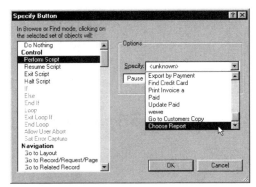

Figure 9.47 Format the field as a button that runs the Reports script.

Figure 9.48 Add instructions to the layout to clarify what the button does.

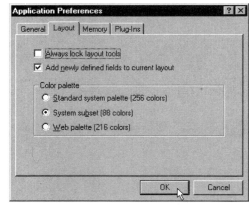

Figure 9.49 This choice automatically adds new fields to whatever layout is in use.

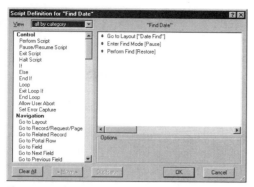

Figure 9.50 This script goes to a layout, enters Find Mode and performs a new search.

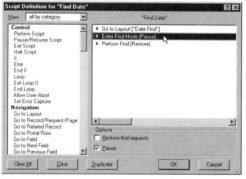

Figure 9.51 New steps are inserted after the selected step.

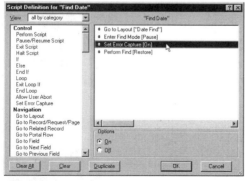

Figure 9.52 Use Set Error Capture to turn off FileMaker's own messages.

Creating Interactive Error Messages

When a script runs and encounters an error , FileMaker usually displays an error message on the screen. Using the script step Set Error Capture, you can replace this generic statement with a message that not only alerts you to the problem, but provides options for a solution. For this example, we create a message prompt that appears when no records are found by a search script.

To show error messages with customized choices:

1. Choose Scripts > ScriptMaker. Double-click a script with a Perform Find step in it, or create a new one. Our example is called Find Date (**Figure 9.50**).

2. In the assembly window, select the script step above the steps you want. In our example, we select the step above the Perform Find step (**Figure 9.51**).

3. From the step list on the left, double-click Set Error Capture. By default, the On option is selected in Options (**Figure 9.52**).

    Turning on Error Capture tells FileMaker to take note of the error code for any error that occurs.

4. While the Set Error Capture step is selected in the assembly window, double-click Loop in the step list on the left.

    continues on next page

5. Click and drag the double arrow to the left of the step to move End Loop to the end of the script (**Figure 9.53**).

The Loop step will indent anything you put between it and End Loop so you can easily see that it takes place inside the Loop.

6. In the assembly window, select the Perform Find step. In the step window on the left, double-click Exit Loop If (**Figure 9.54**). Click Specify to access the Specify Calculation window.

7. In the Specify Calculation dialog box, choose Status Functions in the View drop-down list to access the detailed list of status functions (**Figure 9.55**).

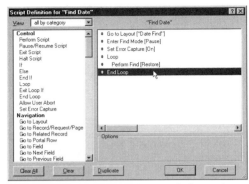

Figure 9.53 Loop will repeat the steps before End Loop.

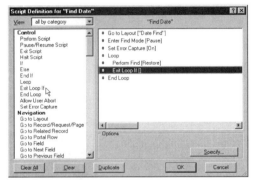

Figure 9.54 Exit Loop If must occur after the step or steps that might create an error.

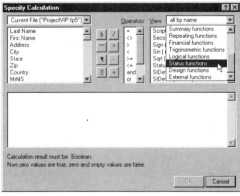

Figure 9.55 Choose Status to see only the Status functions.

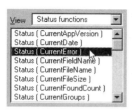

Figure 9.56
Status(CurrentError) looks to see if anything has gone wrong.

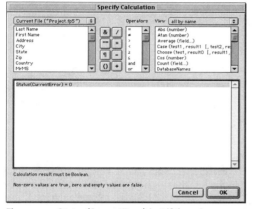

Figure 9.57 Status(CurrentError) is 0 if there is no error.

Figure 9.58 You can customize the message and the buttons that will appear in the error dialog box.

Figure 9.59 Your message will appear when a user uses search criteria that don't match the records in the file.

8. Double-click Status(CurrentError) (**Figure 9.56**). Click to the right of the formula and type =0 (**Figure 9.57**). Click OK.

   The script is now set to exit the loop if there is no error.

9. From the Miscellaneous section of the step list on the left, double-click Show Message. In Options, click Specify.

10. When the Specify Message dialog box appears, type what you want your custom message dialog box to say in the Message Text box.

11. Double-click in the First (default) box and replace the OK with "Try Again," or another short phrase that will fit on the button. Leave Cancel in the Second box. Click OK (**Figure 9.58**).

    When you create a search that turns up no records matching your Find criteria, your error message will display (**Figure 9.59**).

12. From the step list on the left, double-click If. In Options, click Specify to access the Specify Calculation window.

    continues on next page

CREATING INTERACTIVE ERROR MESSAGES

13. In the View drop-down list, choose Status functions, then double-click Status(CurrentMessageChoice) (**Figure 9.60**).

Figure 9.60
Double-click a function to transfer it to the formula box.

14. Click to the right of the parentheses and type =2. Click OK.

The second message button is Cancel, so this script step says that if you choose Cancel in the dialog box, the If step will end.

15. From the Sort/Find/Print section of the step list on the left, double-click Show All Records.

16. From the Navigation section of the step list on the left, double-click Go to Layout.

17. From the step list on the left, double-click Exit Script (**Figure 9.61**).

These last three steps say that if you don't choose Cancel, the script will reset the file, return you to the layout, and exit the script so you can try again.

After the End Loop, you can add any commands you want to take place after a successful find.

18. When you've finished, click OK, then Done.

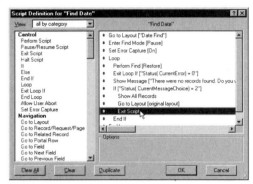

Figure 9.61 If the second button (Cancel) is clicked, the script will exit the loop and return you to the original layout, with all records displayed.

CREATING INTERACTIVE ERROR MESSAGES

SCRIPT TROUBLESHOOTING

A script may look fine while you're working on it, but when you run it the results may surprise you: The wrong records print out in the wrong format, the script quits without doing anything, or refuses to quit at all. Sometimes an error is merely an easily fixed annoyance, like forgetting to sort a small found set before creating the script. Other times it wastes reams of paper and printing time, abandons an untrained user in an unfamiliar layout, or permanently corrupts a good database by altering records.

Although scripting looks easy (and often is), the more steps you add, the more likely it is that you've overlooked something. This is particularly true if you have conditional statements and loops. The debugging process can be challenging, especially if you're relatively new to the concept of scripting in general. The best way to prevent script errors is to assume that you're fallible. Build error-checking steps into your process, and the script will give you debugging feedback as it runs. If an error does occur, a well-written script gives you action options, branches to another part of the script or simply exits before something irretrievable happens.

Testing Finished Scripts

It's wise to test a script you've written to see if it performs as intended. However, even test runs can be dangerous if you don't take precautions. Procedures like modifying data in fields or deleting records can't be undone. Follow good testing procedures and you'll never experience the sinking feeling that comes with a misplaced or missing step.

After the script is run, check to see that the proper records were found, that you end up at the correct layout, that the records are properly sorted, or any other results that you intended are properly done.

To test a new script:

1. Choose File > Save a Copy As to make a copy of the database before running the script.

   This first step is the most critical one. You should never, ever test a script on your only copy of a current database. If all goes as planned, you can delete the copy of the file right after the test.

2. In the Create Copy (Windows)/Create a copy named (Mac) dialog box, choose copy of current file in the Save a (Windows)/Type (Macintosh) drop-down menu (**Figure 10.1**). Click Save.

3. Choose Scripts > ScriptMaker.

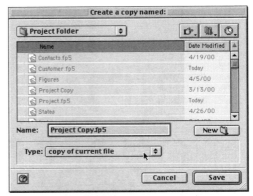

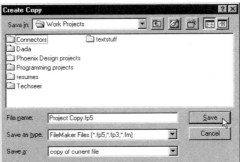

Figure 10.1 The Create a copy named (Mac) or Create Copy (Windows) dialog box lets you save a copy of your file before testing scripts that can alter data.

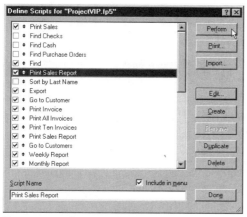

Figure 10.2 Perform runs the selected script.

4. In the Define Scripts dialog box, highlight the script in the window and click Perform to test it by running it in the original file (**Figure 10.2**).

If the script itself seems to run without errors, check the result—layout, printouts or records—to make sure they're correct.

5. If everything is OK, you're finished. If you find anything wrong, close the file or quit FileMaker. Delete the altered original file. Rename the copy with the original file name.

6. Choose Scripts > ScriptMaker and see "Debugging Scripts" below.

✔ Tip

■ Making a copy of your database is really only necessary if the script carries out commands that alter the data in ways that cannot be undone. If there are no such steps, you can simply run the script and check to see if the results are what you intended. However, unless your database is very large or you feel very confident with scripting, it's far better to err on the careful side than to assume that a step can be undone when it can't.

Fixing Typical Errors

Some errors are classics: They crop up in every new scripter's efforts and are all very easily fixed. Before you try troubleshooting your scripts from scratch, check this group of suggested problems and their solutions.

To fix missing or wrong records:

1. If the troublesome script is supposed to find a certain set of records, recreate the find, then choose Scripts > ScriptMaker.

2. In the Define Scripts dialog box, double-click the script you want to check.

3. In the Script Definition dialog box, click OK.

4. In the dialog box, click the Replace radio button in Find Requests (**Figure 10.3**).

5. Click OK, then Done.

To fix an incorrect sort:

1. If your script has any Find steps, make sure your Find pre-sets are done before the Sort command, then redo your Sort.

2. Sort the records, then choose Scripts > ScriptMaker.

3. In the Define Scripts dialog box, double-click the script you want to check.

4. In the Script Definition dialog box, click OK.

5. In the dialog box, click the Replace radio button in Sort Order (**Figure 10.4**).

6. Click OK, then Done.

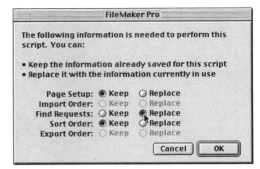

Figure 10.3 Update the restored Find and choose Replace for the Find request.

Figure 10.4 Click Replace for the Sort after you've updated it, or the script definitions won't change.

Figure 10.5 Set the Print/Page Setup options, open the script and choose Replace when closing.

To fix an incorrect print format:

1. Choose File > Print/Page Setup.

2. Set the print options you want, click OK, then choose Scripts > ScriptMaker.

3. In the Define Scripts dialog box, double-click the script you want to check.

4. In the Script Definition dialog box, click OK.

5. In the dialog box, click the Replace radio button in Print/Page Setup (**Figure 10.5**).

6. Click OK, then Done.

✔ Tip

- The Restore option of the Print/Page setup step also restores the setting in the Print dialog box that determines what will print—just the current record, or each of the records being browsed. If your script is printing more files than you expect, check your printing pre-sets as well as your find and sort settings.

To make a script end on a different layout:

1. Choose Scripts > ScriptMaker.

2. In the Define Scripts dialog box, double-click on the script.

3. In the Script Definition dialog box, highlight the last script step in the assembly window (**Figure 10.6**).

4. In the Navigation section of the step list on the left, double-click Go to Layout.

5. In Options, choose the layout you want the script to end on from the drop-down Specify list (**Figure 10.7**). If you want the script to end in the same layout you were in before you ran the script, leave the default, "original layout," specified.

6. Click OK, then OK again in the Keep/Replace dialog box, then Done.

✔ Tip

■ If you end a script with a sub-script, the sub-script, in effect, becomes the main script. This can be confusing if the sub-script calls information from another file, because it will leave you in the external file, not the one you ran the script from in the first place. The solution is simple: add a Navigation script step to the end of the main script. We recommend Go to Layout, using the default option of original layout (**Figure 10.8**).

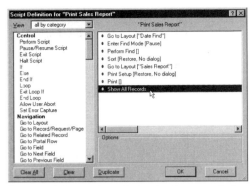

Figure 10.6 You need to select a step to ensure that your new command is inserted in the right place.

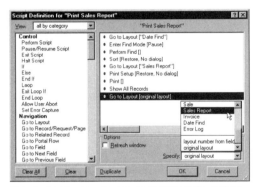

Figure 10.7 You can choose any layout as the ending place for the script.

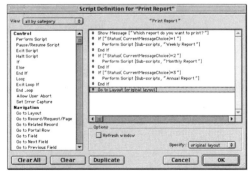

Figure 10.8 If there are no steps after a Perform Script step, the script will not return to the original.

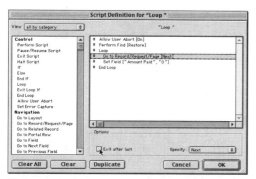

Figure 10.9 Make sure that the script exits after the last record.

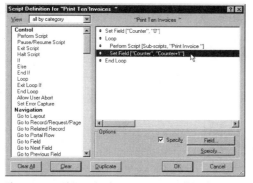

Figure 10.10 This script has no step to tell it when to end.

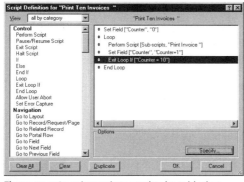

Figure 10.11 Looping scripts need to be told when to exit.

To fix a loop that won't end:

1. Choose Scripts > ScriptMaker.

2. In the Define Scripts dialog box, double-click on the script.

3. In the Script Definition dialog box, look for a Go to Record/Request/Page step. If you see one, click to select it.

4. In Options, check the "Exit after last" check box (**Figure 10.9**). Click OK, then OK again if the Keep/Replace dialog box appears, then Done.

5. If you have no Go to Record/Request/Page step, look for an Exit Loop If step. If you don't find one, click to select the step above the End Loop step (**Figure 10.10**).

6. In the step list on the left, double-click Exit Loop If.

7. In Options, click Specify to bring up the Specify Calculations dialog box and specify the circumstances under which you want the script to end.

   In our example, we have the loop exit when the counter reaches 10 (**Figure 10.11**).

8. Click OK, then OK again if the Keep/Replace dialog box appears, then Done.

continues on next page

FIXING TYPICAL ERRORS

✔ Tips

■ The Allow User Abort script step (**Figure 10.12**) controls whether you can cancel a running script. When you are creating and testing scripts that contain loops, add it as the first line of your script and set its option to On. When the script runs, you can stop it by pressing Escape (Windows) or Command-period (Macintosh). If you have sub-scripts in your script that call steps you might want to cancel, you'll need to place an Allow User Abort step in them and turn it on as well.

■ You can cause yourself problems if you cancel a script before it finishes. Caught in mid-stream, an unfinished script leaves an inconsistent database with some records processed and some untouched. To avoid creating problems instead of solving them, remember to turn the Allow User Abort option to Off after you've finished troubleshooting. Otherwise, if your script has a step in it that already includes a pause for input (like a Find request), a Cancel button will appear in the status area and someone could push Cancel instead of Continue (**Figure 10.13**).

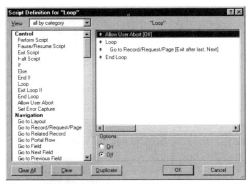

Figure 10.12 This Loop has no Exit condition, so it will never end unless you can manually cancel the script.

Figure 10.13 When Allow User Abort is on, the Cancel button appears in Find Mode.

Creating an Error Trap Script

FileMaker doesn't always tell you that a scripting error has occurred, or what the error is. For example, if a script has a restored Sort that uses a field that is no longer in the database or a Go to Layout step that calls for a deleted or renamed layout, the script will behave unpredictably. Not having a clue to what's wrong with the script, you can waste precious time just narrowing down the nature of the error. To avoid this exasperating experience, create a script that reacts when it finds an error, looks up the error number and uses the information to give you feedback on what happened.

This script relies on Status functions for its effectiveness. A Status function takes the pulse of what's happening on your computer at any given time. The Status (CurrentError) function specifically identifies any error code FileMaker generates. FileMaker offers a complete list of Status (CurrentError) numbers in its Help file. We'll use this to create the database of error numbers and descriptions the error trap script displays.

Once we have the database, we'll create a connection between it and the file whose scripts you want to check, a layout for error codes to display, and the script you add to existing scripts to test them. Although this process is specific to capturing error codes, parts or all of it can be adapted to create online help for new users or supply read-only information from a rolodex or customer database in another file.

To create an error trap database from tabular text:

1. Choose Help > Contents and Index.

2. In the Index tab of the Help Topics dialog box (**Figure 10.14**), type err in the box. This jumps you to the error messages topic in the index.

3. Double-click "error messages" in the index. On the Mac, this will open a list of subtopics below "error messages." In Windows, this brings up the Topics Found dialog box. Double-click Status (CurrentError) function (**Figure 10.15**).

4. When the Reference page appears, scroll down to the Error Codes listing (**Figure 10.16**). Select all the error codes in the list.

5. Copy the list, then close the Help window and launch a word processing program.

6. Create a blank document in the word processor, and paste the list into it.

7. Save the file with Text Only as the file type (**Figure 10.17**) to create a file with no formatting in it, just text and numbers, which can be imported into FileMaker as data for fields.

— Index tab

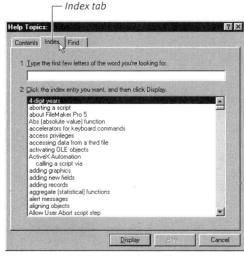

Figure 10.14 Click the Index tab to bring up an alphabetical list of Help topics.

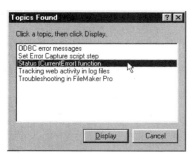

Figure 10.15 Double click Status (CurrentError) to see the list of error numbers and descriptions.

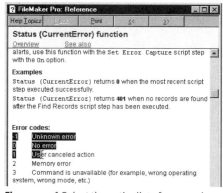

Figure 10.16 Select the entire list of error codes by dragging the mouse down to the end.

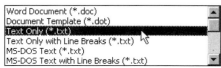

Figure 10.17 Save the file as Text Only so that you can import it into FileMaker.

Figure 10.18 Create the field for the error codes and make it a number type.

Figure 10.19 Choose Tab-separated text to keep the error numbers separate from their explanations.

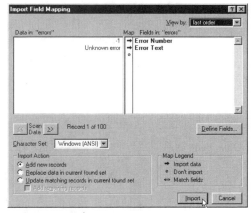

Figure 10.20 Click Import to bring the text file into the database file.

Figure 10.21 The error codes and their matching descriptions will appear in each record.

8. In FileMaker, choose File > New Database. If the template dialog box appears, choose the empty file radio button. Give the file a name and click Save.

9. When the Define Fields dialog box appears, name the field you'll use for the error code (we use Error Number). Select Number as the field type and click Create (**Figure 10.18**).

10. Name the field you'll use for the error description (we use Error Text) for the next field name. Select Text as the field type and click Create. Click Done to finish.

11. FileMaker will add these two fields to Layout #1.

12. Choose File > Import Records.

13. In the Open File dialog box, navigate to the text file that holds your error codes and click to select it. Choose Tab-Separated Text Files in the drop-down list. This file type eliminates all text formatting except the tabs between the error numbers and their text (**Figure 10.19**). Click Open.

14. When the Import Field Mapping dialog box appears, click Import (**Figure 10.20**).

   The Errors database now contains a record for each Status (CurrentError) code, along with the text description of each error (**Figure 10.21**).

To relate the data of one file to another file:

1. In the database whose scripts you want to check for errors, choose File > Define Fields (Ctrl+Shift+D/Command-Shift-D).

2. Enter a field name (we use gError Number), select Global as the field type, and click Create.

continues on next page

CREATING AN ERROR TRAP SCRIPT

3. When the Options for Global Field dialog box appears, choose Number as the data type (**Figure 10.22**). Click OK, then Done to finish.

4. We need to create a relationship to look up the error number description. Choose File > Define Relationships.

5. When the Define Relationships dialog box appears, click New.

6. When the Open File dialog box appears, navigate to the database of error codes and double-click to select and open it (**Figure 10.23**).

7. From the list on the left side of the Edit Relationship dialog box (**Figure 10.24**), click the global field you just created (ours is gError Number). From the list on the right, click the Error Number field. Click OK and then Done.

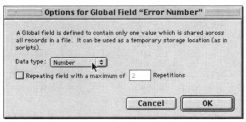

Figure 10.22 Since the gError Number field will contain an error code, choose Number as its type.

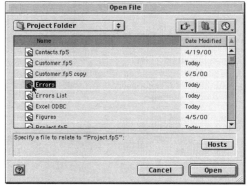

Figure 10.23 The relationship will look up the descriptions in the Errors database.

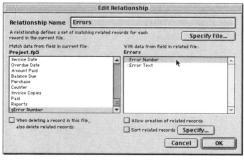

Figure 10.24 The match field for this relationship is gError Number.

Figure 10.25
Add the gError
Number field to
the Errors layout
to see the error
number.

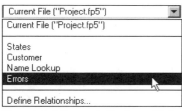

Figure 10.26 Change to the Errors file to add the Error Text field to the layout.

Figure 10.27
The Error Text field
will display the
error description
for the code in the
global field.

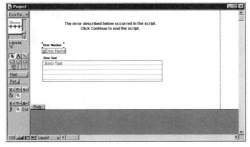

Figure 10.28 Allow enough room for the Error Text field to display the longest error description.

8. To display the script errors, you need a layout. Choose View > Layout Mode (Ctrl+L/Command-L).

9. Choose Layouts > New Layout (Ctrl+N/Command-N).

10. In the New Layout dialog box, type a layout name (we use Error Description). Click Blank Layout in the Select a layout type list. Click Finish.

11. Click the Header tab and drag up until it disappears. Repeat with the Footer tab to leave your layout with Body as the only part.

12. Drag the Field tool onto the layout. When the Specify Field dialog box appears, double-click the global field (**Figure 10.25**).

13. On the layout, Ctrl/Option drag the global field to duplicate it. In the Specify Field dialog box, click the Current File drop-down list and choose Errors (**Figure 10.26**).

14. In the Specify Field dialog box, double-click the Error Text field (**Figure 10.27**). You can resize the Error Text field to allow enough room to read the error description. Use the Text tool to add instructions for anyone else who might need to check scripts (**Figure 10.28**).

To create an error trap script:

1. To create the actual error-trapping script, choose Scripts > ScriptMaker.

2. In the Define Scripts dialog box, type a name for the script. (We use Error Trap.) Click Create.

3. When the Script Definition dialog box appears, delete the default script in the assembly window by clicking Clear All.

4. From the step list on the left, double-click If.

   An If step allows you to test whether or not an error exists.

5. In Options, click Specify to bring up the Specify Calculation dialog box. In the field list on the left, scroll to gError Number and double-click.

6. In the operators list, click <>. Type a zero in the formula box (**Figure 10.29**). Click OK.

   This step tells FileMaker to follow certain instructions if the error code number is anything other than zero. (An error code of zero means that there is no error.)

7. From the step list on the left, double-click Go to Layout. In Options, choose the layout you just created from the drop-down list (**Figure 10.30**).

8. From the step list on the left, double-click Pause/Resume Script (**Figure 10.31**).

   This step pauses the script to allow you to read the description of the error.

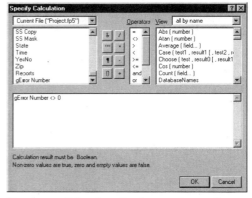

Figure 10.29 If the gError Number equals zero, then no error occurred and none of the subsequent steps will be executed.

Figure 10.30 If an error has occurred, the script will go to the Error layout.

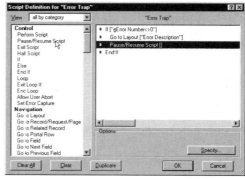

Figure 10.31 Pause/Resume step waits to let you read the description.

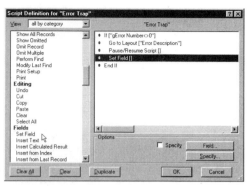

Figure 10.32 After the script displays the error description, you'll want to reset gError Number to 0.

Figure 10.33 Choose gError Number as the field to reset.

9. From the step list on the left, scroll down to Fields and double-click Set Field (**Figure 10.32**).

10. In Options, click the Field button to bring up the Specify Field dialog box; then choose your global field (**Figure 10.33**).

11. In Options, click Specify to bring up the Specify Calculation window. In the formula box, type a zero. Click OK (**Figure 10.34**).

    This Set Field step resets the global field so the old error won't still be displayed after it's no longer relevant.

12. From the step list on the left, scroll up to Navigation and double-click Go to Layout. In the Specify drop-down list, choose a layout that you want to switch to after the script finds an error.

13. From the step list on the left, double-click Halt Script to stop all scripts from running (**Figure 10.35**). Click OK and then Done to finish.

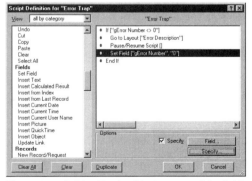

Figure 10.34 "gError Number" is the name of the field, and "0" is the value that clears the field.

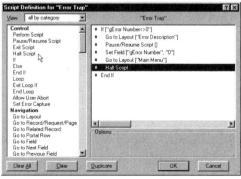

Figure 10.35 The Halt Script step stops both the Error Trap script and the script that called it.

CREATING AN ERROR TRAP SCRIPT

215

Now that you've created a script to explain errors, you need another script that captures the errors themselves and runs the error trap script when they occur.

To use an error trap script in another script:

1. Choose Scripts > ScriptMaker.

2. In the Define Scripts dialog box, double-click a script that you have created and want to test.

3. Click the first step in the Script Definition assembly window. From the step list on the left, double-click Set Error Capture and move it up until it's the first line of the script (**Figure 10.36**).

4. Select the step in the assembly window that may be causing an error. For this example, we use the Sort step.

5. Scroll down to the Fields section of the step list on the left and double-click Set Field.

6. In Options, click the Field button (**Figure 10.37**). When the Specify Field dialog box appears, choose the global field created in "To relate the data of one file to another file" on page 211, then click OK.

7. In Options, click the Specify button to bring up the Specify Calculation dialog box.

8. In the View drop-down list on the right, scroll down to Status functions and click to select it.

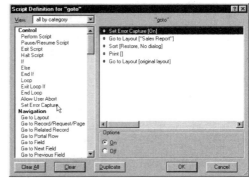

Figure 10.36 In the original script, Set Error Capture must be set to On for the Error Trap script to work.

Figure 10.37 Specify the field to set by clicking Field or checking the Specify check box.

CREATING AN ERROR TRAP SCRIPT

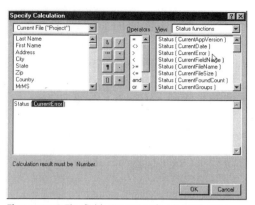

Figure 10.38 The field gError Number is set to Status (CurrentError) before the Error Trap script is run.

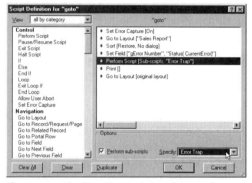

Figure 10.39 The Error Trap script can be run after any step that might generate an error.

9. Double-click Status (CurrentError) (**Figure 10.38**). Click OK.

This Set Field step replaces whatever is in the global field with the error number FileMaker finds.

10. From the step list on the left, double-click Perform Script. In Options, choose the Error Trap script (**Figure 10.39**).

11. Click OK, then OK again to keep your pre-sets.

12. Highlight the script you just added the Error Trap to, and click Perform to run it.

If everything goes well, the script will run without an error code, meaning that there's nothing functionally wrong with your script. If there's a problem that causes a FileMaker error, you'll see it in the Error layout and the script will end.

✔ Tip

■ Sometimes a perfectly good script goes bad because one of the elements it needs—like an external file—has been moved. To guard against such problems, you can use Show Message (see Chapter 9, "To show error messages with customized choices"). This step allows you to offer the option of manually locating the missing file in the Open File dialog box if the script doesn't initially find it.

Debugging Scripts

Debugging is the process of figuring out what the error message you're getting actually means, how it relates to what you've done in your script, and what you need to do to correct it. Although an error capture script can help you with the first step, you have to apply that knowledge to your specific situation.

In addition, not all script problems generate error codes. Everything in the script can be technically correct (no missing fields, no endless loops, no problem sorts) and still not do what you want it to do. When that happens, you need to debug the script from scratch.

There are three major places to check when a script goes wrong:

◆ The pre-sets. The easiest error to make is forgetting to set your sort, find or print options before creating the script. Checking your pre-sets is the first debugging step if you have no error codes but your script doesn't give you the records you expect.

◆ Step order. It's easy to add a step in the wrong place, particularly if you're adapting an existing script. Using the Pause Script, Halt Script and Exit Script steps, you can stop a script at any stage to isolate the problem.

Pause Script stops everything until you click Continue or Exit in the status area. You can set several Pause Script steps in strategic places in a long script to help you figure out where to concentrate your debugging efforts. The Exit step stops a running sub-script and returns you to the main script. This helps you figure out whether your problems are in the main script or are really based in the sub-script it uses. The Halt step brings all scripts to

an end at whatever point you place it. Halt is particularly useful for troubleshooting loops.

◆ Conditional statements. Even the best script makers occasionally put the item they want as the Else condition into the If step instead. When you have a nested If script (one If step inside another), it's all too easy to get confused. An error-trapping script is particularly useful in troubleshooting an If statement.

To see pre-sets in existing scripts:

1. Run the script through to the end.

2. Choose Records > Sort (Ctrl/ Command-S).

3. When the Sort Records dialog box appears, the setting that appears in Sort Order (**Figure 10.40**) is the one that was used by the script.

You can also use this technique to view restored settings for Page/Print Setup, Find, Import and Export by replacing Step 2 with the relevant menu choices.

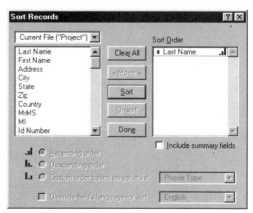

Figure 10.40 When you do a manual Sort, the default sort order will be the same as the last Sort.

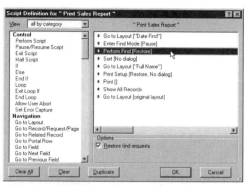

Figure 10.41 Highlight the script step you want to check.

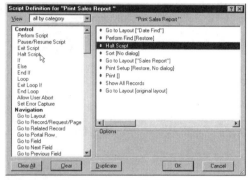

Figure 10.42 The Halt command will stop a script where ever you place it.

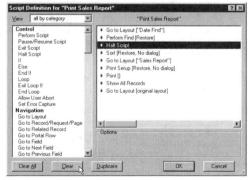

Figure 10.43 After you have debugged the script, remove the Halt step.

To use the Halt, Pause or Exit Script commands:

1. Choose Scripts > ScriptMaker.

2. Double-click on the script you want to check. Our example, Print Sales Report, has a restored Find, and we want to check on which records the script found.

3. In the assembly window in the Script Definition dialog box, click to select the step that you want to check. In our example, it's Perform Find (**Figure 10.41**).

4. Double-click Halt Script in the step list on the left (**Figure 10.42**). Click OK, and then OK again in the Keep/Replace dialog box.

5. In the Define Scripts dialog box, click Perform to run the script.

   The script will end where you inserted the Halt step. Check the conditions at that point to see if there is a problem.

6. Choose Scripts > ScriptMaker and return to the Script Definition dialog box to make any changes.

7. Repeat Steps 5 and 6 until your script runs perfectly.

8. When you're finished, return to the Script Definition dialog box. Click the Halt step that you inserted. Click Clear (**Figure 10.43**).

9. Click OK and then Done.

✔ Tips

- To use Pause or Exit Script, substitute these commands for the Halt step.

- There is no way to see the restored find request in ScriptMaker. But you can insert an Exit Script step after the Perform Find (Restore) and then use the Modify Last Find command manually to see what the restored find criterion is.

Printing Scripts

Once you've debugged a script, particularly if it's a long and complex one, you can print it out for future reference. Having printed copies makes it easier to locate a script you want to use as a basis for a new script, particularly if you run several related files or different databases. It also makes it easy to reconstruct a complicated script if something nasty happens to your database and you have to reconstruct it from an earlier version. You can print scripts individually or all at once.

To print a script in Windows:

1. Choose File > Print.

2. In the Print drop-down list, choose "Script definition for" (**Figure 10.44**).

3. In the script drop-down list, leave the default "all scripts" or choose a specific script to print (**Figure 10.45**).

4. Click OK to print the script(s).

To print a script on the Macintosh:

1. Choose File > Print.

2. In the Print: section at the bottom of the dialog box, click the Script radio button (**Figure 10.46**).

3. In the Script drop-down list, leave All scripts as the default or choose a specific script to print (**Figure 10.47**).

4. Click OK to print the script(s).

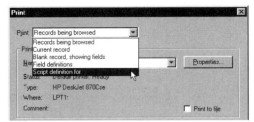

Figure 10.44 Set the Print option to Script definition for.

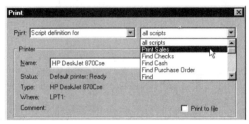

Figure 10.45 You can choose to print all of the scripts in the database or just one.

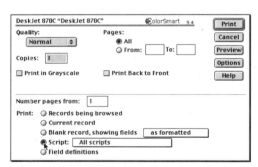

Figure 10.46 The Print Script radio button will print the script definitions.

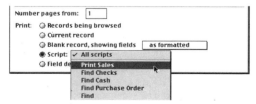

Figure 10.47 You can choose to print all of the scripts in the database or just one.

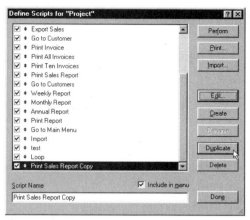

Figure 10.48 When you duplicate a script, it will create a script with the same name plus Copy.

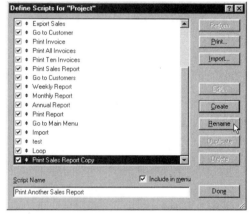

Figure 10.49 Make sure that you click Rename and not Create.

Figure 10.50 Click Replace for the restored settings that you want to change.

Changing and Adapting Scripts

There are only so many different ways you can sort and print a report. Rather than recreate the scripting wheel every time, it makes a lot more sense to duplicate an already debugged script, then adapt it for new uses.

To change pre-sets for a script:

1. Create new Find, Sort or Print settings.

2. Choose Scripts > ScriptMaker. In the Define Scripts dialog box, double-click the script you want to change.

3. In the Script Definition dialog box, click OK.

4. In the dialog box that appears, choose which settings to keep and which to replace, and click OK. Click Done to finish.

To adapt an existing script:

1. If the new script involves restored Find, Sort or Print settings, set these manually before working on the script.

2. Choose Scripts > ScriptMaker. In the Define Scripts dialog box, click to select the script on which you want to base the new script. Click Duplicate (**Figure 10.48**).

3. Type a new name for the script and click Rename (**Figure 10.49**).

4. Double-click the new script name to bring up the Script Definition dialog box. Make any changes that are required.

5. Click OK when you're finished. If there are restored settings in the script, choose which settings to keep and which to replace in the dialog box, and click OK (**Figure 10.50**). Click Done to finish.

FileMaker and Other Programs

Whenever you import or export a spreadsheet file, you're using FileMaker to communicate with other software. This transfer of information is important, but it's limited and indirect. You're forced to create a new file in a format that both programs can read, and only unformatted text and numeric information is transferable. Sometimes that's enough, like when you just want to export a list of names and numbers. But when tempting data sits out of reach in industrial-strength databases while you recreate the parts you need, you can really feel hemmed in by these limitations.

Rest assured—there are work-arounds for many applications. In some cases FileMaker itself provides links to other information, either with its built-in flexibility or through plug-ins that come with it. Scripting is also key to unlocking access to other programs, their formats and their data. Using scripting and enhancements added in FileMaker 5.0, you can not only transfer files to and from other programs, you can embellish the information with formatting and manipulate the programs themselves.

Using Scripts to Send Email

FileMaker isn't an email program, but you can make it act as if it is. If you're using one of the following email applications as your default email software, FileMaker can access it from within your database.

MACINTOSH	WINDOWS
Claris Emailer	Eudora
Eudora	Exchange
	Outlook (or any other email program that is MAPI compliant)

You'll notice a glaring omission. Unfortunately, AOL software does not work directly with FileMaker's Send Mail scripting command. However, Macintosh AOL users can use Claris Emailer to send mail from FileMaker. There are also third-party FileMaker add-ons that can circumvent the need to use a mailer program. See Appendix A for download information.

If you have fields for an email address and an Internet URL (Web address) in a contact database, FileMaker scripting can give you direct access to your customers. First you need to set up an email message layout, then set up the script that will actually send the message.

Before you follow these instructions, add three additional text fields to the database file you plan to use: cc:, Subject, and Body. With these fields, you'll be able to create a FileMaker layout similar to the window you use to send mail in your email software.

To create an email layout:

1. Choose View > Layout Mode (Ctrl+L/Command-L).

2. Choose Layouts > New Layout/Report (Ctrl+N/Command-N).

3. When the New Layout/Report dialog box appears, give the layout a name. (We use Email.) Click Blank layout in the Select a layout type list. Click Finish.

4. Drag the Header and Footer tabs up until they disappear. Drag the Body tab down to fill the screen.

5. Drag the Field tool onto the layout. Choose your email address field from the Specify Field dialog box (**Figure 11.1**). Click OK.

6. Holding the Ctrl/Option key, drag the Email Address field to duplicate it.

7. When the Specify Field dialog box appears, double-click to choose the cc: field (**Figure 11.2**).

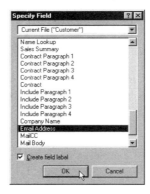

Figure 11.1 Add the email address field to the Email layout by choosing it in the Specify Field dialog box.

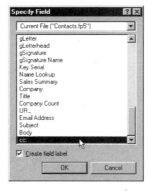

Figure 11.2 After duplicating the first field, specify a different field for the copy.

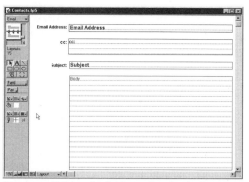

Figure 11.3 Enlarge the fields to allow for the longest sections you expect to need.

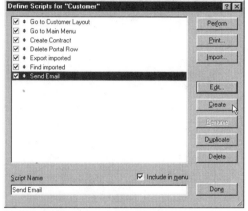

Figure 11.4 Type a name that describes what the script does.

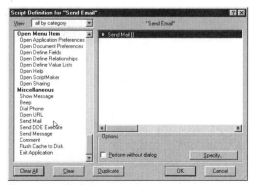

Figure 11.5 Add the Send Mail step to the script.

8. Repeat Steps 6 and 7 for the Subject and Body fields.

   When creating the Body field, uncheck the Create field label check box.

9. Resize all the fields as necessary to allow enough room for addresses and the text of an email message (**Figure 11.3**).

   To use these fields to compose and send a message, see "To create an email script" below.

To create an email script:

1. Choose Scripts > ScriptMaker.

2. In the Define Scripts dialog box, enter a name for your script. (We use Send Email.) Click Create (**Figure 11.4**).

3. In the Script Definition dialog box, click Clear All to clear the default script.

4. In the script step list on the left, scroll down to Miscellaneous and double-click Send Mail (**Figure 11.5**).

5. In the script assembly box, double-click the Send Mail step to bring up the Specify Mail dialog box.

6. In the To: section, click the Field Value radio button (**Figure 11.6**).

continues on next page

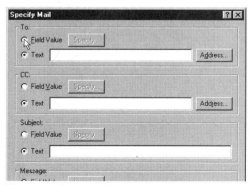

Figure 11.6 Choose Field Value to use an email address from your database.

7. When the Specify Field dialog box appears, choose your email address field from the scrolling list. In the Records box, click the Use current record radio button (**Figure 11.7**). Click OK.

8. Repeat steps 6 and 7 for the cc:, Subject, and Message sections, choosing the appropriate fields from the Specify Fields dialog box (**Figure 11.8**). Click OK to finish.

When you return to the Script Definition dialog box, the Send Mail script line will include your Subject field in quotes (**Figure 11.9**).

9. Check Perform without dialog in Options to queue or send the messages without having to interact with the email program itself (**Figure 11.10**).

If you leave this box unchecked, the message will open in your email program and wait for you to manually send it. If you expect to send attachments occasionally, you might prefer to leave the box unchecked so you can do this selectively in the email program.

10. Click OK, and then Done to finish. When you run the script, FileMaker will send the data you entered into the appropriate fields in your email program.

✔ Tip

■ To add a Send button so you can run the script with one click from the email layout, follow the instructions in "To create a button for a script" in Chapter 9.

Figure 11.7
Since you'll only want to send email to the person in the open record, choose the Use current record setting.

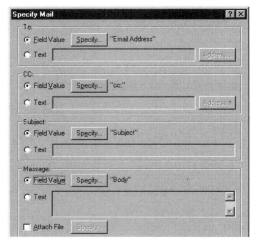

Figure 11.8 To use the contents of the fields to fill in the email data, specify each field.

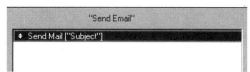

Figure 11.9 Send Mail selects your subject line as the email reference information.

Figure 11.10 If you want to review the contents of the message in your email program before it is sent, leave the Perform without dialog box unchecked.

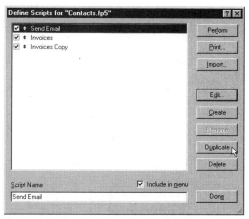

Figure 11.11 Since this script is very similar to an existing one, it's easier to duplicate the original and edit it than to create a new script from scratch.

Figure 11.12 Use Show Message to add a dialog box prompt to confirm that you want to send bulk email.

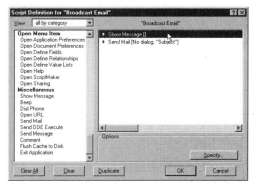

Figure 11.13 Your message should appear before your Send Mail step takes place.

Using Scripts to Send Bulk Email

By adapting the script created in "To create an email script" on the previous page, you can create a script to send email to every person in an entire database or within a found set.

To send bulk email:

1. Follow the steps in "To create an email script."

2. If you want to send bulk email to only a subset of people, do a Find to create a found set of the contacts you want to reach.

3. Choose Scripts > ScriptMaker.

4. In the Define Scripts dialog box, click the script you just created, then click Duplicate (**Figure 11.11**).

5. Rename the script, then click Rename. We call our new script Broadcast Email.

6. Double-click on the new script to open the Script Definition dialog box.

7. In the script assembly window on the right, click the Send Mail step.

8. Because bulk email can be interpreted as spam (junk email) or cause embarrassment if you run this script by mistake, we'll insert a dialog box to confirm that you really want to run this script. In the script step list on the left, scroll down to Miscellaneous and double-click Show Message (**Figure 11.12**).

9. Move the Show Message step above Send Mail, then double-click on it (**Figure 11.13**).

continues on next page

10. When the Specify Message dialog box appears, type a message like "Are you sure you want to send this email to everyone?" in the Message Text box (**Figure 11.14**).

11. In the Button Captions section, type **No** in the First (default) box and **Yes** in the Second box (**Figure 11.15**). Click OK.

12. In the script step list on the left in the Script Definition dialog box, scroll up to the Control section and double-click If (**Figure 11.16**). In Options, click Specify.

13. When the Specify Calculation dialog box appears, click the View drop-down list on the right and choose Status functions.

14. From the list of status functions, double-click Status (CurrentMessageChoice) (**Figure 11.17**).

Figure 11.14 The message text warns that the email will be sent to everyone in the found set.

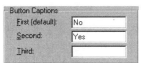

Figure 11.15 The default is set to No, the least dangerous choice.

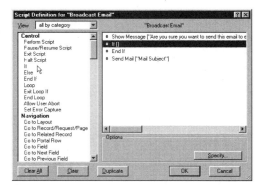

Figure 11.16 The If step will check which button the user clicked and act accordingly.

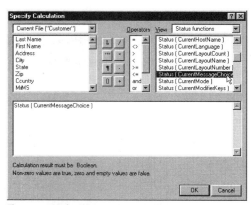

Figure 11.17 The CurrentMessageChoice status function returns a number corresponding to the button you click in the message box.

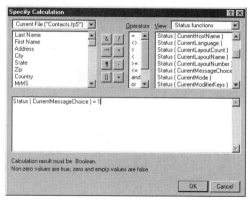

Figure 11.18 The value for the No button is 1.

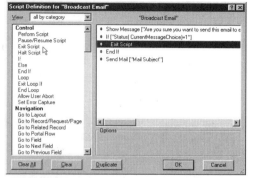

Figure 11.19 If the choice is No, the script ends without sending the email.

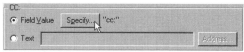

Figure 11.20 The Field Value for the cc: option is where you'll put the bulk mail addresses.

15. Click to the right of the parentheses. Double-click the = operator button, then type 1 (**Figure 11.18**). Click OK.

This step sets the default choice to No, so you won't send bulk email unless you are certain you want to.

16. In the script step list on the left of the Script Definition dialog box, double-click Exit Script (**Figure 11.19**). In the script assembly window, double-click the Send Mail step.

17. When the Specify Mail dialog box appears, click the Specify button in the cc: section (**Figure 11.20**).

18. When the Specify Field dialog box appears, choose your email address field from the scrolling list.

19. Click the "Use all records in found set" radio button (**Figure 11.21**).

continues on next page

Figure 11.21 "Use all records in found set" will insert all the current email addresses into the cc: section of the email.

USING SCRIPTS TO SEND BULK EMAIL

20. Click OK to save the change. Click OK to close the Specify Mail dialog box, OK again and then Done.

When you run this script, the Show Message dialog box appears (**Figure 11.22**). If you click No, nothing will happen. If you click Yes, FileMaker creates an email message addressed to the person in the current record with the addresses of everyone else in the found set entered in the cc: section (**Figure 11.23**).

✔ Tips

■ If you have already added a Send button to the Email layout, add a "Broadcast" button to the same layout to make it easy to choose between the two scripts.

■ Sometimes when you're sending bulk email, you need to attach a spreadsheet or HTML page. If you do this all the time, return to the script and double-click on the Send Mail step to reopen the Specify Mail dialog box. Click the Attach File dialog box in the Message section (**Figure 11.24**). When the Open dialog box appears, navigate to the file you want to attach, click OK to save the change, then exit ScriptMaker.

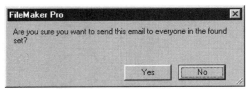

Figure 11.22 Without the message, you could send bulk email by mistake.

Figure 11.23 The cc: section contains all the addresses except the current record.

Figure 11.24 You can bulk-mail attachments by choosing the Attach File check box.

USING SCRIPTS TO SEND BULK EMAIL

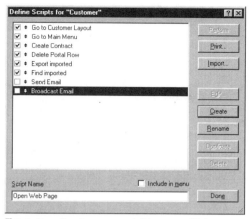

Figure 11.25 Create a new script to open a Web page in a browser.

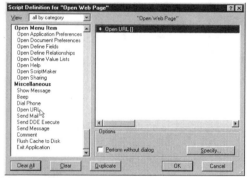

Figure 11.26 The Open URL step tells your default browser software to open.

Figure 11.27 The Specify URL dialog box will open the URL for the current record.

Using a Script to Open URLs

Many of the companies and people in your contact list have a Web page. If it lists pricing, products, or other useful data, you might want to have easy access to it when you examine the customer accounts. If you have a URL field for the entry, you can create a script to open the Web page in your default browser.

To use a script to open a Web page:

1. Choose Scripts > ScriptMaker.

2. In the Define Scripts dialog box, name the new script (we use Open Web Page) (**Figure 11.25**). Click Create.

3. In the Script Definition Dialog box, click Clear All to delete the default script.

4. In the step list on the left, scroll down to Miscellaneous and double-click Open URL (**Figure 11.26**).

5. In Options, click the Perform without dialog check box, then click the Specify button.

6. When the Specify URL dialog box appears (**Figure 11.27**), click the Field Value radio button.

continues on next page

7. In the Specify Field dialog box, double-click the field that contains Web addresses (ours is URL) (**Figure 11.28**). Click OK.

If necessary, you can click the Define Fields button to create a URL field.

8. Click OK to save the script, then Done to finish.

✔ Tips

■ To add a convenient button that will run the script, follow the instructions in "To create a button for a script" in Chapter 9. Although you can name this button anything you'd like, "Go" is short, sweet, and familiar to anyone using the Internet (**Figure 11.29**).

■ Although we have used a Web URL in this example, you can use this script to open an FTP site or any other type of address that an Internet utility (like Fetch or Gopher) understands. As long as the field data is properly formatted, the script will open the appropriate application.

Figure 11.28
Specify the field that contains your Web addresses.

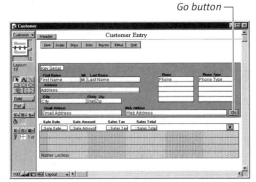

Go button

Figure 11.29 The Go button appears on many Web pages.

Figure 11.30 Choosing HTML Table Files formats the field contents with an HTML <TABLE> tag.

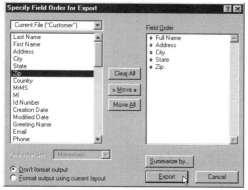

Figure 11.31 Choose the fields you want to export to the table.

Full Name	Address	City	State	Zip
Gary Lambusta	2105 Community Way	Brick	NJ	08997
Denise Lambusta	2105 Community Way	Brick	NJ	08997
Megan McCalla	2105 Community Way	Brick	NJ	08997
Caitlin McCalla	2105 Community Way	Brick	NJ	08997
Dan Peck	113 Hancock Ave	Hoboken	NJ	07030
Enoch B. Rutherford	121 Old Time Lane	Gold Hill	VA	20048
Henry H. Sapoznik	6250 Rovna Lane	Olive Bridge	NY	10647
Moira Sessa	15 Thistle St.	Kearny	NJ	07320
Elizabeth Sessa	15 Thistle St.	Kearny	NJ	07320
Merlin Shepard	210 Sackbutt Lane	Brighton	MA	20135
Lorin Sklamberg	234 Matics Ave.	Brooklyn	NY	11201

Figure 11.32 The exported file appears with the HTML <TABLE> tag defaults.

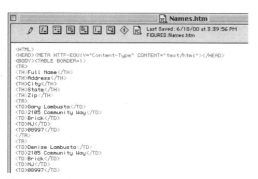

Figure 11.33 The new file contains field data surrounded by HTML code.

Exporting Data to Static HTML Tables

In Chapter 15, we show you how to use FileMaker directly on the World Wide Web. But sometimes you just want to export data from FileMaker to a simple HTML table. If that's all you need to do, you can create a file with data and HTML Table tags using the Export command.

To create an HTML table:

1. In the database with the table data, sort the records as you want them to appear.

2. Choose File > Export Records.

3. In the Export Records to File dialog box, type a name for the export file and choose HTML Table Files as the Save as type (**Figure 11.30**). Click Save.

4. The Specify Field Order for Export dialog box will appear. In the field list on the left, double-click to choose the fields you want to include in the table (**Figure 11.31**). Click Export.

If you open the exported HTML file in your Web browser, it will appear as a table (**Figure 11.32**). The actual contents of the file is HTML code that can be inserted into any other Web page (**Figure 11.33**).

Exporting Formatted Text

When you use the Export command in FileMaker, you create a text file without any of the formatting specifications that you may have created on your layouts.

Using calculation fields, you can embellish that raw data if you are exporting the text to a program like QuarkXPress that supports formatting tags. Being able to control typographic setup when you export records can improve your communication with a designer who is using the material to create an annual report, or simply save your own precious time by not having to redefine basic hierarchies of information in a page layout program.

As an example of how to export Quark style tags, we'll add tags to name and address fields to make the names bold and the addresses italic.

To include format tags in exported text:

1. In the file you want to use to export formatted text, choose File > Define Fields (Ctrl+Shift+D/Command-Shift-D).

2. In the Define Fields dialog box, type a field name (We use Formatted Name). Click the Calculation radio button for field type (**Figure 11.34**). Click Create.

3. When the Specify Calculation dialog box appears, click the quotes operator button. Double-click the <> operator (**Figure 11.35**). Insert your cursor within the <>'s and type B.

    The <> operator is also the universally recognized symbol for a font formatting tag. Formatting tags act as toggles, so this <B> turns on the bold style.

4. Click to the right of the quotes and click the ampersand button (**Figure 11.36**).

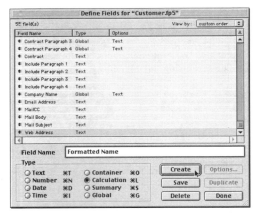

Figure 11.34 You need a calculation to specify markup tags.

Figure 11.35 The <> symbol can be found in the scrolling operators list.

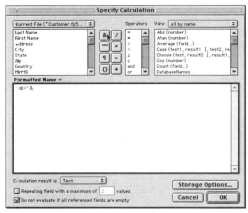

Figure 11.36 Use the & button to connect different portions of a formula.

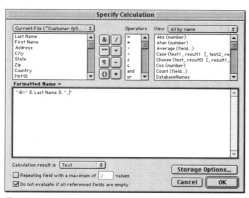

Figure 11.37 The comma and space must be inside quotes.

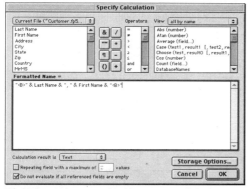

Figure 11.38 The second bold tag turns off the bold format.

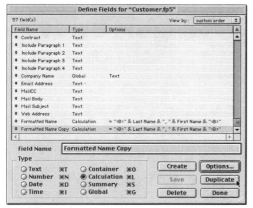

Figure 11.39 Duplicating and changing the Formatted Name field is easier than creating the second field from scratch.

5. Click to the right of the ampersand. Double-click the Last Name field in the field list.

6. Click the ampersand button and then the quotes button. Type a comma and a space between the quotes (**Figure 11.37**).

You need to put quotes around any non-field characters so they won't be mistaken for a field or formula.

7. Click to the right of the quotes and click the ampersand button. Double-click the First Name field in the field list.

8. Click the ampersand button and then the quotes button. Double-click the <> operator. Insert your cursor within the <>'s and type B (**Figure 11.38**). This second formatting tag toggles the Bold style to off. Click OK.

This first formula creates a format that will make the field text export like this: **Smith, Patti**

9. When the Define Fields dialog box returns, click on the Formatted Name field and click Duplicate (**Figure 11.39**).

continues on next page

10. Change the field name to Formatted Address and click Save (**Figure 11.40**). Double-click on the Formatted Address field.

11. In the Specify Calculation dialog box, change both <B>s to <I>s (**Figure 11.41**). Doing this changes the toggled style to Italic.

12. Select the Last Name field in the formula and double-click the City field in the field list (**Figure 11.42**).

13. Select the First Name field in the formula and double-click the State field in the field list (**Figure 11.43**). Click OK, and then Done to finish.

The address information will export in this format:

New York City, NY

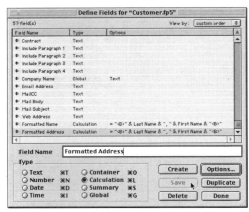

Figure 11.40 Save your edited changes.

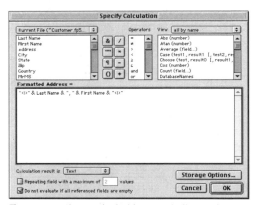

Figure 11.41 Change the bold tags to italic tags by editing the letter inside the angle brackets.

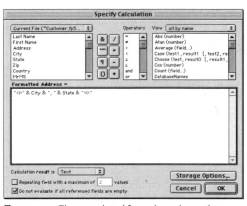

Figure 11.43 The completed formula replaces the markup tags and fields with new ones.

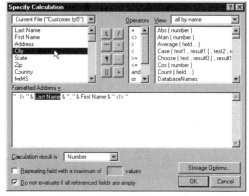

Figure 11.42 Select only the field name, then replace it with a different field.

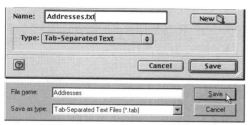

Figure 11.44 Choose Tab-Separated text in Mac (upper) or Windows (lower) to insert tabs, not spaces, between each field.

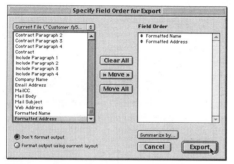

Figure 11.45 Specify the formatted fields, not the original ones, for export.

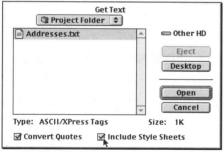

Figure 11.46 Include Style Sheets will interpret the markup tags properly when the text is placed in a Quark document.

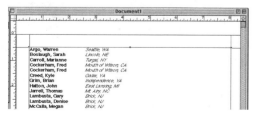

Figure 11.47 This is how the imported text will appear in Quark.

To export formatted fields to a text file:

1. Once you have a calculation to add format tags to your data, choose the records to export and sort them.

2. Choose File > Export Records.

3. In the Export Records to File dialog box, type a name for the export file. Click in the file type drop-down list and choose Tab-Separated Text (**Figure 11.44**). Click Save.

4. In the Specify Field Order for Export dialog box, double-click on the Formatted Name and Formatted Address fields in the field list on the left. Click Export (**Figure 11.45**).

You now have a text file that you can import into Quark just as you would any other text document. When you place the text in QuarkXPress, make sure that the Include Style Sheets option is checked (**Figure 11.46**).

When placed in Quark, the list will automatically be formatted in bold and italics (**Figure 11.47**).

✔ Tip

■ You can expand this technique to include any formatting options. Consult the documentation of the page layout program you use for a complete list of available tags.

Using Excel Data in FileMaker

FileMaker Inc. has done a great job of making FileMaker and Excel files easily interchangeable. For example, in Chapter 5 in "To export summary data," we show how easy it is to save FileMaker databases as worksheet files using the File > Export Records command.

But did you know that you can also open Excel files directly in FileMaker to create a new database? This allows you to create a new FileMaker file with all of the spreadsheet data included. You can use column headers from the Excel file to automatically create FileMaker field names. Use the drag-and-drop feature in both Windows and the Mac OS, and the whole process can be virtually effortless.

To create a FileMaker database from an Excel file:

1. In Windows Explorer or Macintosh Finder, arrange your windows or desktop so that you can access the Excel file and the FileMaker program icon (or a shortcut/alias) at the same time (**Figure 11.48**).

2. Drag the Excel file icon on top of the FileMaker program icon (**Figure 11.49**). Doing this launches FileMaker and automatically opens the First Row Option dialog box.

   If you don't have a FileMaker program icon on your desktop, start FileMaker and choose File > Open. Choose Microsoft Excel Files in the drop-down list (**Figure 11.50**). Double-click the name of the Excel file.

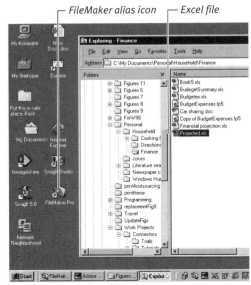

FileMaker alias icon — *Excel file*

Figure 11.48 Windows Explorer is open to the Excel file, and the FileMaker program alias is on the desktop.

Figure 11.49
Use drag-and-drop to launch the Excel spreadsheet as a FileMaker file.

Figure 11.50 Choose Excel as the file type to see all the available Excel files.

Using Excel Data in FileMaker

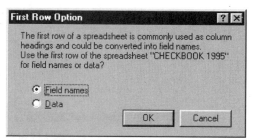

Figure 11.51 Choose Field names to use data in the first row of the spreadsheet as the field names in the new database.

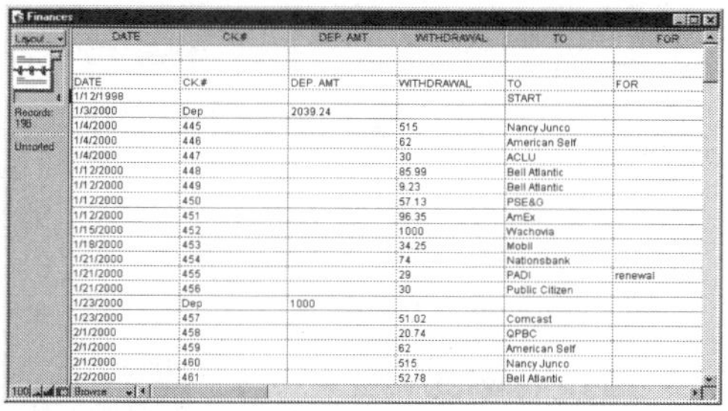

Figure 11.52 The field names will be the same as the first row in the spreadsheet if you chose that option.

3. In the First Row Option dialog box, click the Field names radio button if you want to use the first row in the spreadsheet as your field names (**Figure 11.51**). If not, click the Data button. Click OK.

4. In the Name converted file dialog box, type a name for the new database. Click Save.

5. The new FileMaker database will open with all of the data from the spreadsheet.

If you choose the Field names option in Step 3, the field names will be created from the first row of the spreadsheet (**Figure 11.52**). Otherwise, your fields will be given generic letter/number codes (F1, F2, F3, etc.) as field names that you can edit in the Define Fields dialog box.

✔ Tip

■ If you convert an Excel spreadsheet that contains formulas into a database, the formula results will display in the fields, not the formulas themselves. Alas, Excel formulas don't translate into FileMaker calculations.

USING EXCEL DATA IN FILEMAKER

Working with ODBC

FileMaker users with access to large corporate databases like Oracle can use ODBC to access data. ODBC is an application interface that gives all databases that support it a common "language" for record sharing; it is also the method for importing database information from Microsoft Access files. Before you can import, you must have the proper ODBC drivers installed on your computer. Because each database configuration is different, you should consult with the network manager to find out what you need and what resources are available.

To import ODBC data:

1. Open the FileMaker database into which you want to import ODBC source data.

2. Choose File > Import Records.

3. When the Open File dialog box appears, select ODBC Data Sources from the Files of type drop-down list (**Figure 11.53**).

4. In the Select ODBC Data Source dialog box, choose the type of data source that you want to import from (**Figure 11.54**).

5. If the data source requires a user name and password, enter them in the Enter Password dialog box. If no password is required, just click OK (**Figure 11.55**).

Figure 11.53 Choose ODBC as the import file type to see the available ODBC sources.

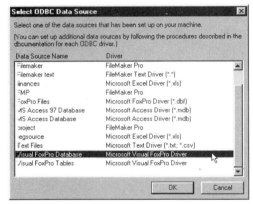

Figure 11.54 Choose the data source to use.

Figure 11.55 If it's required, enter your user name and password for access to the data source.

WORKING WITH ODBC

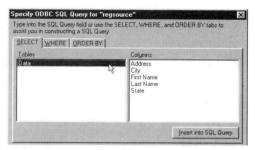

Figure 11.56 Choose the table you want to import.

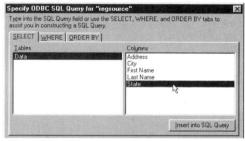

Figure 11.57 Choose the table fields from the column list.

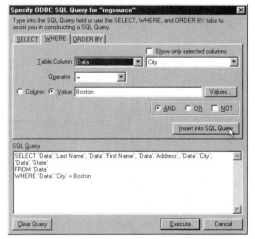

Figure 11.58 The Where tab is used to create a filter for imported records.

6. In the Select tab of the Specify ODBC SQL Query dialog box, click on the table you want to import (**Figure 11.56**).

7. In the columns list, double-click the fields to include in the import. The query builder will add the fields to the SQL Query scrolling window (**Figure 11.57**).

8. If you want to limit the import to certain records, click the Where tab and create a filter using SQL commands (**Figure 11.58**). Click the Insert into SQL Query button to add the filter to the query.

continues on next page

WORKING WITH ODBC

9. If you want to import the records in a sorted order, click the Order By tab and select the fields to sort by (**Figure 11.59**). Click the Insert into SQL Query button to add the sort to the query.

10. Click Execute when you're ready to begin the import (**Figure 11.60**).

When the import finishes, the Import Field Mapping dialog box will appear because you still need to connect the imported data to the fields in your FileMaker database.

11. In the Import Field Mapping dialog box, select the FileMaker fields on the right and move them so they're next to the matching query fields on the left.

12. Click the arrow in the map column to indicate that the data is flowing into the FileMaker fields (**Figure 11.61**). Click Import.

The records from the imported file will flow smoothly into your database.

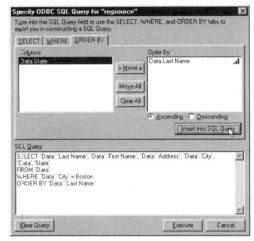

Figure 11.59 You can import the records in a sorted order using the Order By tab.

Figure 11.60 The Execute button begins the import process.

Figure 11.61 Import Field Mapping matches the imported fields to the existing FileMaker fields.

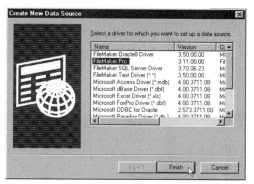

Figure 11.62 Specify the FileMaker ODBC driver to make your file available to other ODBC programs.

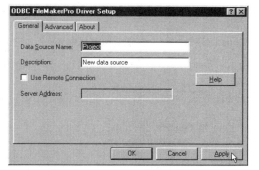

Figure 11.63 Other programs will identify your database by the name you enter.

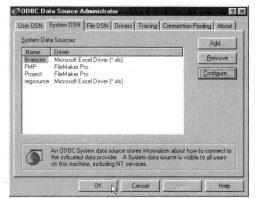

Figure 11.64 Your database will be available to other ODBC applications when it's listed as a data source.

Sharing Databases Using ODBC

Not only can you import ODBC data into your FileMaker database, you can share your FileMaker databases with ODBC client applications. To make it possible for others using ODBC to access your files, you must first register the FileMaker database on your computer as a data source, then turn on the Data Access plug-ins. The registration process is a bit different on Windows and Macs.

To register a database in Windows:

1. Open the FileMaker database you want to register.

2. From the Windows taskbar, choose Start > Settings > Control Panel. Double-click ODBC Data Sources.

   The ODBC Data Source Administrator dialog box appears with the User DSN tab selected. You should see FileMaker listed as a user data source. If it isn't listed, click Add and follow the instructions that appear.

3. Click the System DSN tab, then click the Add button.

4. In the Create New Data Source dialog box, click the FileMaker Pro driver. Click Finish (**Figure 11.62**).

5. In the ODBC FileMaker Pro Driver Setup dialog box, type the name of your database in the Data Source Name box. You can add a description if you'd like, but it's not required (**Figure 11.63**). Click Apply, and then OK.

6. Your database will now be listed in the System Data Sources window and will be available to other ODBC applications (**Figure 11.64**). Click OK to finish.

To register a database on the Macintosh:

1. Open the FileMaker database you want to register.

2. Choose Apple Menu > Control Panels > ODBC Setup.

   The ODBC Setup control panel is installed with your FileMaker application.

3. The ODBC Data Source Administrator dialog box appears with the User DSN tab selected. Click Add (**Figure 11.65**).

4. In the Create New Data Source dialog box, double-click the ODBC 3.11 FileMaker Pro driver (**Figure 11.66**).

5. In the driver dialog box, type the name of your database in the Data Source Name box. You can add text in the Description box if you'd like, but it's not required (**Figure 11.67**). Click OK.

6. Your database will now be listed as a data source and will be available to other ODBC applications (**Figure 11.68**). Click OK to finish.

   The FileMaker file that you register as a data source must be open in FileMaker to be available to other programs.

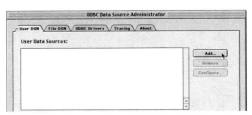

Figure 11.65 This dialog box is empty if you've never used ODBC before.

Figure 11.66 Choose the ODBC FileMaker driver.

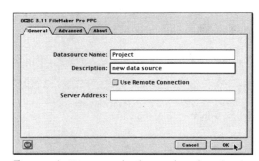

Figure 11.67 Name your database to broadcast it as an ODBC data source.

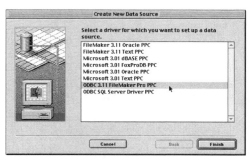

Figure 11.68 Your database is available as a data source to other applications.

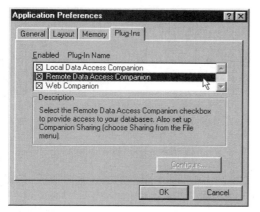

Figure 11.69 The Remote Data Access Companion plug-in creates access to your FileMaker database over a network.

To turn on Data Access plug-ins:

1. Choose Edit > Preferences > Application.

2. Click the Plug-Ins tab of the Preferences dialog box.

3. Click the check box next to Local Data Access Companion if you are going to use a program on your own computer to access FileMaker files.

4. Click the check box next to Remote Data Access Companion to allow other users on the network to access the databases (**Figure 11.69**). Click OK to save the settings.

Using AppleScript with FileMaker Scripting

Although AppleScript itself is outside the scope of a FileMaker Pro book, it's definitely worth a mention because it allows you to combine FileMaker scripting with almost limitless ability to affect Macintosh Finder functions (like automatically backing up FileMaker databases at specific times of day), and to initiate actions in other AppleScript-aware programs—from simply cutting and pasting text between applications to mining your Netscape cache for interesting GIF files.

This example uses a simple script that copies the contents of a FileMaker field, switches to Microsoft Word, and pastes the text into a document.

To send an Apple Event to another Mac application:

1. Choose Scripts > ScriptMaker.

2. In the Define Scripts dialog box, name the new script (we use Paste Into Word). Click Create (**Figure 11.70**).

3. When the Script Definition dialog box appears, click Clear All to delete the default script.

4. In the script step list on the left, double-click Go to Layout. From the Specify drop-down list in Options, choose the layout that holds the field data you want to copy. Our example uses the Contract layout (**Figure 11.71**).

5. In the step list on the left, scroll down to the Editing section and double-click Copy.

Figure 11.70 This script name describes what its AppleScript does.

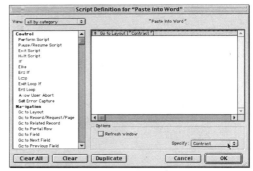

Figure 11.71 For the Copy step to work properly, the field whose contents you want to copy must appear on the layout you specify.

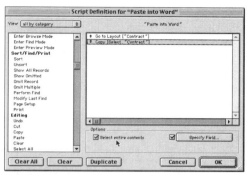

Figure 11.72 Leave Select entire contents checked to copy the entire contents of the field.

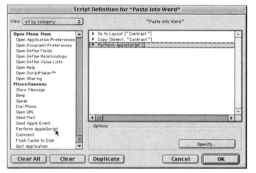

Figure 11.73 The Perform AppleScript step allows you to enter commands that are executed by AppleScript.

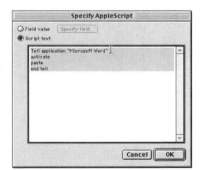

Figure 11.74 These AppleScript commands switch to Microsoft Word and paste data into its current document.

6. Click Specify Field to bring up the Specify Field dialog box and double-click Contract to choose it from the field list. Leave "Select entire contents" checked unless you want to edit the field (**Figure 11.72**).

7. In the script step list on the left, scroll down to Miscellaneous and double-click Perform AppleScript (**Figure 11.73**).

8. In Options, click Specify.

9. When the Specify AppleScript dialog box appears, type your AppleScript (**Figure 11.74**).

10. Click OK, and then Done to finish.

✔ Tips

■ Although AppleScript is a very powerful tool for connecting FileMaker with other applications, it is not cross-platform. If you open a database file that uses AppleScript on a Windows computer, the scripts won't work.

■ To learn more about how to use FileMaker with AppleScript, check *AppleScript for the Internet: Visual QuickStart Guide*, by Ethan Wilde, published by Peachpit Press.

DATA IMPORTING AND REPAIRING

12

The world is full of information and comparatively little of it is in perfect, ready-to-use FileMaker 5.0 format. Foreign data can be sprinkled with useless formatting and unreadable characters. Tabular text and spreadsheets may be easy to import, but seem to require so much editing that you're tempted to start from scratch. Perhaps you've been given the task of incorporating a file whose data overlaps with your own, but hesitate to corrupt your own files with duplications and inconsistencies. Even existing FileMaker databases can present problems. They may not have been created in a recent version, or have been so poorly designed that they need emergency care.

There are several strategies you can use to overcome these problems. Some take advantage of word processors and spreadsheets to clean up the problems before you import. Others are elegant applications of scripting that mold the new data into clean, useful records.

Migrating to FileMaker 5.0

Databases created in FileMaker versions 3 or 4 are very easy to convert to FileMaker 5. Before converting, you'll want to open the file in the earlier version and save a compressed copy just in case you (or someone else) may still need to examine the database in its original format.

To compress a copy of a file:

1. Open your database in FileMaker 3 or 4.

2. Choose File > Save a Copy As.

3. In the Create Copy/Save dialog box, choose compressed copy in the Type/Save a drop-down list (**Figure 12.1**). Click Save.

To convert earlier databases to FileMaker 5:

1. Start FileMaker 5.

2. Choose File > Open.

3. In the Open File dialog box, double-click the file you want to convert.

4. In the Conversion dialog box, you will see the default name under which FileMaker will save a copy of the file in its original version. You can either type a new name, or just click OK to accept the default name in the box (**Figure 12.2**). Click OK.

5. In the Name converted file dialog box, click Save (**Figure 12.3**).

   The file will open in FileMaker 5. There will also be a backup copy saved with the name chosen in Step 4.

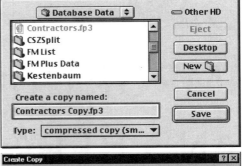

Figure 12.1 You should save a compressed copy of the old file before you convert to FileMaker 5.

Figure 12.2 FileMaker saves a backup copy of the old file.

Figure 12.3 Click Save in the Name converted file dialog box to convert the old file into FileMaker 5 format.

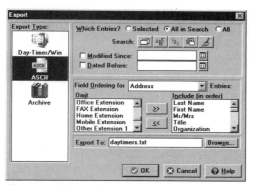

Figure 12.4 This Day-Timer database has the option for saving an ASCII file.

6. A file converted from earlier versions of FileMaker will be exactly the same in version 5 as it was in the original. All calculations, layouts, relationships and scripts will be intact. However, this new file is no longer compatible with older FileMaker versions. If this database is used by other people on your network, make sure that they all have FileMaker 5 installed or they won't be able to use the new file.

About Data File Types

Although FileMaker can import a variety of file types, the most common are text files. Not all word-processed document files are text files—in fact, most of them aren't. Text files are a special subset of files that contain only ASCII text. ASCII text contains only text, numbers and basic punctuation—no special characters, font format, or layout information. Because they're so simple, ASCII text files are readable on every type of computer, and virtually every application that works with data can produce text files. This universal readability makes text format the best choice for transferring data between different applications.

By convention, text file names end with .txt on most operating systems. Although the Macintosh doesn't add a file extension at the end of its file names, it still recognizes .txt files.

Although text files can't contain real formatting, they can carry a couple of special characters that make them useful for data transfer as well as straight text. These characters allow for line returns and tabs. Most programs that support ASCII text as well as their own formatting have an option for saving files with these two important characters (**Figure 12.4**). Some programs call this file type "Tab-delimited text," while others use "Text Only with Line Breaks." (Delimited text is another name for letters and numbers separated by tabs—or commas—for the fields, and returns for the records.)

Other common file formats you are likely to encounter when importing data are DIF and DBF, both of which FileMaker recognizes. DBF and DIF file names should end with .dbf and .dif, respectively.

DIF files are usually created by spreadsheets. Unlike plain text files, DIF files retain any field names they contain. DBF files are created in a format that dates back to the venerable grandparent of all modern databases, Dbase. Many database programs can both export and import DBF files. Like DIF files, DBF files retain the field name information.

MIGRATING TO FILEMAKER 5.0

Importing Data from Other Sources

Some files from other applications (like Microsoft Excel) can be imported into FileMaker without much fuss. But to import data from most programs, you need to create intermediate files in a format readable by both FileMaker and the original program. (See "About Data File Types" on the previous page, and refer to your software's documentation for instructions on exporting files.)

Although text files are a universal output format, they don't usually contain field names. You have to determine field order either by looking at the data in the original program, or by examining the data after you import it. Fortunately, FileMaker has a wonderful field mapping feature right in the Import dialog box that allows you to match imported data to your existing FileMaker fields.

To import text data files:

1. With the database you want to import into open, choose File > Import Records.

2. When the Open File dialog box appears, choose the format of the exported file from the Files of type drop-down list. Navigate to the file and double-click to import it (**Figure 12.5**).

3. If the export file includes field names, you will see them in the Import Field Mapping dialog box (**Figure 12.6**). If not, you will see the data from the first record (**Figure 12.7**). Click the field names on the right and move them up or down to match the data (or field names) on the left (**Figure 12.8**).

Figure 12.5 When you choose a file type, only files of that type will appear in the Open File dialog box.

Figure 12.6 If there are field names in the import file, they will appear as the data of the first record, although they may not match up with your fields on the right.

Figure 12.7 If there are no field names in the import file, you will see the data in the first record instead.

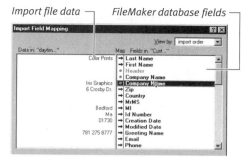

Import file data ┐ *FileMaker database fields* ┐

Figure 12.8 Drag the FileMaker field names to correspond to the data that will be imported into them.

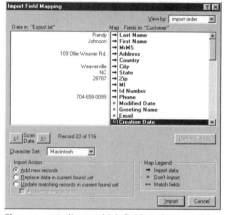

Figure 12.9 Indicate which fields to import with the arrows in the Map column.

Figure 12.10 The Scan Data buttons let you see any records in the import file.

4. For each field that you want to import, turn on the arrow in the Map column by clicking on it. If there are fields that you don't want to import, click the arrow off (**Figure 12.9**).

To help you locate all the match fields, examine the rest of the data in the import file by clicking the Scan Data buttons (**Figure 12.10**). If you find information that doesn't match any current fields, click the Define Fields button (**Figure 12.11**). This will bring you to the Define Fields dialog box, where you can create a new field to hold the data.

5. When you are satisfied that the field mapping is correct, click Import.

continues on next page

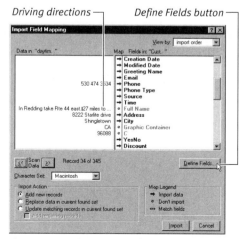

Driving directions ┐ *Define Fields button* ┐

Figure 12.11 Define additional fields for data that doesn't match your current database. In this example, we need to add a "Directions" field.

IMPORTING DATA FROM OTHER SOURCES

6. In the Import Options dialog box, click the Perform auto-enter check box if you want the database to do lookups or add serial numbers to the new records (**Figure 12.12**). Click OK to start the import.

When the import is complete, the database will show the imported data as a found set. Check the data carefully. If you find that all the fields didn't match up properly, choose Records > Delete Found Records to delete all the imported records and try again.

7. If the imported file had field names, the first record will display them. Delete this record (**Figure 12.13**).

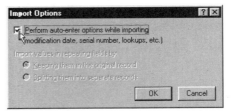

Figure 12.12 You can have the imported data update any lookups or other auto-enter settings.

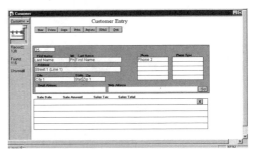

Figure 12.13 If the field names were imported with the data, delete that record.

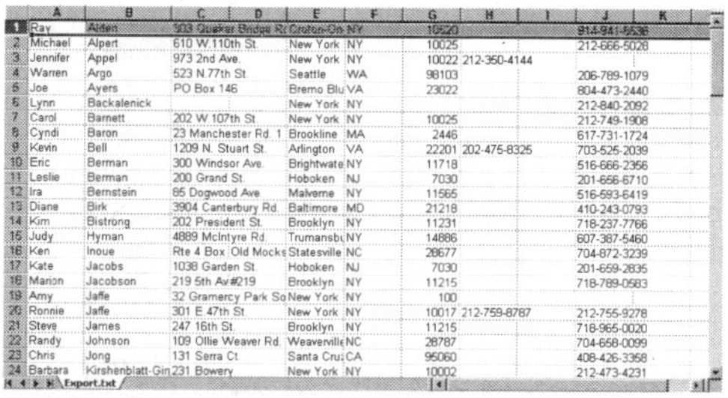

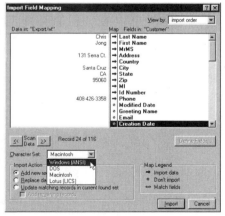

Figure 12.14 In a spreadsheet, columns are the fields and rows are the records.

Figure 12.15 If you want to create field names in a spreadsheet, insert a row at the top and type the field names.

Figure 12.16 The Character Set should be the same as the operating system running the FileMaker database.

✔ Tips

- If the data in a file you're importing doesn't match your existing FileMaker structure, give the information a thorough looking-over in a spreadsheet program like Excel before you continue. Spreadsheet programs display tab-delimited data in columns. Each column corresponds to a field and each row to a record (**Figure 12.14**). You can insert a row at the top of the spreadsheet to create field names, making the match-up process a little easier (**Figure 12.15**). You can also make global search-and-replace changes, then save the data as an Excel file to retain the field names when you import.

- If you're using Excel, you'll import your data with Excel's import wizard. Look at the data in the wizard to see if any of the fields is a Zip code. If so, use the wizard to set that field to text format or else Excel will strip the leading zeroes when you import.

- For Windows users: If you're importing a text file from a Mac or an old DOS application, FileMaker can usually determine the correct character set automatically. If it doesn't, you can manually set the correct Character Set in the Import dialog box (**Figure 12.16**).

Cleaning Up Text Data Before Importing

Sometimes the data you want to import looks promising, but the text file has a consistent quirk that is sure to cause problems. Although most people work with fairly recent versions of software, there are isolated holdouts who use programs so antiquated that their software doesn't use either of the delimiter standard characters (commas or tabs). Problems also occur with text files that contain extra return characters: The extra return produces a blank record, which can throw the database import structure off.

If you have a text file that contains extra returns or other single-character anomalies, there is a relatively painless method for removing them before you import the file, using Microsoft Word. Be sure to work on a copy of your text file, not the original, so that you can recover if you make a mistake. Not all of these changes are easy to undo.

To delete formatting characters in Word:

1. Open the text file in Word.

2. Choose Tools > Options (Windows)/ Preferences (Macintosh).

3. When the Options dialog box appears, the View tab will be selected. In the Nonprinting characters section, click the check boxes next to Tab characters and Paragraph marks (**Figure 12.17**). Click OK.

   In Word 2000, the section you need in the View tab is called Formatting marks.

4. Tab and return characters that are usually hidden will now appear in the text file. If you see extra returns that need removing, choose Edit > Replace (**Figure 12.18**).

Figure 12.17 To see the formatting in a text file, use Tools > Options to make the nonprinting characters visible.

Figure 12.18 These extra return characters need to be stripped out of a file before it's imported.

Figure 12.19 Formatting characters are available from the Special drop-down list.

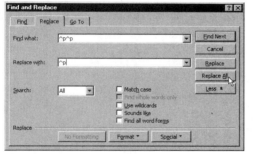

Figure 12.20 Replace All examines the entire document and replaces every double return with a single return.

5. In the Find and Replace dialog box, click the More button to display more dialog box options.

6. Click Special and select Paragraph Mark from the drop-down list (**Figure 12.19**). Do this a second time, so that you have two paragraph marks in the Find what box.

7. Tab to the Replace with box, click Special and select Paragraph Mark from the drop-down list.

8. Click Replace All (**Figure 12.20**).

   Word searches for any two consecutive returns and deletes one of them. Repeat the Replace All command until Word indicates that no replacements were made, then save the file.

   You can now import the file into FileMaker without creating extra blank records.

✔ Tips

- When editing text files before importing, be very careful about deleting tabs and returns. If you accidentally remove one of these characters, you can throw off the structure of the file. If the file structure is changed, all your data from that point on could import into the wrong fields.

- You can also use Word's Find and Replace dialog box to globally correct misspellings, wrong tab characters and other data errors.

CLEANING UP TEXT DATA BEFORE IMPORTING

Finding and Eliminating Duplicates

Duplicate records are a constant problem in databases, particularly if you have to merge data from different sources to update or create them. Even if you're diligent in updating the unavoidable changes in contact person, address, phone and email information, if you have duplicate records you can never be sure that you've edited the right one.

Calculated fields offer a clean and relatively simple way to find and dump the duplicates. They do, however, depend on your having a good definition of what constitutes a duplicate file. In this example, we define a duplicate by the simplest criteria: two records with the same first and last name. In a larger database, however, you'll probably want to expand that definition to include some or all of the address as well, to take into account the fact that more than one individual can have the same name.

Because setting up a calculation is time-consuming and you'll probably want to weed for duplicates periodically, we'll create a script to automate the process.

To find duplicate records:

1. In the file you want to weed, choose File > Define Fields.

2. In the Define Fields dialog box, type Dupe Finder for the field name and click the Calculation radio button. Click Create.

3. When the Specify Calculation dialog box appears, scroll down in the function list on the right to Trim, and double-click to select it (**Figure 12.21**).

   The Trim function deletes any spaces at the beginning or end of a record.

4. In the field list on the left, double-click Last Name (**Figure 12.22**).

Figure 12.21 Select Trim to delete initial and trailing spaces around an entry.

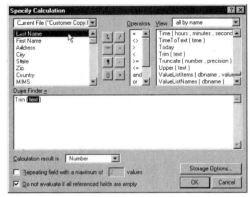

Figure 12.22 The first field the Dupe Finder calculation trims is Last Name.

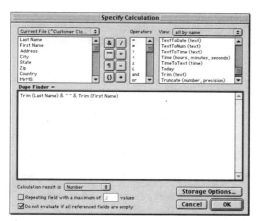

Figure 12.23 The second half of the calculation trims the First Name field.

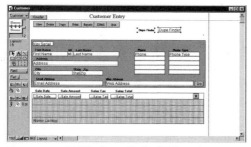

Figure 12.24 Add the Dupe Finder field to a layout.

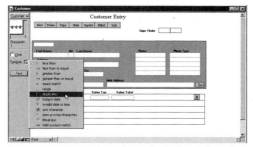

Figure 12.25 The exclamation point is the Find symbol for duplicates.

5. Click to the right of the parentheses and click the ampersand operator button.

6. Click the quotes button and type a space between the quotes.

You need a space placed between quotes so it can be read as part of the function. Otherwise the extra space would be ignored.

7. Click to the right of the quotes and click the ampersand operator button.

8. In the function list, double-click Trim.

9. In the field list on the left, double-click the First Name field (**Figure 12.23**).

We chose the Last Name field before the First Name field because that's how they appear in the layout we use. You should adapt the field choices and add text characters (like commas) as necessary to fit your needs.

10. From the Calculation result pop-up list, choose Text. Click OK, and then Done to finish.

11. To use this calculation, you need to put the Dupe Finder field on a layout. Go to a layout that displays the records in a form that allows you to check them. Choose View > Layout Mode (Ctrl+L/Command-L).

12. Drag the Field tool to the layout. When the Specify Field dialog box appears, double-click Dupe Finder (**Figure 12.24**). The field will be placed on your layout.

13. Choose View > Find Mode (Ctrl+F/Command-F).

14. Click in the Dupe Finder field. Click the Symbols drop-down menu and choose the exclamation point (duplicates) (**Figure 12.25**).

continues on next page

15. Click the Find button.

If there any duplicate values in the Dupe Finder field, those records will become the found set and display on the layout.

16. If there were no records found, make a duplicate copy of any record (Ctrl+D/ Command-D) and click Find again.

If the Find you just tried still doesn't turn up any duplicate records, you'll have to create one and run the Find again. The next step will be to write a script to automate this process, and unless the search successfully locates a found set with your criteria, the script won't have any criteria to restore, and therefore won't work.

17. Choose Scripts > ScriptMaker.

18. Name the script "Dupe Finder" and click Create.

19. When the Script Definition dialog box appears, click Clear All to delete the default script.

20. In the script step list on the left, scroll down to the Sort/Find/Print section and double-click Perform Find (**Figure 12.26**). Click OK, and then Done to finish.

You can remove the Dupe Finder from the layout because you no longer need it. If you duplicated a record to create a find criterion, delete it as well.

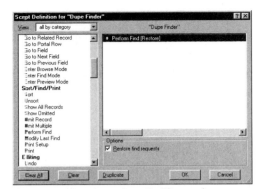

Figure 12.26 Use the Perform Find (Restore) step to automatically find duplicates.

✔ Tips

■ The best way to look at the duplicate records you've found is with a column layout format. This lets you see all the data in the same layout.

■ Be careful not to choose Delete Found Records when you run the Dupe Finder. Dupe Finder will display both copies of the record so you can compare them. If you delete the found set, you delete both the duplicate and the original.

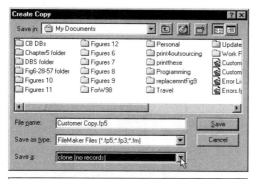

Figure 12.27 A saved copy (clone) will have the same structure as the original file, but no records.

Importing Data without Duplications

Although it's good to clean up a database after you've imported records, it's even better to avoid duplication to begin with.

To compare your new data with your old data and avoid importing duplicates, you'll need to have the field and script created in "To find duplicate records" above. You'll also want to create a clone of the main file first. You can then import the data into the clone, manipulate it in perfect confidence and safety, then import the results into the main file.

To clone a database:

1. Open the main file in FileMaker.

2. Choose File > Save a Copy as.

3. In the Create Copy/Create a Copy named dialog box, choose Clone (no records) in the Type/Save a drop-down list (**Figure 12.27**). Click Save.

This clone has all the fields, scripts and other elements from your database, but contains no records. It's a perfect place to import your new data and strip it of duplicates before adding it to the main file.

To import data without duplicates:

1. In the database clone, choose File > Define Relationships.

2. In the Define Relationships dialog box, click the New button.

3. In the Open File dialog box, navigate to your original database and double-click to open it.

4. When the Edit Relationship dialog box appears, type a name in the Relationship Name box (we use Dupes).

continues on next page

5. Select the Dupe Finder field for both databases (**Figure 12.28**). Click OK and then Done to finish.

6. In the cloned file, choose File > Define Fields. In the Define Fields dialog box, name the field (ours is Dupe Lookup). Click Create.

7. In the field list, double-click the Dupe Lookup to bring up the Options dialog box. In the Auto-Enter tab click the Looked-up value check box.

8. When the Lookup for Field dialog box appears, click the Lookup a value drop-down list and choose Dupes (**Figure 12.29**).

9. In the scrolling field list, click the Dupe Finder field. In the If no exact match, then area, verify that the do not copy radio button is selected (**Figure 12.30**). Click OK twice, and then Done to finish.

So far, we've created a relationship between the original and clone files that will compare the data in them based on the calculation field Dupe Finder. Only duplicate records will have a value copied to the Dupe Finder field in the clone.

10. Choose File > Import Records. In the Open File dialog box, navigate to the file you want to import and double-click to open it.

11. When the Field Mapping dialog box appears, follow the instructions in "To import text data files" to map the fields, then click Import.

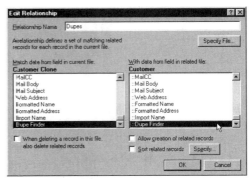

Figure 12.28 The Dupes relationship uses the Dupe Finder field in both the main and clone files.

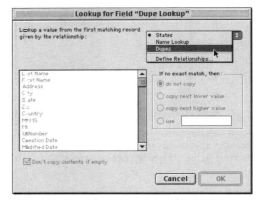

Figure 12.29 Use the Dupes relationship for the lookup in the Dupe Lookup field.

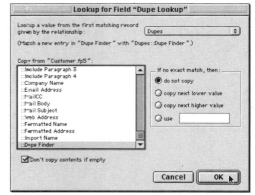

Figure 12.30 If there's no match, the Don't copy contents if empty option will put nothing in the Dupe lookup field.

Figure 12.31 The Perform auto-enter option will do the lookup when you import the data.

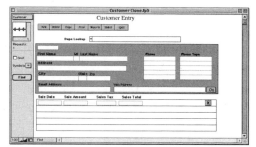

Figure 12.32 Before importing into the main file, find all records that don't have an entry in the Dupe Lookup field.

12. When the Import Options dialog box appears, check the Perform auto-enter options check box (**Figure 12.31**). Click OK.

13. Choose View > Layout Mode (Ctrl+F/Command-F). Drag the Field tool onto the layout. In the Specify Field dialog box, choose the lookup field you just created (ours is Dupe Lookup).

14. Choose File > Find Mode (Ctrl+F/ Command-F).

15. Click in the Dupe Lookup field and choose = from the Symbols drop-down list. Click Find (**Figure 12.32**).

    The = symbol tells FileMaker to find records with no value in the Dupe Lookup field. Since the Dupe Lookup field only contains a value if it is a duplicate record, it will be blank if the imported data doesn't match any records in the main file.

16. When the Find finishes, none of the records in the found set are duplicates of those in the main database. Open the main database file and choose File > Import.

17. Navigate to the database clone and double-click to select it as the file to import. The Import command in the main file will only import records from the clone's found set.

✔ Tip

- Although the Dupe Finder/Dupe Lookup process prevents you from importing records that duplicate your existing database, it doesn't close the door to duplicates within the data you want to import. If you suspect that the new records aren't clean, you can run the Dupe Finder script on the imported file to check it before you follow the steps to compare it to the main database.

IMPORTING DATA WITHOUT DUPLICATIONS

Troubleshooting Problem Data

Some data problems can't be anticipated, so they find their way into your database even after you've taken basic precautions. These errors usually have to do with inconsistencies in data entry, misspellings and missing data. FileMaker's Replace command can be of immense help in correcting these problems. The Replace command allows you to set a field in every record in the database (or in a found set) to a particular value or the result of a calculation.

To show how Replace cleans up inconsistencies, we'll use the example of inconsistent entries in a database's State field. Some records might have no state name entered, while others might have entries like N.Y. or n.y. when you want NY.

Before you use Replace, make a backup copy of your file. This command cannot be undone.

To replace inconsistent data:

1. Create a Search that finds all the versions of the state that you've observed in the records.

   You can search by using Requests > Add New Request, or see Chapter 5 for ways to use search operators to fine-tune your text search.

   This will capture as a found set every record whose State field you want to change.

2. Enter the correct entry in the field for any one of the incorrect records. In our example, we'd enter the correct state abbreviation. Leave the cursor in the field.

3. Choose Records > Replace.

4. When the Replace dialog box appears, click Replace (**Figure 12.33**). A warning will display asking if you really want to replace the records. Click OK.

   The field in all of the records will now contain the text you entered in Step 2.

You can repeat these steps for any other state, as well as any set of records with some common element, such as name or address, that you need to replace.

✔ Tip

■ If you don't want to look through your data for variations on a State field, consider doing a search for a range of Zip codes instead. Since Zip codes are assigned according to state, you'll still get a found set you can work with, then use the Replace command to clean up the State field.

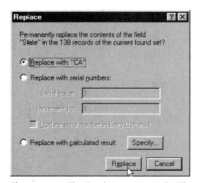

Figure 12.33 The Replace command will change all of the entries in the selected field to the data in the current record.

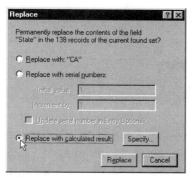

Figure 12.34 Replace with calculated result allows you to replace formatting, not just text.

Figure 12.35 The Upper function changes the type style to capital letters.

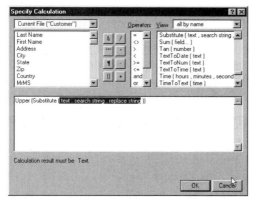

Figure 12.36 The Substitute function changes all occurrences of one piece of information with another.

Replacing Inconsistent Formatting

A straight Replace puts new data where old information once was. Sometimes, however, you only want to edit a portion of a record while leaving the rest of the field contents intact. That's when you need a calculation using the Substitute function.

For example, suppose you have a State field containing a variety of formats, like NY, N.J., Ca, and R.i. Searching for each state's variations would take so long you might as well input them by hand. The Substitute function replaces a letter, word or any other piece of data with another, leaving the rest of the field intact.

To replace inconsistent formatting:

1. Go to a layout containing the field whose data you want to improve. Click in the field. Our example uses the State field.

2. Choose Records > Replace.

3. Click the Replace with calculated result radio button (**Figure 12.34**).

   Replace with calculated result replaces the data in the field with a calculation instead of text or numbers.

4. When the Specify Calculation dialog box appears, scroll down in the function list on the right to Upper, and double-click it (**Figure 12.35**).

   The Upper function turns all text within the field you specify into uppercase characters.

5. In the function list, double-click the Substitute function (**Figure 12.36**).

   The Substitute function searches for characters in a field, then replaces them with whatever other characters you specify.

continues on next page

6. Highlight the word "text" in the formula builder and double-click the State field in the field list (**Figure 12.37**).

This tells the Substitute function to make its changes in the State field.

7. In the formula builder, highlight "search string" and click the quotes button. Type a period between the quotes (**Figure 12.38**).

The Substitute function will search for periods in the State field.

8. In the formula builder, highlight "replace string" and click the quotes button. Don't type anything between the quotes (**Figure 12.39**). Click OK.

This tells the Substitute function to delete any periods it finds in the State field.

9. In the Replace dialog box, click Replace.

The information in the State field won't change, but it will all be in capital letters without periods.

You can apply this technique to any field containing characters that you want to get rid of. For instance, if you import address data that includes unwanted commas, you can leave out the Upper function and use a comma instead of a period for the search string.

✔ Tip

■ If you want to do a Find and Replace for a single record, you can do a Find to isolate that record. Then you can use a Replace with the Substitute function to search for all instances of a piece of text in a field and replace them with other text (or with nothing). This is especially handy for fields with long text blocks.

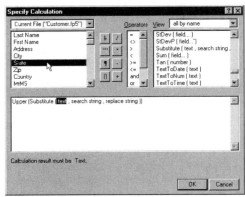

Figure 12.37 Enter the State field for the text argument.

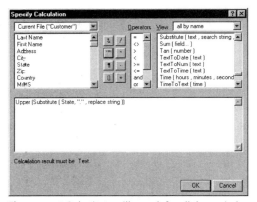

Figure 12.38 Substitute will search for all the periods in the field.

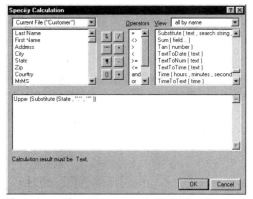

Figure 12.39 The empty quotes indicate that the periods will be deleted.

Figure 12.40 Match the Import Name field with the full name data.

Separating Parts of Data

If you are faced with importing a file with badly structured data, you may have to separate parts of a single field into smaller parts. For example, if your text file has one field for first and last names or city, state and Zip code but your database has them as separate elements, you need to separate the data into its constituent parts. The process of doing this is called *parsing*, and it can be complex because each set of text combinations can present its own problems. No one script can be used for all parsing situations, but the concept we show here is adaptable for a wide range of parsing needs. These steps show how to parse a Full Name field:

Name = John J. Jones
into first, middle and last names.

First Name = John
MI = J
Last Name = Jones

To parse imported data:

1. Clone your main file. (See "To clone a database" above.)

2. In the original database, choose File > Define Fields (Ctrl+Shift+D/Command-Shift-D).

3. You need to create a field into which you will temporarily import the name data from the import file, so you can then parse it into separate fields. Type a name for the field (we use Import Name). Click Create and Done.

4. Open the database clone. Follow the steps in "To import text data files" above, matching the names (or the name field) in the import file to the Import Name field (**Figure 12.40**).

continues on next page

SEPARATING PARTS OF DATA

5. Choose Scripts > ScriptMaker. Type a name for the script (we use Parse Name) and click Create.

6. When the Script Definition dialog box appears, click Clear All to delete the default script.

7. In the step list on the left, double-click Go to Record/Request/Page. Leave the option set to First (**Figure 12.41**).

8. In the step list on the left, double-click Loop.

9. In the step list on the left, double-click If to insert it between Loop and End Loop (**Figure 12.42**). In Options, click Specify to bring up the Specify Calculation dialog box.

10. In the function list on the right, scroll down to WordCount and double-click it.

The WordCount function counts the number of words in the field you choose.

11. In the field list on the left, double-click the Import Name field (**Figure 12.43**).

12. Click to the right of the parentheses and double-click the equal operator. Enter 3 (**Figure 12.44**). Click OK.

This calculation tells the script to look at the Import Name field to see if it has three words in it.

13. In the step list, scroll down to the Fields section and double-click Set Field. In Options, click the Field/Specify Field button (**Figure 12.45**). When the Specify Field dialog box appears, double-click MI.

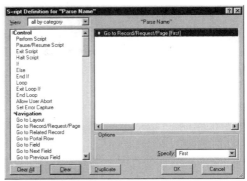

Figure 12.41 The Go to Record/Request/Page step starts the script in the first record in the database.

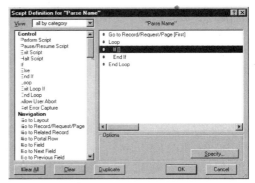

Figure 12.42 If and End If are inserted between Loop and End Loop.

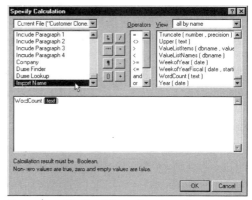

Figure 12.43 The Word Count function will count words in Import Name.

SEPARATING PARTS OF DATA

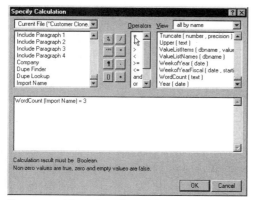

Figure 12.44 The script will act if the Import Name field has three words in it.

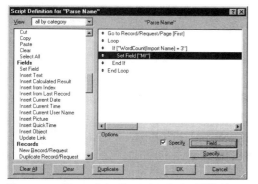

Figure 12.45 The script will put data in the MI field.

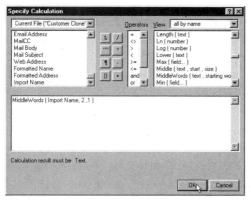

Figure 12.46 The MiddleWords function extracts the second word in the Import Name field.

14. In Options, click the Specify button to bring up the Specify Calculation dialog box.

15. In the function list on the right, scroll down to MiddleWords and double-click.

16. In the formula box, highlight "text" inside the parentheses. In the field list, double-click Import Name.

17. In the formula box, highlight "starting word" and type 2. Highlight "number of words" and type 1 (**Figure 12.46**). Click OK.

The script now says: If there are three words in Import Name, find word number 2 and place it into the MI field.

18. In the script assembly box, click the End If step. In the step list, double-click Set Field (**Figure 12.47**).

19. In Options, click the Field/Specify Field button. When the Specify Field dialog box appears, double-click First Name.

20. In Options, click the Specify button to bring up the Specify Calculation dialog box.

continues on next page

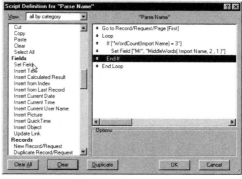

Figure 12.47 Highlight End If in the assembly window to insert the Set Field step above it.

SEPARATING PARTS OF DATA

21. In the function list on the right, scroll down to LeftWords and double-click.

The LeftWords function looks at the field you choose and counts from the left to find the number of words you specify.

22. In the formula box, highlight "text" inside the parentheses. In the field list, double-click Import Name.

23. In the formula box, highlight "number of words" and type 1 (**Figure 12.48**). Click OK.

24. In the script assembly window, click the Duplicate button to duplicate the last Set Field script step (**Figure 12.49**). Double-click the new Set Field step.

25. When the Specify Field dialog box appears, double-click Last Name.

26. In Options, click the Specify button to bring up the Specify Calculation dialog box.

27. In the formula box, highlight "Left" in LeftWords. Type Right to change the function to RightWords (**Figure 12.50**). Click OK.

RightWords is exactly like LeftWords, except that it counts from the right, not the left.

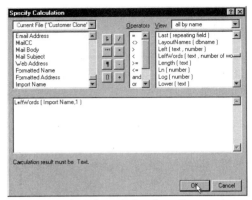

Figure 12.48 The LeftWords function will return the first word in the Import Name field.

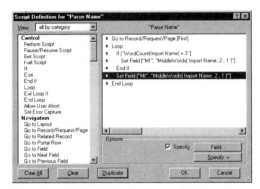

Figure 12.49 It's easier to duplicate and edit a script step with a calculation.

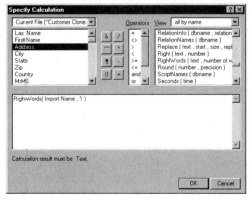

Figure 12.50 Change LeftWords to RightWords.

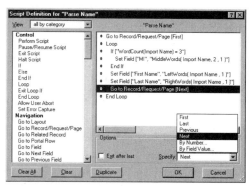

Figure 12.51 The script will go to the next record in the file until it's changed them all.

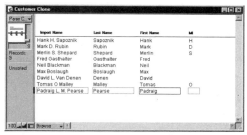

Figure 12.52 A column layout with the name fields makes it easy to correct any problems that the Parse Name script couldn't handle.

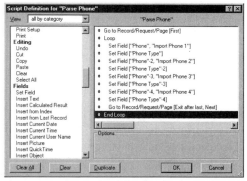

Figure 12.53 The number following the name of a field indicates which repetition of the field each phone number should be placed in.

28. In the step list on the left, double-click Go to Record/Request/Page. In Options, choose Next from the Specify drop-down list (**Figure 12.51**). Click the Exit after last check box.

This step tells the script to go to the next record it finds, then stop after the last one.

29. Click OK, and then Done to finish.

When you run this script, it marches through the clone database putting the first word of Import Name into the First Name field, the last word into the Last Name Field and, if there are three words in Import Name, the middle word into the MI field.

✔ Tips

- If any of the records have more than three words (like James J. Jones Jr.), some data won't parse correctly. To double-check your work before you import the clone data into the main database, create a column layout with the fields Import Name, First Name, MI and Last Name. You'll quickly see the names that weren't parsed correctly and can edit the records (**Figure 12.52**).

- You can adapt the script-parsing strategy for times when the data structure of the import file and main database are different. For example, many handheld devices have separate phone fields for home, work, fax, etc., but your database may have one phone field with several repetitions. Create several Import Phone fields (1 through however many phone repetitions you have). Keep track of which number imports into which field. Then create a script loop with a Set Field (Phone) to Import Phone 1 (the home number), Set Field (Phone/repetition 2) to Import Phone 2 (the work number), and so on (**Figure 12.53**).

MULTI-USER FILES ON A NETWORK

13

Although many people create single-user databases for their own purposes, in general databases are maintained and used by more than one person. Frequently, that means that several users will have an urgent need to use this information at exactly the same time. If you have networked computers no one has to wait in line. One of FileMaker Pro's strengths is its ability to allow file sharing on a network by both Windows and Macintosh users simultaneously. While one person is entering new data, another can be printing reports while a third person is searching for particular records. This basic capability is enhanced and turbo-charged with FileMaker Server, which eliminates the major limitations placed on the standard version and supports more extensive LAN and Internet access. FileMaker Server is covered in the next chapter.

Setting Network Protocols

In order to share your database, you need to tell FileMaker what protocol your network uses. If you choose the wrong protocol you won't be able to access multi-user files or do any other network-related tasks with FileMaker. Check with your network administrator if you're not sure what protocol your network supports.

To set network protocols:

1. Choose Edit > Preferences > Application to bring up the Application Preferences dialog box with the General tab displayed.

2. Click the Network Protocol drop-down list and choose your protocol (**Figure 13.1**).

3. Click OK.

   You must quit FileMaker and start it again for the change to take effect.

✔ Tip

■ Each IP (Internet Protocol) address is a unique number that identifies the computer on a TCP/IP network. If the computers on your network are already using TCP/IP, they have addresses. On the other hand, if you are setting up TCP/IP for the first time and the computers don't have an Internet connection, you can assign IP numbers to them that begin with 192.168 (following the standard IP address format, like 192.168.0.1) This series of numbers is reserved for internal computer use and isn't accessible on the Internet, but it's perfect for allowing you to test your connections before you go online, or if your FileMaker network will remain local.

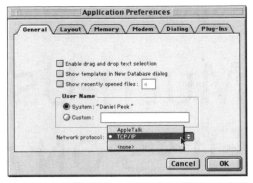

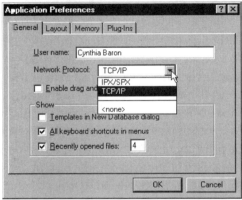

Figure 13.1 Set the network protocol by choosing it from the drop-down list.

Network Speed and Network Protocols

The more people using your databases at the same time, the more important the network speed becomes. There are many things you can do when you configure your network to improve the way your networked FileMaker database performs.

FileMaker's minimum practical network is a 10-Base-T Ethernet architecture. If you anticipate more than 10 or 12 users, 100-Base-T is a better choice.

"Why such a high requirement?" you might ask. FileMaker is a disk-based database program. That means that data is constantly accessed from the server's disk rather than loaded into memory on each guest computer. As a result, FileMaker constantly goes back and forth between guest computer and server while a database is in use. A slow network will make people wait for their files to open, and operations like Find and Sort could become frustratingly slow.

Other network hardware can make a speed difference as well. Most small networks use a hub as their central point for sending and receiving information. If you anticipate that the number of users will grow, consider replacing the hub with a switch, which is more expensive but much faster at moving information back and forth.

Last but not least is the network protocol you choose. Protocols are like a set of language rules for computer communication. Computers that share these rules and settings are like people who share a common language—they can communicate successfully. Computers using different protocols cannot. FileMaker is capable of supporting a variety of network protocols, ranging from TCP/IP (the Internet protocol) to IPX/SPX and Macintosh's AppleTalk, but every computer that will be accessing a FileMaker database must run the same protocol. FileMaker can use TCP/IP on any operating system. Since TCP/IP is faster on most computers than the alternatives, if you can use it as your protocol, you should. On a mixed Windows and Mac network, you won't usually have a choice, because it's the only protocol that both types of computers can recognize.

Setting Up Multi-User Files

Once you have set your network protocols, you can either share files on your computer or access files on other computers. In FileMaker networking lingo, if your computer holds the database file, it's called the host. If you are accessing other files, your computer is a guest.

When you set files to be shared, FileMaker blocks both host and guest from certain actions to preserve the integrity of the database and prevent contradictory changes from being made. For example, when a user of a shared database is editing a record, that record is locked. Other users can view the data but can't edit it until the first user finishes the edit or switches to another record. Everyone can create and edit layouts and scripts, but only one user can do so at any time.

There are other actions that neither host nor guest can do to a shared file while someone else is using it:

◆ Define fields.

◆ Change the sharing status or group access privileges.

◆ Save copies of the database.

In addition, the host can't close a shared file until all other users have closed it.

To host a file:

1. Open the database that you want to share, then choose File > Sharing.

2. In the File Sharing dialog box, click the Multi-User radio button (**Figure 13.2**). Click OK.

3. Repeat Steps 1 and 2 for all files that are related to the first database.

The file(s) will now be available to other users on your network.

Figure 13.2 Share database files by setting them to Multi-User.

✔ Tip

■ Make sure that you set the same passwords and access level for all related files you want to host. If you don't, the main file will open, but the related files won't be accessible. When a file is opened through a relationship, the related files accept the master file's password by default and don't require you to enter the password for each file.

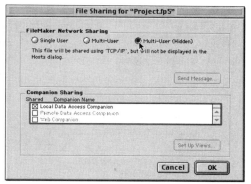

Figure 13.3 A file to set to Multi-User (Hidden) won't appear in the hosts list, but will be available if opened by a relationship or script.

Hiding Related Files

The Hosts dialog box (refer to Figure 13.5) is fairly small, and after you've opened only a few files the window becomes full and you have to scroll to find the one you want. Rather than clutter up the Hosts dialog box with files that will be opened automatically by relationships, you can set just one file (like a Main Menu) to be visible in the hosts dialog box and set the rest to be hidden.

To hide related files:

1. Open the related database that you want to hide, then choose File > Sharing.

2. Click the Multi-User (Hidden) radio button (**Figure 13.3**). Click OK.

3. Repeat Steps 1and 2 for all related files that you want to hide.

The related files won't appear in the Hosts file list, but they will open on guest computers along with the main file.

Creating an Opening Script

Automating repetitive tasks is always good, particularly if they involve several steps that would keep you glued to the screen instead of doing something productive. Although you can wade through FileMaker's startup screens and dialog boxes, it's more efficient to create a single startup script to open several multi-user files automatically.

To create an opening script:

1. Start FileMaker. When the Open File dialog box appears, click Cancel. Choose File > New Database.

2. When the Create New File dialog box appears, give the new database a descriptive name like NetStart (**Figure 13.4**). Click Save.
   When the Define Fields dialog box appears, just click Done.

3. Choose File > Open (Ctrl+O/Command-O). In the Open File dialog box, click the Hosts button.

4. When the Hosts dialog box appears, make sure that all of the databases you want the script to open are available on the network (**Figure 13.5**). Open them if they're not. To close the dialog boxes, click Cancel twice.

5. Choose Scripts > ScriptMaker. In the Define Scripts dialog box, type a name for the script (ours is called Opener). Click Create.

6. In the Script Definition dialog box, click Clear All to clear the default script.

7. In the script step list on the left, scroll down to Files and double-click Open (**Figure 13.6**). In Options, click the Specify/Specify File button (**Figure 13.7**).

Figure 13.4 You can create a new database that only opens files from the network.

Figure 13.5 All the files you want to open must be available before you create the script.

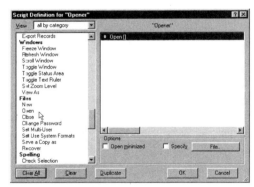

Figure 13.6 The Open step can open files from the host or server.

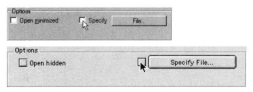

Figure 13.7 Specify the file you want to open by clicking the Specify (Win)/Specify File (Mac) box.

Figure 13.8 In the Hosts dialog box, select files for the script will open.

Figure 13.9 Choose Status functions from the View list to see the complete set of status functions.

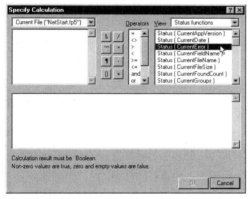

Figure 13.10 This status function captures any error FileMaker encounters while running the script.

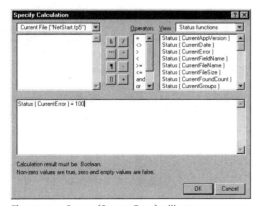

Figure 13.11 Status (CurrentError) will return error 100 if the specified file is not found on the network.

8. In the Open File dialog box, click the Hosts button. When the Hosts dialog box appears, double-click the name of the first file you want to have the script open (**Figure 13.8**).

9. In the script step list on the left, scroll up to the Control section and double-click If.

10. In Options, click the Specify button to bring up the Specify Calculation dialog box.

11. Click the View drop-down list on the right and choose Status functions (**Figure 13.9**). In the Status functions list, double-click Status (CurrentError) (**Figure 13.10**).

12. Click to the right of the parentheses. From the Operators list, double-click the = sign. Type 100 to the right of the equal sign (**Figure 13.11**). Click OK to return to the Script Definition dialog box.

    The error code 100 is the "File is missing" error.

13. In the script step list on the left, scroll down to Files and double-click Open.

    This If statement says that if the file you want to open is missing, the Open File dialog box will appear so you can manually locate the file.

continues on next page

CREATING AN OPENING SCRIPT

14. If there are other files you want this script to open, you'll have to duplicate this first group of steps and edit them. Click on the first step, hold the Shift key down and click on the last step to select the group (**Figure 13.12**). Click the Duplicate button (**Figure 13.13**).

15. Double-click the new Open step (**Figure 13.14**). In the Open File dialog box that appears, click the Hosts button. When the Hosts dialog box appears, double-click the name of the next file you want to have the script open.

16. Repeat Steps 14 and 15 for as many other files as you need to open at startup.

17. In the step list on the left, scroll to the Files section and double-click Close (**Figure 13.15**).

The Close step closes whatever file you specify. If you don't specify a file name, it closes the database of the script in which it was used.

18. In Options, click Specify/Specify File. When the Open Files dialog box appears, double-click the name of the new database in which you are creating the script (**Figure 13.16**).

If you are not sure how the script will work, you can leave out this Close script step (Steps 17 and 18) so you can more easily return to the script to make changes.

19. Click OK to save the script and then Done to finish.

20. Choose Edit > Preferences > Document. The Document Preferences dialog box will appear with the General tab selected. In the When opening section, click Perform script. In the script drop-down list, choose the script you just created (**Figure 13.17**). Click OK.

Figure 13.12 Select multiple steps by holding down the Shift key while selecting.

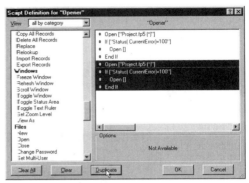

Figure 13.13 Duplicate the selected steps so you don't have to add them manually.

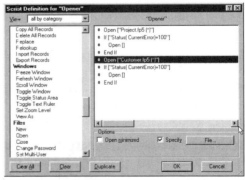

Figure 13.14 The new Open step can be edited to open another file.

Figure 13.15 The Close step will close any open file you specify.

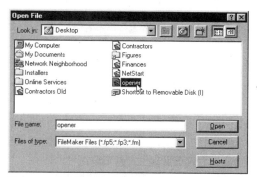

Figure 13.16 Select the database you just created.

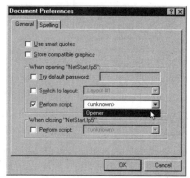

Figure 13.17 Set the script to run on startup in the Preferences > Document options.

When you want to open your network files, double-click to launch the database you just created. The script will run automatically, opening the specified files and then closing itself. If you open a database that has related files, the related files will open automatically, too.

✔ Tips

- If you include the Close step but discover when the script runs that you need to change it, hit Escape (Windows) or Command-period (Macintosh) repeatedly as the database opens. This will cancel the script and leave the file open so you can access ScriptMaker. If you think this might happen frequently, you can give yourself enough time to cancel the script by inserting a short pause in the script itself.

- If you want a particular file to be the active window when all of the files open, make it the last file to open.

Internet Speed and Internet Databases

There is a big difference between making a database available for searching on the Internet and having that same database be editable and shared. The first is not much different from any other Web page accessing information from an Internet server. The second is doable, but frankly less than ideal unless both host and guest computers use a high speed connection like a T-1 or DSL line. Dial-up modems are really much too slow for satisfying communication. Opening a single file can take several minutes and large stores of patience. Finding and editing records will take noticeably longer than the same actions on a local network. Even when both computers have reasonably good bandwidth, sharing a FileMaker database over the Internet isn't zippy. For this reason, if you must share your database this way, keep your layouts as simple as possible. Don't use any unnecessary graphics or backgrounds. Avoid complex calculated fields and summary fields whenever possible.

Accessing Databases Over the Internet

You can open a FileMaker database hosted by another computer even if you aren't on the same network as long as both the host computer and the guest are connected to the Internet and the host computer has a fixed IP address. Both host and guest machines must have FileMaker set to use TCP/IP.

To open a FileMaker database over the Internet:

1. Establish your Internet connection and start FileMaker.

2. Choose File > Open.

3. In the Open files dialog box, click Hosts.

4. In the Hosts dialog box, click Specify Host (**Figure 13.18**).

5. In the Specify Host dialog box, type the IP address of the computer hosting the database you want to open (**Figure 13.19**). Click OK.

   When you return to the Hosts dialog box, you will see a list of all the open shared files on the host computer (**Figure 13.20**).

6. Double-click the file you want to open.

   There will probably be a delay after you enter the IP address of the host and after you double-click the file to open (see the sidebar "Internet Speed and Internet Databases" on page 281).

Figure 13.18 When you click Hosts, you look for files outside your local computer.

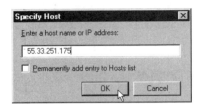

Figure 13.19 To open a FileMaker database over the Internet, enter the host computer's IP address.

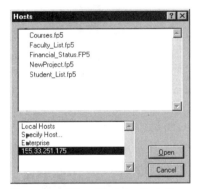

Figure 13.20 When FileMaker finds the computer, it will list the host's available databases.

✔ Tips

- FileMaker 5 databases can only be opened with FileMaker 5. You have to convert databases created in earlier versions of FileMaker before they can be used in FileMaker 5. Consequently, anyone who wants to open a shared FileMaker 5 file must have this version of the software installed on their computer.

- If you don't see any files listed on the host after entering an IP address, check the network settings on both computers. If the host computer's network has a firewall between the network and the Internet, you may have to have the network administrator open a port. FileMaker uses port 5003 for Internet connections.

- You've seen how easy it is to connect to a FileMaker database over the Internet. Keep in mind that anyone in the world (literally) can access your database if they know your host computer's IP address. If you host FileMaker files over an Internet connection, password protection is an absolute must.

ACCESSING DATABASES OVER THE INTERNET

FileMaker Multi-User vs. OS File Sharing

FileMaker uses its own set of rules for sharing files. In fact, Windows or Macintosh OS File Sharing doesn't even have to be turned on for the host and guest machines to share FileMaker files.

Guests should never try to open a shared FileMaker database through their OS's File Sharing dialog boxes. They must always open files by clicking the Host button in FileMaker's Open File dialog box or by using a script that's been written to automate the process.

Testing Scripts for Access Problems

FileMaker allows you to identify users and create groups of users to control how much access you're willing to grant to a database. However, there's a problem with this security that only arises when you use scripts. Ordinarily, if users try to go to a layout they don't have access to, they'll see an Access Denied dialog box message. Unfortunately, when this happens while running a script, FileMaker doesn't know what to do next. Sometimes the dialog box simply freezes on the screen. Other times, the script tries to continue running, fails, and then freezes. To prevent this from happening, you should include an If statement in such scripts that checks to see if the layout you've referenced is one that the individual or group running it can use.

Our example runs this test for a group, but you can substitute references to CurrentGroup with CurrentUser instead.

To test scripts for user access problems:

1. Choose Scripts > ScriptMaker. Double-click a script whose user access you want to control.

2. Click on the first line in the script assembly box.

3. In the script step list, double-click If (**Figure 13.21**).

4. Move the If and End If steps to the top of the script assembly window so they are the first steps in the script (**Figure 13.22**). Select the If step.

5. In Options, click the Specify button to bring up the Specify Calculation dialog box.

6. In the function list on the right, double-click PatternCount (**Figure 13.23**).

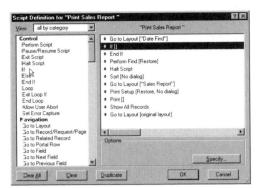

Figure 13.21 The If step allows you to test for two possible situations: if the user is a group member or not.

Figure 13.22 The If step must be located before the rest of the script so it can test for group membership before the rest of the script runs.

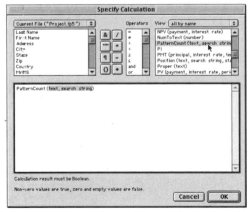

Figure 13.23. PatternCount will return the number of occurrences of a search string.

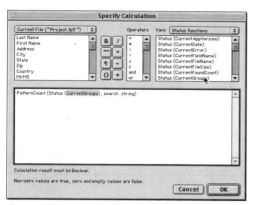

Figure 13.24. Status (CurrentGroups) returns the names of all groups associated with the current password.

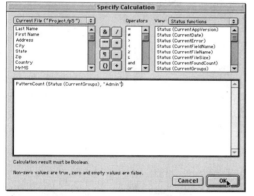

Figure 13.25 For the search string, enter the group name that should access the script.

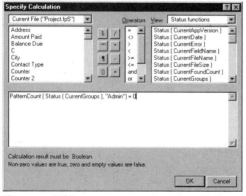

Figure 13.26 If the group name entered is not in the Status (CurrentGroups) search string, PatternCount will return 0.

PatternCount searches for a string of text and tells you how many times it occurs; if it returns the number "0," the specific piece of text is not present.

7. Double-click to select "text" in the parentheses after PatternCount.

8. Click the View drop-down list on the right and choose Status functions. Double-click the Status (CurrentGroups) function (**Figure 13.24**).

   Status (CurrentGroups) identifies which group a user belongs to by examining the current password the user entered to log in.

9. Double-click to select "search string" in the parentheses. Click the quotes button. Type the name of the group that is allowed to access the file (**Figure 13.25**).

10. Click at the end of the formula. In the Operators list, select =, then type 0 (zero) (**Figure 13.26**). Click OK.

    This step looks at the password the user typed, and does whatever you specify in your next script step if the name of the group isn't the one you specified.

continues on next page

TESTING SCRIPTS FOR ACCESS PROBLEMS

11. In the script step list, scroll down to the Miscellaneous section and double-click Show Message (**Figure 13.27**).

12. In Options, click Specify. In the Specify Message dialog box, enter the message to be displayed to a user who does not have access to this script (**Figure 13.28**).

In our example, if the user isn't in the Admin group, they'll receive this message.

13. In the Button Captions section, double-click on Cancel in the Second box and press the Delete key (**Figure 13.29**). Click OK.

We eliminate the Cancel button because the user has no alternative choices.

14. In the script step list, scroll up to the Control section and double-click Halt Script (**Figure 13.30**).

Halt Script ends the script without running it if the user isn't a member of a group authorized to run the script.

15. Click OK and then Done to finish.

✔ Tips

■ FileMaker passwords are not absolute protection for the security of a file. There are "cracker" utilities that can delve into the inner workings of a FileMaker file and reveal the password. For optimum security, proper network security procedures should be observed in addition to password-protecting the file itself.

■ Group privileges take precedence over password privileges. If a user has editing privileges (set by the password), but does not have access to a field (set by the group), he or she cannot edit that field.

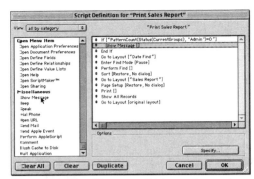

Figure 13.27 Show Message will let users know why they can't get access to a script.

Figure 13.28 Specify Message lets you enter a custom message for the dialog box.

Figure 13.29 You only want to give one choice, so delete the second button text.

Figure 13.30 The Halt Script step will end the script if the user isn't a member of the right group.

USING FILEMAKER PRO SERVER

When there are more than five or six users accessing a shared database simultaneously, performance speed begins to degrade. Although you can partially solve this by designating one computer for file hosting, you'll find this is only a temporary solution. Instead, you should consider using FileMaker Pro Server.

FileMaker Pro Server does just one thing, but does it exceptionally well. It hosts FileMaker databases on a dedicated (single-purpose) computer and allows many users to connect to the same databases with little or no performance loss.

Hosting Files on FileMaker Server

When hosting files, keep them in one location in the server application folder, not scattered around the disk. Centralizing files makes them easier to back up or recover, and can improve access time among files with relationships. In addition, FileMaker Pro Server will automatically open any FileMaker databases that are either in the same folder as the Server application or in a folder inside the Server application folder. You can also use a shortcut (Windows) or alias (Macintosh) of the databases you want to open when Server starts.

To automatically host files in FileMaker Server:

1. Open the FileMaker Pro Server application folder. Create a new folder. You can give it any name you choose (**Figure 14.1**).

2. Create shortcuts/aliases of the databases you want Server to automatically open. Copy those shortcuts/aliases into the new folder.

3. Start FileMaker Pro Server.

   The administration window will open with the Files tab active. In the list you will see a list of the files Server has automatically opened (**Figure 14.2**).

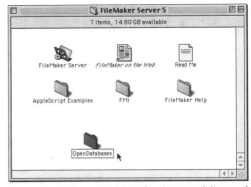

Figure 14.1 Make a new folder for shortcuts/aliases of files you want to open automatically.

Figure 14.2 The Files tab displays all the open files being handled by the Server.

✔ Tips

- Avoid the temptation to toss FileMaker Pro Server on a machine that you already use for other server tasks. If your multi-user database needs are complex enough to warrant running Server, they're complex enough to raise havoc when performance degrades and several access-intensive applications conflict.

- Since you will be running Server on a dedicated computer, you probably want the application to open on startup. On a Macintosh, you can put an alias for the Server application in the Startup Items folder (in the System Folder). On Windows, you add the shortcut to the Startup folder.

- Opening a file in FileMaker Server is not the same as opening the file in FileMaker Pro. You can't use Server to access the file or make changes to it. To make changes to a FileMaker database, you must open it in FileMaker Pro.

- When accessing files hosted by FileMaker Pro or earlier versions of FileMaker Server, you can't modify or add field definitions. In FileMaker Server 5 (with the version 5.0.3 update), as long as you are the only guest in a shared file, you can make changes to the field definitions. This is a wonderful improvement, since it saves you from having to go to the server computer and open the file in FileMaker Pro just to make a simple change.

FileMaker Server Requirements

- FileMaker Pro Server will only run on the Macintosh or Windows NT operating systems. There is no version for Windows 95/98.

- FileMaker Pro Server must be run on a dedicated computer. The server must not be used as a mail or Web server and should not even have file-sharing turned on.

- Ideally, the computer running FileMaker Pro Server should have the fastest hard drive (preferably SCSI) and use the fastest processor speed you can provide. Database file serving is not a trivial task for a computer, and hardware that works beautifully for other server tasks may not be sufficient for FileMaker Server.

HOSTING FILES ON FILEMAKER SERVER

Optimizing Server Settings

You can change some of the Server settings to maximize performance or make it easier for you to administer. In many cases the settings you'll need will be specific to your own database uses, hardware configuration and number of users, so you'll probably have to experiment with some of the settings before you have everything working to perfection. Optimizing requires restarting the Server to enable your changes, so be careful to do these steps when no files are being hosted to avoid damaging database files.

To optimize FileMaker Pro Server:

1. In the Server application, choose Edit > Preferences. The Preferences dialog box will appear, with the Guests tab active.

2. In the Guests tab, enter (or use the up or down arrows to set) the maximum number of users that you expect to be accessing the shared databases at the same time (**Figure 14.3**).

   Set the number a little higher than the current number of users to allow for growth, but don't compensate too much. The more users you specify the slower your database access will be.

3. Check the Disconnect Idle Guests check box.

   People often forget to disconnect when they leave for the day, but if they're still connected they're wasting network and server resources.

4. Enter or use the up and down arrows to set the maximum amount of time a user connection can be idle before the server automatically disconnects it (**Figure 14.4**).

Figure 14.3 Adjust the number of users; add an extra three to five if you expect your users to grow in number.

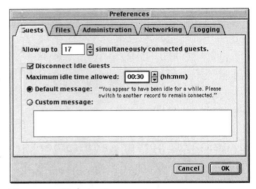

Figure 14.4 You can disconnect users who aren't actively using the server.

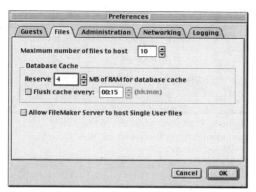

Figure 14.5 Improve performance by lowering the maximum number of open files.

Don't worry that you'll accidentally cut someone off in the middle of a Find. Idle time is determined by the guest's actual use of the shared file. Clicking in a field, doing a Find or switching records resets the idle time countdown to zero.

5. In the Preferences dialog box, click the Files tab.

6. Enter the maximum number of files that Server will host (**Figure 14.5**).

The default value of 50 might be higher than you need. Lowering the value can increase performance.

7. Increase the Database Cache to 10 MB.

The Database Cache has a default setting of 4 MB. This is the size of the memory block your operating system will dedicate to your database, but if you have sizable files that number is probably woefully small. The 10 MB we recommend is only a starting point. You'll probably have to experiment to find the right amount for your specific needs.

8. Click OK to close the Preferences dialog box when you're done.

9. Restart Server to put your changes into effect.

✔ Tips

■ The Flush cache setting in the Files tab controls how often Server will save everything in the cache to the hard drive. A lower number (flush more often) will minimize the possibility of losing changes but can compromise performance. Practically speaking, lost changes are rare and usually limited to the most recently input record. You can usually start low and raise the Flush setting if problems arise. Like the cache setting, you can experiment to find your optimum value.

continues on next page

OPTIMIZING SERVER SETTINGS

- You can check the "Allow FileMaker Server to host Single User files" check box. This allows Server to serve files that are set to single user, so only one user at a time can use them. Hosting single-user files is useful when you want to store a file on the server, but not open it to multiple uses while it's there.

- Macs and PCs handle memory for applications very differently. Windows handles memory assignment automatically. On the Mac, the user has the option of making changes. When you close the Preferences dialog box after optimizing FM Server, the application will tell you exactly how your changes have affected it, how much memory it now needs, and it will offer you the option of upping the memory or resetting the Server preferences (**Figure 14.6**).

For optimal performance, don't allocate more memory to the server than it really needs. The default setting can adequately serve 25 guests and 50 files. If you think you're going beyond that or your files are few in number but very large, watch your cache hits in the Usage Statistics window. Only allocate more RAM if this number drops below 90.

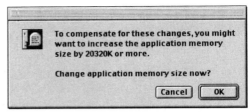

Figure 14.6 On a Mac you can see how much additional memory the Server will need for your optimized changes.

OPTIMIZING SERVER SETTINGS

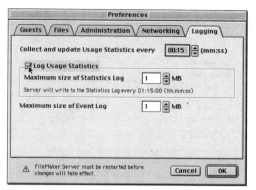

Figure 14.7 You create a log of server activity using the Log Usage setting.

Setting Up a Usage Log

You can have Server keep track of its activity and monitor usage by enabling the Usage Log option. Usage logs note any error situations that occur and keep track of server usage. When you're trying to optimize your server, this log can be invaluable. For example, the log shows the maximum number of users who have been connected to the server at one time, as well as the average number. Since Server runs most efficiently when the number of users allowed closely matches the number of actual users the database has to support, this figure can be a great help in increasing performance. The logs are text files that can be opened in any text or word processor software.

To set up a server usage log:

1. Choose Edit > Preferences.

2. When the Preferences dialog box appears. click the Logging tab.

3. Click the Log Usage Statistics check box to create a log file (**Figure 14.7**).

   If you are running a network with a large number of users, you can set the size of the log to more than the default 1 MB.

4. When you're done, click OK.

5. Quit the Server application and restart it to enable your changes.

✔ Tip

■ Make use of FileMaker's ability to convert .txt docs into files on the fly and 5.0's ability to display layouts in a table. In a snap you'll have a searchable database to look for key words like "error" or a specific file name.

Managing Server Remotely

You can configure FileMaker Pro Server so that you can change settings from another computer. There are many good reasons for not making your changes directly on the computer you're using as a server. The most important, however, is that the computer you've set up as the FileMaker Server may not be sitting right next to your desk. If you have to race around the building every time you want to tweak performance, you'll tend let things slide instead of fixing them. Remote administration makes it much more convenient to maintain and troubleshoot networked databases.

After installing the Remote Administration plug-in (found on your server installation CD) on any computers you want to use for Server administration, you can use FileMaker Pro to open and close files, send messages to connected users, disconnect users and see the usage statistics. In fact, the only things you won't be able to do remotely are those functions that relate to the Server computer itself, like setting preferences and quitting the Server software.

To set up remote administration:

1. In the FileMaker Server application, choose Edit > Preferences.

2. When the Preferences dialog box appears. click the Administration tab.

3. In the Remote Administration section, click Requires password. Enter the password you'll use to log into the FM Server from another computer (**Figure 14.8**).

4. Check the Maximize performance check box (**Figure 14.9**). When you're done, click OK.

   The Maximize Performance setting will give CPU priority to Server at the expense of other applications.

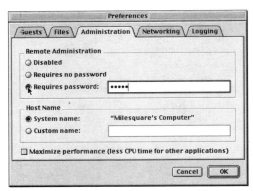

Figure 14.8 Server settings can be changed from another computer on the network if the Remote Administration setting is set on.

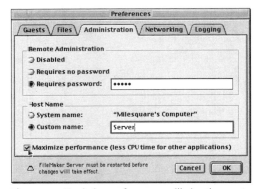

Figure 14.9 Maximize performance will give the most computer processing time to the Server application.

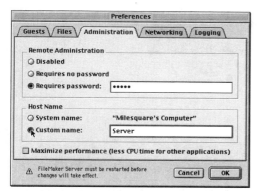

Figure 14.10 You can use a custom name for the Server on your network with the Host Name option.

Figure 14.11
Choose the name of the computer you're using as your server from the Hosts dialog box.

5. Quit the Server application and restart it to enable your changes.

6. Install the Remote Administration plug-in (on your installation CD) on any computer you'll use for remote administration.

To administer Server remotely:

1. Start FileMaker. Choose File > Open.

2. When the Open File dialog box appears, click the Hosts button.

3. In the Hosts dialog box, double-click the name of the Server (**Figure 14.11**).

   If you've set up a password for remote administration, you'll need to type it to continue.

   FileMaker will open three databases from the Server: Server_Admin, Server_Data and Server_Usage.

continues on next page

Naming Your Server

Sometimes the name that's been assigned the computer you're using to run FileMaker Server isn't particularly descriptive. In large organizations, for example, computers might be called by their location number rather than by what they do. If that's the case for you, you'll want to set a different name for users to recognize the server easily.

In Preferences, in the Host Name section of the Administration tab, click the Custom name radio button and enter the name in the box (**Figure 14.10**). Restart the computer and the new name will broadcast as the server name.

---

4. Choose Window > Server_Admin to open the Server_Admin dialog box.

5. You can use the buttons in the Admin window to open and close files and send Messages, just as you do in the Server Admin window (**Figure 14.12**). If you click the Usage button you'll see the server's usage statistics (**Figure 14.13**).

6. When you are finished with your administration tasks, either quit FileMaker or close all three Server_ windows.

✔ Tip

■ Although you can't run Server on a Windows 95/98 computer, if you insert the FileMaker Pro Server installer CD in a Windows 95/98 computer, the installer will give you the option of installing the Remote Administrator plug-in.

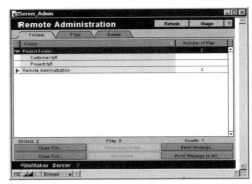

Figure 14.12 You can do most of the same things as a remote administrator as you can right on the server.

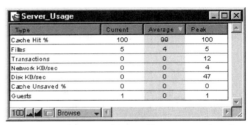

Figure 14.13 The Usage button allows you to view the usage log you created.

15

WEB PUBLISHING

In Chapter 13, we used FileMaker to access FileMaker databases over the Internet. Although useful, it's actually not the best and most flexible way to combine FileMaker and the Web. FileMaker lets you use a Web browser to access your databases, which means you can make your files available to anyone even if they don't own FileMaker themselves.

If you are not a crackerjack HTML or XML programmer and your needs are simple, the best way to get your databases on the Web is by using FileMaker's Instant Web Publishing. IWP is the ultimate in user-friendly. Just by enabling one plug-in and making a few menu choices, you can put actual files on the Web with almost no prior Web experience.

Although delightfully easy to set up, IWP has significant limitations. There are very few stylistic looks for displaying the data, and if you have to allow for older Web browser versions that don't support Cascading Style Sheets, JavaScript and XML, the choices boil down to only one or two styles. If you want to incorporate FileMaker data into more complex Web pages or an already-existing Web site, you will need Custom Web Publishing instead of IWP. CWP allows you to display data, and to fully control your FileMaker database and the way it is visually and functionally presented. However, it relies on CDML (Claris Dynamic Markup Language), which is similar to HTML but considerably more complex, and requires that you already be familiar with HTML to use it effectively. In this chapter we cover the most important elements for using either method. Bear in mind, though, that explaining Custom Web Publishing alone could fill several books, so this chapter will only cover enough to get you started.

Instant Web Publishing

Most of the same requirements we mentioned in Chapter 13 for FileMaker applications on the Internet apply for Web browsing as well. At the very least, you must have a full-time, high-speed connection to the Internet with a fixed IP address.

Consider how many users will access the database once it is published on the Web. The standard FileMaker version only allows access to ten different computers (defined by their IP addresses) in any 12-hour period. If you limit access to just a few people, the standard version is all you need.

However, if you intend to invite the world to your database, you will need FileMaker Pro Unlimited. This version of FileMaker is identical to the standard one, but has no upper limit on the number of people who can use it at one time.

✔ Tip

■ Anyone using a dial-up connection will probably have a different IP address each time they connect. Keep this in mind if you're considering FileMaker Pro Unlimited instead of Standard, but you're not sure you absolutely need it.

Web-Savvy File Planning

If you'll be publishing a database on the Web, consider these technical requirements before you begin:

◆ File names should adhere to the 8.3 convention.

◆ File, field, and layout names should not contain spaces. Use underscores (Shift-hyphen) instead.

◆ Pop-up lists and drop-down menus may not display correctly on older browsers, so avoid them in your layouts when possible.

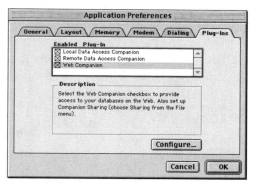

Figure 15.1 The Web Companion plug-in makes FileMaker files available over the Web.

Configuring Databases for Web Access

The FileMaker Web Companion plug-in is your key to making databases available on the Web. This plug-in acts as a CGI gateway, translating requests between a Web browser and FileMaker Pro into the appropriate code for each, allowing a user to seamlessly interact with your database. Once you've enabled Web Companion, you'll also need to open your files with a password that allows records to be exported.

To enable Web Companion:

1. In FileMaker Pro, choose Edit > Preferences > Application.

2. When the Application Preferences dialog box appears, click the Plug-Ins tab.

3. Click the Web Companion check box (**Figure 15.1**).

   If the Web Companion plug-in does not appear in the list, you can install it from your original FileMaker installation CD.

4. Click OK.

To configure file sharing privileges:

1. In the database to be published on the Web, choose File > Sharing to open the File Sharing dialog box.

2. In the FileMaker Network Sharing section, click the Multi-User radio button (**Figure 15.2**).

3. In the Companion Sharing area, click the Web Companion check box (**Figure 15.3**).

4. Click OK.

Repeat these steps for any other databases you want to publish and for any related databases. Your databases are now ready for Web access.

✔ Tip

■ If you want to have related databases available for Web publishing but don't want them to appear as separate files, click the Multi-User (Hidden) radio button instead of Multi-User in the FileMaker Network Sharing section (**Figure 15.4**).

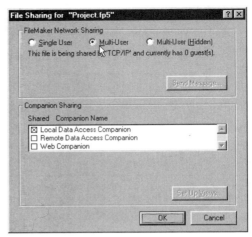

Figure 15.2 To publish a database with the Web Companion, you must specify it as Multi-User.

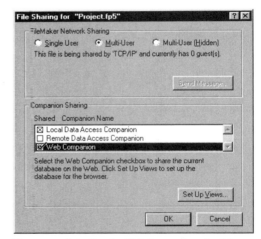

Figure 15.3 Selecting the Web Companion check box starts the Web Companion.

Figure 15.4 The Multi-User (Hidden) option prevents an open database from displaying on the home page.

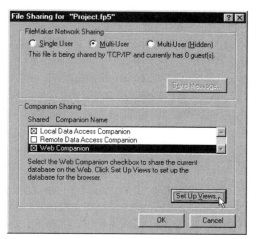

Figure 15.5 Set Up Views lets you select Web Styles for each database.

Choosing a Layout Style

Layout Styles determine what your database looks like in a Web browser. Colors, text styles and graphics are all determined by the style you select. Styles are similar in appearance to the Themes that are used to create layouts in the Layout Assistant.

To choose a layout style:

1. In the database to be published, choose File > Sharing to bring up the File Sharing dialog box.

2. In the Companion Sharing area, click the Web Companion plug-in check box.

3. Click the Set Up Views button (**Figure 15.5**).

continues on next page

Browser Versions and FileMaker Styles

Unfortunately, not all browsers are created equal, and some are more unequal than others. Despite their being free to download, not everyone updates Web browsers to the latest version. In fact, a surprisingly large number of people—those with older computers or slow Web access—are still using browsers that can't understand JavaScript or Cascading Style Sheets (CSS).

The range of capabilities in browsers is an important consideration when you're choosing a Web Style. Styles depend on CSS to render them. If the user accesses your database with a browser that supports CSS, the layouts will appear much as they do in FileMaker itself. On the other hand, someone using an older browser will see the layouts in Fern Green. That's because all styles except Fern Green and Blue and Gold 2 depend on CSS.

If you can't be reasonably sure that the only people who will access your database are using browser versions at least as new as Internet Explorer 3 and Netscape 4, choose only one of these two "safe" styles.

4. In the Web Style tab, click the Styles drop-down list and select the Web style you want to use for that database (**Figure 15.6**). Click Done, then OK.

✔ Tip

■ While you're in Web Style, consider how you want people to use your database. You might want to choose Search Only or Entry Only. Search Only allows a user to search for and view data, but not enter new files or change old ones. Entry Only allows a user to enter a new record in the database, but not to view existing records. Entry Only comes in handy if you want visitors to add their names to a mailing list or guest book (see "Creating a Guest Book," page 309). It augments FileMaker's password restriction capabilities and is an easy way to improve your Web data security.

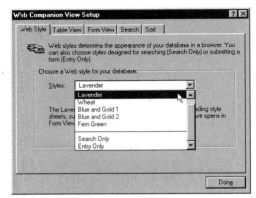

Figure 15.6 Web Style determines the colors and layout you'll see in a Web browser.

Accessed database IP address

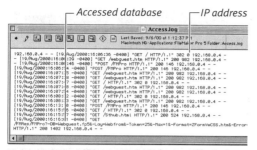

Figure 15.7 The Access log tracks the IP address of each user who signs in to the databases.

Figure 15.8 If any errors occur while a user is accessing your databases, they will be recorded in the Error log.

Figure 15.9 The Access, Error, and Information logs need to be enabled before they will record data.

Tracking Activity and Access

You can use FileMaker's log files to keep track of who has accessed your database and when they did so. You can also track any errors that may occur, which is a good way to debug a problem before too many people experience it. These three log files are in text format, which means you can easily print them out. You can also import them into FileMaker, making it possible to perform keyword searches to display errors or info on specific files. The log files are saved in the same folder as your FileMaker Pro application:

◆ The Access log file (access.log) records every user's IP address as well as the pages looked at (**Figure 15.7**).

◆ The Error log (error.log) records any errors that occur while a user is accessing the databases (**Figure 15.8**).

◆ The Information Log (info.log) is only needed if you are using CDML replacement tags in the HTML code of a Web page. For example, the CDML tag [FMP-Log] will enter any data after the tag; [FMP-Log: Access was granted.] will enter the date and time with "Access was granted." in the info.log file.

To track activity with log files:

1. Choose Edit > Preferences > Application.

2. In the Application Preferences dialog box, click the Plug-Ins tab.

3. In the list of Plug-Ins, click Web Companion to highlight it.

4. Click the Configure button.

5. In the Web Companion Configuration dialog box (**Figure 15.9**), click the check boxes for Access log file, Error log file and/or Information log file.

6. Click OK, then OK again to finish.

Accessing a File with a Browser

Once you've set up Instant Web Publishing, your databases are available and accessible to anyone with Internet access. All that's necessary is a basic understanding of how to use a Web browser.

To access a database with a browser:

1. In your Web browser's address box, type the IP address of the computer that is hosting the databases (**Figure 15.10**). Press Enter.

   For this example, we are using an intranet with an IP address. If your database is published using a domain name, the user can enter the URL (e.g., http://domain-name.com).

2. The FileMaker home page will appear (**Figure 15.11**). Click on any of the links displayed to access a database (**Figure 15.12**).

3. If the hosted databases are password-protected, you will be prompted for a user name and password (**Figure 15.13**).

✔ Tip

■ You can publish databases for Web access even if you open the files from FileMaker Pro Server, as long as the regular FileMaker application is running on your computer. FileMaker Pro Server alone cannot publish databases for Web access.

Figure 15.10 To access published databases with a Web browser, type in the IP address of the host computer.

Figure 15.11 Unless you specify a custom home page, the built-in home page will appear when a user accesses the databases.

Figure 15.12 Databases are accessed by clicking the links on the home page.

Figure 15.13 If a database has a password, you'll need to enter it with your user name to gain access.

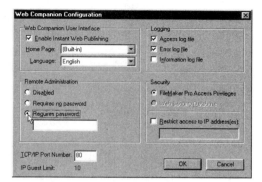

Figure 15.14 Remote administration should always be enabled with a password to protect the files.

Enter password

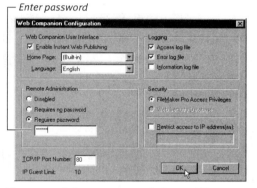

Figure 15.15 Enter your password after enabling Remote Administration.

Enabling Remote Administration

You can administer your Web-published databases from computers other than the one holding your database. Remote administration allows you to open and close databases and use HTTP commands to upload and download files to your Web folder.

To enable remote administration:

1. Choose Edit > Preferences > Application.

2. In the Application Preferences dialog box, click the Plug-Ins tab.

3. In the list of Plug-Ins, click Web Companion, then click the Configure button.

4. In the Web Companion Configuration dialog box's Remote Administration section, click the Requires Password radio button (**Figure 15.14**).

5. Type the password in the box below the radio button (**Figure 15.15**). Click OK, then OK again to finish.

✔ Tip

■ Although you have the option to enable remote administration without a password, it is not a good idea. Without a password, all of your databases are open to anyone.

Restricting Database Access

Password protection for a FileMaker Web database is set within the application. In addition, you can limit access to your published databases to specific IP addresses. This is a handy feature if you are publishing the databases only for the use of people in your company.

To restrict access by IP address:

1. Choose Edit > Preferences > Application.

2. In the Application Preferences dialog box, click the Plug-Ins tab.

3. In the list of Plug-Ins, click Web Companion, then click the Configure button.

4. In the Web Companion Configuration dialog box's Security section, click the Restrict access to IP address(es) check box (**Figure 15.16**).

5. In the box below the check box, type the IP addresses to which you want to grant access. If you want to use more than one IP address, separate the addresses with commas. If you want to allow access to a range of IP addresses, use an asterisk as a wild card (**Figure 15.17**). Click OK, then OK again to finish.

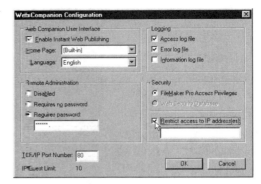

Figure 15.16 You can restrict database access to the IP addresses you enter.

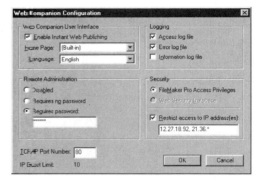

Figure 15.17 By using an asterisk as a wild card, you can grant access to a range of IP addresses.

Creating a Custom Home Page

Unless you specify a custom home page, users accessing your database will see the default home page FileMaker generates. Your alternative is to create a custom Web page that will serve as your gateway to the published databases.

To create a custom home page:

1. Using an HTML editing program or Web page layout program, create the Web page that you want to use as a custom home page.

2. To create links on the home page to the databases that you plan to publish, launch your Web browser and access the first of your published databases (refer to Figure 15.11).

3. In the browser, click the link to the first database. The URL for the database will appear in the address line. Select and copy the full address (**Figure 15.18**).

4. Paste the copied address into your HTML code as the link to that database (**Figure 15.19**).

continues on next page

Figure 15.18 Copy the full URL from the Web browser.

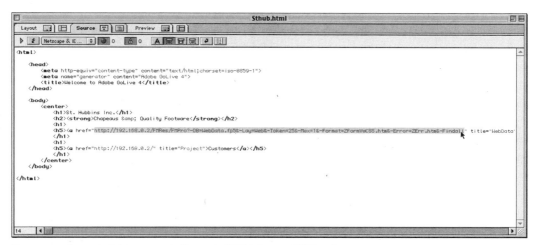

Figure 15.19 For each database, paste the copied URL into your HTML code.

CREATING A CUSTOM HOME PAGE

5. Repeat Steps 3 and 4 for each database that will be listed on the custom home page.

6. After you have inserted URLs for all of your links, save the custom home page and move it to the Web folder (in the same folder as the FileMaker Pro application).

7. Choose Edit > Preferences > Application.

8. In the Application Preferences dialog box, click the Plug-Ins tab.

9. In the Plug-In list, click Web Companion, then click the Configure button.

10. In the Web Companion Configuration dialog box's User Interface section, choose the name of your custom home page from the Home Page drop-down list (**Figure 15.20**). Click OK, then OK again to finish.

When a user accesses your databases with a browser, they will see the custom Web page you created, rather than the default home page (**Figure 15.21**).

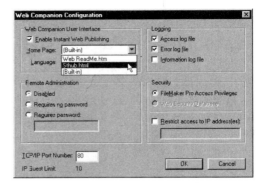

Figure 15.20 Configure FileMaker to use the custom page instead of the built-in page.

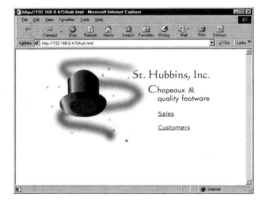

Figure 15.21 Users will see your custom Web page displayed in their browser programs.

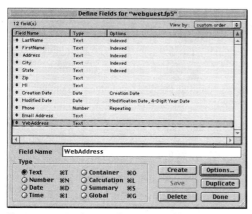

Figure 15.22 For best performance, add only the fields you need.

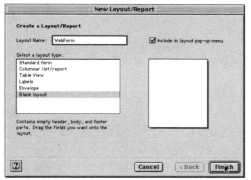

Figure 15.23 Use a blank layout to create your guest book.

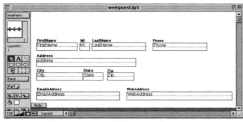

Figure 15.24 The layout fields will appear as you placed them if the browser supports CSS.

Creating a Guest Book

Web-published FileMaker databases are perfect for collecting names and addresses for a mailing list. In this example, visitors see a screen that allows them to enter their data, but don't see other records in the database.

When creating Web layouts for online data input, make your fields in your FileMaker layout larger than you would ordinarily. Web browsers tend to display entry fields smaller than you see them in FileMaker.

To create a guest book:

1. Create a FileMaker database with the data fields that you want visitors to fill out (**Figure 15.22**).

2. In the new database, choose View > Layout Mode.

3. Choose Layout > New Layout (Ctrl+N/ Command-N).

4. Type a name for the layout and click Blank layout. Click Finish (**Figure 15.23**).

5. Click on the Header and Footer tabs and move them up until they disappear.

6. Add the fields to the Body part of the layout in the order that you want them to appear in the browser (**Figure 15.24**).

7. Choose File > Sharing to bring up the File Sharing dialog box. Make sure that the Web Companion plug-in is checked.

continues on next page

309

8. In the Companion Sharing section, double-click Web Companion (**Figure 15.25**).

9. In the Web Companion View Setup dialog box, choose Entry Only from the Styles pop-up list (**Figure 15.26**).

10. Click the Form View tab.

11. Choose the layout you created in Steps 3 through 6 from the layout pop-up list (**Figure 15.27**).

12. Click Done, then OK to finish.

To check your guest book, launch your Web browser and enter the host computer's IP address. When you click on the database name in the home page, the entry form will appear. Fill in the form, click the Submit button, and the record should be added to the database (**Figure 15.28**).

✔ Tip

■ If a user accesses your guest book database with an older browser that doesn't support CSS, they will see the Fern Green style instead of the layout you created. In addition, they will be able to see the other records entered. To deal with this weakness, import the entered records into a separate mailing list database and then delete them from the guest book. Do this frequently enough to avoid a backlog of entries.

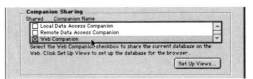

Figure 15.25 Use the Web Companion plug-in to configure the database for the Web.

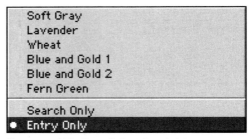

Figure 15.26 The Entry Only style only lets a user enter a new record.

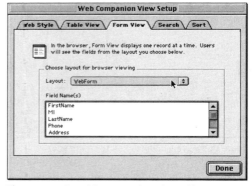

Figure 15.27 Form View uses the selected layout to display the layout in a browser.

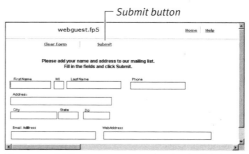

Figure 15.28 When a user enters data in the fields and clicks the Submit button, a new record is created.

Figure 15.29 Typing Localhost instead of an IP address will access the hosted databases on the same computer you're working on.

Testing Your Web Database

Before you publish your databases, test them first with your own browser to make sure they work the way you expect. In fact, you should try to test them with the latest versions of both Internet Explorer and Netscape, and at least one older version. By checking with several browsers, you can make sure that no major problems will appear when a wide range of visitors access your pages.

To test published databases:

1. Open the databases configured for Web sharing in FileMaker.

2. On the same computer, start your Web browser.

3. Open a blank browser page.

4. Type http://localhost/ in the address line (**Figure 15.29**).

   The default start page (or the custom one, if designated) will appear in your browser.

5. Use your browser to view the layouts.

6. Switch back to FileMaker to make any changes necessary (like widening fields).

7. Switch back to the browser and click the Refresh/Reload button to see the changes.

About Custom Web Publishing

Instant Web Publishing is easy to set up and implement, but it sure is limited. Enter Custom Web Publishing. Using CDML tags, Custom Web Publishing lets you insert FileMaker data into standard Web pages. CDML tags are commands that a Web page sends to FileMaker, which interprets them through the Web Companion plug-in. Based on the requests it receives, FileMaker will either carry out a command (through CDML's action tags) or display data on the Web page (through CDML's replacement tags).

Using CDML tags, you can do much more than just display data. You can write HTML code to search, sort, and add data to a FileMaker database from a Web page.

Don't toss those IWP Styles yet, though. Although temptingly powerful, CDML is not something you can master overnight. It is somewhat similar to HTML (which should already be an old friend before you start working with CDML) but has its own, more complicated syntax.

CDML Tags

There are three categories of CDML tags: action tags, variable tags, and replacement tags.

- Action tags carry out commands within a database like adding, searching, and editing records.

- Variable tags are used with action tags to specify the names of database, layout, and results format files (results files are the place where the result of an action is displayed).

- Replacement tags are placeholders. They're used to display data from a FileMaker database in appropriate places on a Web page.

Action and variable tags begin with a hyphen (-):

```
NAME="-format"
```

Replacement tags are enclosed with within square brackets ([ ]):

```
[FMP-CurrentFormat]
```

Figure 15.30 The Web Companion plug-in must be enabled to use Custom Web Publishing.

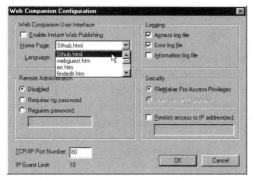

Figure 15.31 When users access your database, the default Web page will be the first thing that they see.

Setting Up Custom Web Publishing

Custom Web Publishing, like Instant Web Publishing, requires the Web Companion and a default home page. The home page can be a standard Web page, but it will require links to the format files for each action you want database users to carry out. We show you how to set up a CDML format file below.

Your home page, format files, and any other Web pages you want connected to your FileMaker database should be placed in the Web folder inside your FileMaker Pro folder.

To set up Custom Web Publishing:

1. Create your default Web page. Save or copy it to the Web folder.

2. Open the FileMaker database to be published and choose File > Sharing.

3. Make sure that the Web Companion plug-in is checked (**Figure 15.30**). Click OK.

4. Choose Edit > Preferences > Application.

5. Click the Plug-Ins tab. Make sure the Web Companion plug-in is checked.

6. Double-click the Web Companion plug-in.

7. In the Web Companion Configuration dialog box, uncheck the Enable Instant Web Publishing check box if it is checked.

8. In the Home Page drop-down list, choose the default home page you want to use .(**Figure 15.31**). Click OK, then OK again.

✔ Tip

■ When you publish FileMaker databases on the Web, any files placed in the Web folder can be accessed by Web users. Never put any important or sensitive files in the Web folder.

Creating a Template Format File

Format files are specialized HTML pages. They determine how data from your FileMaker database appears in a Web browser. Each individual action a user needs to carry out on your database (add, edit, delete, etc.) requires an individual format file written with CDML tags.

A format file contains both CDML tags and HTML code.

Most format files include two modular pieces: HTML coding for a standard Web page, and HTML information that acts as a "header" to identify the FileMaker elements. Once you have these pieces, you can add custom CDML scripting to describe actions you want performed.

We'll build a complete CDML format file in two stages. First, we'll create the basic HTML for a Web page and the header information required by most of the format files we'll show you here. Second, we'll create a CDML action that prompts a user to enter information and gives feedback in response. For this example, we use the Guest Book file from the Instant Web Publishing example above.

To create a basic Web page:

1. Open a blank page in your text editor.

2. In the blank document, type the following lines, replacing "Web Page Title" with a descriptive name.

   ```
   <HTML>
   <HEAD>
   <TITLE>Web Page Title</TITLE>
   </HEAD>
   <BODY>
   </BODY>
   </HTML>
   ```

This is a very bare-bones, simple Web page we've created to hold our CDML heading. You can create a very complex Web page with style sheets and frames instead of this example, as long as the CDML information always appears inside the <BODY> tags.

✔ Tip

■ If you use a text editor that has been designed for HTML coding (like BBEdit) it will open a new file that automatically includes all of this information. All you'll have to do is choose a title for your Web page and insert it between the <TITLE> tags (**Figure 15.32**).

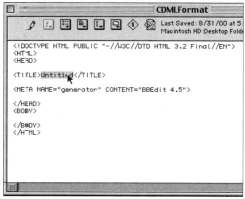

Figure 15.32 BBEdit opens new Web pages with basic formatting in place.

To create a CDML form header:

1. In the HTML Web page you just created, insert your cursor between the <BODY> and </BODY> tags. Type this line of code to indicate that you'll be posting a form using FileMaker:

   `<FORM ACTION="FMPro" METHOD="POST">`

   This line must always be the first line of a Web form because it tells the browser that the next section relates to the form.

2. Although you'll add them one by one, the following four <INPUT> lines can appear in any order. The next line identifies the database you'll use:

   `<INPUT TYPE="hidden" NAME="-db" VALUE="webguest.fp5">`

3. This CDML line locates the layout in the database:

   `<INPUT TYPE="hidden" NAME="-lay" VALUE="Webform">`

4. This line tells the browser to display a standard response to the user when he/she has finished entering information. To create this response Web page, see "To create a response message format file" on page 318.

   `<INPUT TYPE="hidden" NAME="-format" VALUE="response.htm">`

5. If an error occurs while visitors are entering information, you should alert them. You'll need to create the "err.htm" HTML page this line requires.

   `<INPUT TYPE="hidden" NAME="-error" VALUE="err.htm">`

6. This last line is the HTML closing tag for the form (**Figure 15.33**).

   `</FORM>`

7. Save the template format file.

8. When you're ready to use this file for a project, resave the file with a descriptive name, then position your cursor just before the </FORM> tag. Additional CDML code for the form should be added just after the <INPUT TYPE> tags.

   To customize this code for other projects, substitute the name of your database for "webguest.fp5" in the second line, your FileMaker layout name for "Webform" in line three, the name of the format file you'll use to display the data for "response.htm" in line four, and the name of the format file to display if an error occurs for "err.htm" in the last line of code.

✔ Tip

■ Although your HTML and CDML code will work just fine even if you run all the codes together, you'll find it a lot easier to check your code and follow what it does if you put each piece of code on its own line. HTML ignores the Return key on your keyboard, so you can organize your code without adding extra blank lines to your Web page.

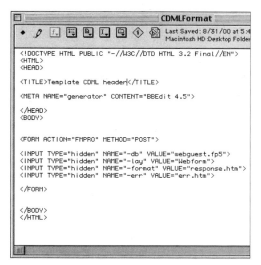

Figure 15.33 This Web page includes the header information needed to turn it into a CDML format file.

Prompting User Input with CDML

The database we used to set up the format file header above (webguest.fp5) contains name and address information, plus fields for email and Web addresses on a layout named Webform. We want this format file to prompt users to fill in their contact information, so we need to input the code in the format file for this action.

To prompt a user for input:

1. Open the template format file you created above. Change the Web page title and save it as a new file.

2. Position your cursor just before the </FORM> tag (**Figure 15.34**) and type the HTML code for the form's instruction text:

   ```
   <P>Please enter your information to
   be included in our mailing list.
   </P><P></P>
   ```

3. Enter the following code to create the form's data entry fields. Since this is a Web page, all SIZE information is input in pixels. You can change these dimensions if you want.

```
<P>First Name: <INPUT TYPE="text" NAME="FirstName" SIZE=20></P>

<P>MI: <INPUT TYPE="text" NAME="MI" SIZE=5></P>

<P>Last Name: <INPUT TYPE="text" NAME="LastName" SIZE=20></P>

<P>Address: <INPUT TYPE="text" NAME="Address" SIZE=20></P>

<P>City: <INPUT TYPE="text" NAME="City" SIZE=20></P>

<P>State: <INPUT TYPE="text" NAME="State" SIZE=5></P>

<P>Zip: <INPUT TYPE="text" NAME="Zip" SIZE=20></P>

<P>Phone: <INPUT TYPE="text" NAME="Phone" SIZE=20></P>

<P>Email: <INPUT TYPE="text" NAME="EmailAddress" SIZE=20></P>

<P>Web: <INPUT TYPE="text" NAME="WebAddress" SIZE=20></P>
```

Position your cursor here

```
webguest.htm
Last Saved: 9/2/00 at 4:55
Macintosh HD:Projects:Fil...

<HTML>
<HEAD>
<TITLE> St. Hubbins Mailing List</TITLE>
</HEAD>
<BODY>
<FORM ACTION="FMPro" METHOD="POST">
<INPUT TYPE="hidden" NAME="-db" VALUE="webguest.fp5">
<INPUT TYPE="hidden" NAME="-lay" VALUE="Webform">
<INPUT TYPE="hidden" NAME="-format" VALUE="response.htm">
<INPUT TYPE="hidden" NAME="-error" VALUE="err.htm">

</FORM>
</BODY>
</HTML>
```

Figure 15.34 Anything that will be a part of the form must appear before the </FORM> close tag.

4. Now we'll create the CDML code to add the data entered by the user into the FileMaker database.

`<P><INPUT TYPE="submit" NAME="-new" VALUE="submit"></P>`

The Submit command combined with the –new tag tells FileMaker to create a new record from the information that the visitor inputs. It also adds a Submit button to the form.

5. Save this page in your Web folder (**Figure 15.35**). In this example we've named it webguest.htm.

Figure 15.35 After entering the code for a format file, save it in the Web folder.

PROMPTING USER INPUT WITH CDML

Providing Visitor Feedback

To provide feedback to the visitor, we need to create two more Web pages—one that will display after a successful submission, and another that displays if an error occurs.

To create a response message format file:

1. To create a new Web page, follow the steps in "To create a basic Web page" on page 314.

2. Position your cursor between the open and close <BODY> tags (**Figure 15.36**), and type the following HTML code:

   <P>Thanks. Your name has been added to our mailing list.</P>

3. Save this file in the Web folder as "response.htm". It will display if the record is added to the database successfully (**Figure 15.37**).

To create an error message format file:

1. Create another Web page, following the steps in "To create a basic Web page" on page 314.

2. Position your cursor between the open and close <BODY> tags, and type the following HTML code:

   <P>Sorry. There seems to have been a problem. Click your Back button and try again.</P>

3. Save this file in the Web folder as "err.htm". It will display if there's a problem with the submission (**Figure 15.38**).

You have now created the three format files needed for your visitors to enter their contact information and transfer it to the database. The last step is to create a link from your default home page to the webguest format file.

Figure 15.36 Text for the response should be inserted between the open and close <BODY> tags.

Figure 15.37 Response.htm will be displayed after the data has been successfully entered into the database.

Figure 15.38 If there is a problem entering the data, err.htm will be displayed.

Figure 15.39 Add a link to the default Web page to add a record with the webguest format file.

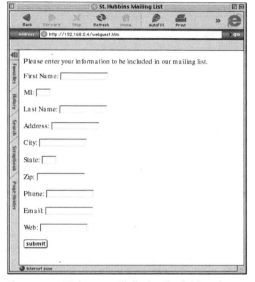

Figure 15.40 Webguest will display the fields to be added to the database.

To link a format file to the home page:

1. Open the default home page in your text editor.

2. Within the <BODY> tags, add a line of HTML text inviting people to join the mailing list, and providing a link to the list itself (**Figure 15.39**):

   Add your name to our exclusive
   <a href="webguest.htm">Mailing
   List</a>

   You can, of course, customize this text with HTML coding to specify its size, position and font.

3. Save the document.

When a visitor inputs the URL for your home page, your default home page will display. When users click the link, they'll see the form your coding created (**Figure 15.40**). They can type data into the fields and click the Submit button. If all goes as planned, they see the response.htm page and the record is added to your database. If not, they see the err.htm page.

Searching for Data with CDML

You can create a format file that searches specified fields in the published database, and returns the results in another format file for editing or viewing. For this example, you'll prompt the user to search by last name or state. Users might want to do this if, for example, their contact information has changed and they need to update the information in the database.

To create a search format file:

1. Open your text editor and follow the instructions in "To create a basic Web page" on page 314.

2. Follow the instructions in "To create a CDML form header" above to add a CDML form header. Since all of the header information is the same except for the name of the format file that will be used after the search format file, customize the information by entering a new file name in the format line (**Figure 15.41**):

    ```
    <INPUT TYPE="hidden" NAME="-format" VALUE="findedit.htm">
    ```

3. Position your cursor just before the </FORM> close tag and insert a line of HTML text prompting the visitor to locate his or her name in the records (**Figure 15.42**):

    ```
    <P>Please find your name.</P>
    <P></P>
    ```

4. Next we'll add the code that prompts the user for the Find criteria. Right after the prompt line you just created and above the </FORM> close tag (**Figure 15.43**), add these lines of code:

    ```
    <P><SELECT NAME="-op">
        <OPTION SELECTED>equals
        <OPTION>not equals
        <OPTION>contains
    ```

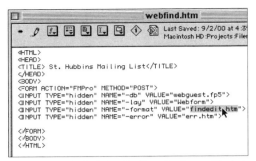

Figure 15.41 "findedit.htm" will be the format file that the search format file calls.

Figure 15.42 You can insert HTML text inside a </FORM> tag.

Figure 15.43 The <SELECT> HTML code creates a pop-up list of the options within it.

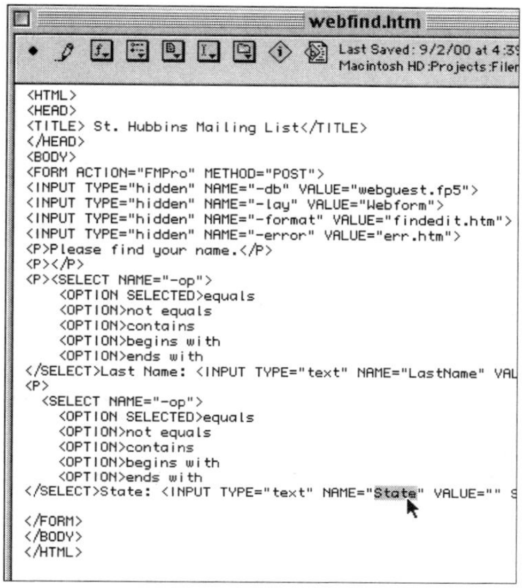


```
<HTML>
<HEAD>
<TITLE> St. Hubbins Mailing List</TITLE>
</HEAD>
<BODY>
<FORM ACTION="FMPro" METHOD="POST">
<INPUT TYPE="hidden" NAME="-db" VALUE="webguest.fp5">
<INPUT TYPE="hidden" NAME="-lay" VALUE="Webform">
<INPUT TYPE="hidden" NAME="-format" VALUE="findedit.htm">
<INPUT TYPE="hidden" NAME="-error" VALUE="err.htm">
<P>Please find your name.</P>
<P></P>
<P><SELECT NAME="-op">
    <OPTION SELECTED>equals
    <OPTION>not equals
    <OPTION>contains
    <OPTION>begins with
    <OPTION>ends with
</SELECT>Last Name: <INPUT TYPE="text" NAME="LastName" VAL
<P>
  <SELECT NAME="-op">
    <OPTION SELECTED>equals
    <OPTION>not equals
    <OPTION>contains
    <OPTION>begins with
    <OPTION>ends with
</SELECT>State: <INPUT TYPE="text" NAME="State" VALUE=""

</FORM>
</BODY>
</HTML>
```

Figure 15.44 Always duplicate and edit code rather than retyping it.

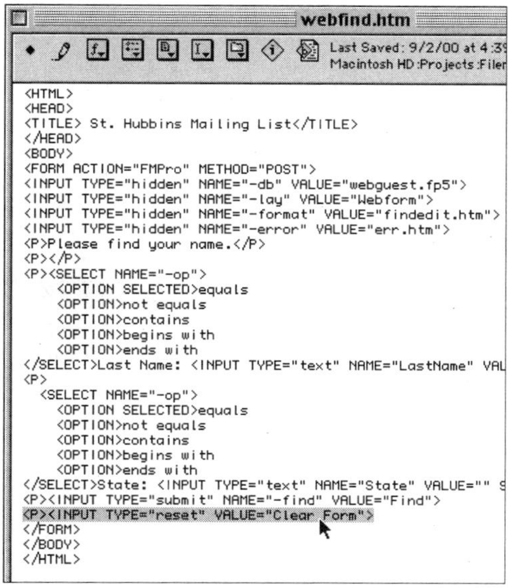


```
<HTML>
<HEAD>
<TITLE> St. Hubbins Mailing List</TITLE>
</HEAD>
<BODY>
<FORM ACTION="FMPro" METHOD="POST">
<INPUT TYPE="hidden" NAME="-db" VALUE="webguest.fp5">
<INPUT TYPE="hidden" NAME="-lay" VALUE="Webform">
<INPUT TYPE="hidden" NAME="-format" VALUE="findedit.htm">
<INPUT TYPE="hidden" NAME="-error" VALUE="err.htm">
<P>Please find your name.</P>
<P></P>
<P><SELECT NAME="-op">
    <OPTION SELECTED>equals
    <OPTION>not equals
    <OPTION>contains
    <OPTION>begins with
    <OPTION>ends with
</SELECT>Last Name: <INPUT TYPE="text" NAME="LastName" VAL
<P>
  <SELECT NAME="-op">
    <OPTION SELECTED>equals
    <OPTION>not equals
    <OPTION>contains
    <OPTION>begins with
    <OPTION>ends with
</SELECT>State: <INPUT TYPE="text" NAME="State" VALUE=""
<P><INPUT TYPE="submit" NAME="-find" VALUE="Find">
<P><INPUT TYPE="reset" VALUE="Clear Form">
</FORM>
</BODY>
</HTML>
```

Figure 15.45 Once a search has finished, clearing the form allows a second search to be done.

```
    <OPTION>begins with
    <OPTION>ends with
</SELECT>
Last Name: <INPUT TYPE="text"
NAME="LastName" VALUE=""
SIZE=20></P>
<P>
```

The SELECT NAME="-op" creates a pop-up list that allows the user to choose a find operator from the options that you specify with the <OPTION> tag.

5. By duplicating and editing the code, you allow a search by State as well as by Last Name. Copy the code from step 4 above and paste it in below the existing lines. Change Last Name to State and NAME="LastName" to NAME="State" (**Figure 15.44**).

6. Add this line below the second block of code:

   ```
   <P><INPUT TYPE="submit" NAME=
   "-find" VALUE="Find">
   ```

   The Submit button code contains the action tag "-find", which tells FileMaker to search for the data entered in the fields and display the results in the findedit.htm file from the format tag in the header.

7. Add this line below the submit line (**Figure 15.45**):

   ```
   <P><INPUT TYPE="reset"
   VALUE="Clear Form">
   ```

   This input command clears the form fields of all previous data. It's the last line we add within the <FORM> tags.

8. Save the file to your Web folder. In this example, we've named it webfind.htm.

You've created a format file to find a record; next you'll need one to edit the record when it is found.

Editing Data with CDML

Once visitors have found the record that holds the desired contact information, they still need to be able to see the record itself, and then be able to edit it. For this, you need a separate format file. This format file uses replacement tags (in addition to the action and variable tags we've already seen) to display data from your database.

To create an edit format file:

1. Open your text editor and follow the instructions in "To create a basic Web page" on page 314.

2. Follow the instructions in "To create a CDML form header" on page 315.

   Since all of the header information is the same except for the name of the format file that will follow this one, customize the information by inputting a new file name in the format line (**Figure 15.46**):

   ```
   <INPUT TYPE="hidden" NAME="-format" VALUE="editresp.htm">
   ```

3. You need this line to tell FileMaker which record can be edited. The replacement tag [FMP-currentrecid] is a placeholder for the current record (the one in the user's found set).

   ```
   <INPUT TYPE="hidden" NAME="-RecID" VALUE="[FMP-currentrecid]">
   ```

4. Position your cursor just before the </FORM> close tag and insert a line of HTML text prompting visitors to edit their record (**Figure 15.47**):

   ```
   <P>Please edit your information.</P>
   ```

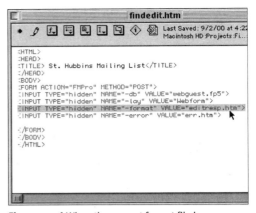

Figure 15.46 When the current format file is completed successfully, the file named in the "-format" tag will run.

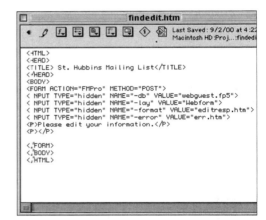

Figure 15.47 Be sure to insert your code before the </FORM> tag, or it won't appear as part of your Web page form.

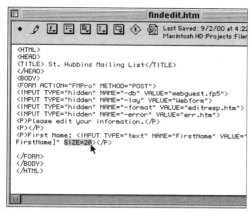

```
findedit.htm                    Last Saved: 9/2/00 at 4:22
                                Macintosh HD:Projects:Filer
<HTML>
<HEAD>
<TITLE> St. Hubbins Mailing List</TITLE>
</HEAD>
<BODY>
<FORM ACTION="FMPro" METHOD="POST">
<INPUT TYPE="hidden" NAME="-db" VALUE="webguest.fp5">
<INPUT TYPE="hidden" NAME="-lay" VALUE="Webform">
<INPUT TYPE="hidden" NAME="-format" VALUE="editresp.htm">
<INPUT TYPE="hidden" NAME="-error" VALUE="err.htm">
<P>Please edit your information.</P>
<P></P>
<P>First Name: <INPUT TYPE="text" NAME="FirstName" VALUE="
FirstName]" SIZE=20></P>

</FORM>
</BODY>
</HTML>
```

Figure 15.48 The SIZE code determines how much space is allotted to display the field.

5. Next we'll add the code that displays the visitor's record in the form. Following the prompt line you just created in the previous step and above the </FORM> close tag, add the lines of code shown below and in **Figure 15.48**.

These <INPUT> tag lines are basically the same as the field code for the webguest.htm format file we created in "To create a search format file" above, with one exception: We add the VALUE= "[FMP-Field:]" command inside the tag. This command prompts FileMaker to display the contents of the fields from the found record in the database.

continues on next page

```
<P>First Name: <INPUT TYPE="text" NAME="FirstName" VALUE="[FMP-Field:FirstName]"
→ SIZE=20></P>

<P> MI: <INPUT TYPE="text" NAME="MI" VALUE="[FMP-Field:MI]" SIZE=5></P>

<P>Last Name: <INPUT TYPE="text" NAME="LastName" VALUE="[FMP-Field:LastName]"
→ SIZE=20></P>

<P>Address: <INPUT TYPE="text" NAME="Address" VALUE="[FMP-Field:Address]"
→ SIZE=20></P>

<P> City: <INPUT TYPE="text" NAME="City" VALUE="[FMP-Field:City]" SIZE=20>
→ State: <INPUT TYPE="text" NAME="State" VALUE="[FMP-Field:State]" SIZE=5>
→ Zip: <INPUT TYPE="text" NAME="Zip" VALUE="[FMP-Field:Zip]" SIZE=20></P>

<P>Phone: <INPUT TYPE="text" NAME="Phone" VALUE="[FMP-Field:Phone]" SIZE=20></P>

<P>Email: <INPUT TYPE="text" NAME="EmailAddress" VALUE=
→ "[FMP-Field:EmailAddress]" SIZE=20></P>

Web: <INPUT TYPE="text" NAME="WebAddress" VALUE="[FMP-Field:WebAddress]"
→ SIZE=30></P>
```

EDITING DATA WITH CDML

6. To create a Submit button, add this line after the <INPUT> tags:

```
<P><INPUT TYPE="submit" NAME=
"-edit" VALUE="Submit">
```

The –edit tag tells FileMaker to update the data in the record with the entries made in the form (**Figure 15.49**).

7. Add this line below the submit line:

```
<P><INPUT TYPE="reset"
VALUE="Clear Form">
```

This will clear the fields on the form, allowing the user to start over.

8. Save the file to your Web folder. We've called our example findedit.htm.

9. You'll need a format file to tell the user that the data was updated successfully. Follow the steps in "Create a response message format file" above. Replace the message text with a message that acknowledges that the changes were made successfully (**Figure 15.50**). In our example, we've inserted:

```
<P>Thanks. Your changes have
been added.</P>
```

10. Save this file to your Web folder. For this example, we'll name it editresp.htm.

11. Open your default home page.

12. Add this line to create a line of text within the Body part containing a link to the find format file:

```
Locate your name and
<a href="webfind.htm">
update your information</a>
```

Format the text line as you'd like.

Figure 15.49 Submit automatically creates a Submit button.

Figure 15.50 The response format file is just a standard HTML page with a text message.

Figure 15.51 With the additional code, the default Web page displays the link to the webfind format file.

Figure 15.52 Webfind searches the database for the data a user enters.

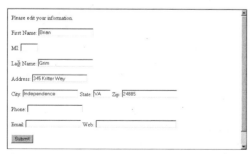

Figure 15.53 The data in the found record is displayed in the findedit format file

13. Save the default page. When you access the default page in your Web browser, you will see the new choice (**Figure 15.51**).

When a visitor clicks Find, the webfind format file prompts for the search criteria (**Figure 15.52**). When he/she enters a last name and clicks the button, the findedit format file displays the data from the found record (**Figure 15.53**). Visitors can make changes to the record and click Submit to update the database.

✔ Tip

■ If you use a graphical Web page editor like Adobe GoLive to create Web pages, make sure that it does not strip out non-standard code. If it does, you can still create the basic layout of pages with the Web page editor, then use a text editor like BBEdit to add the CDML tags to the resulting code.

Browsing Records

Sometimes you don't want users to see the entire database. But what if more than one record meets the search criteria they used to find their file? To allow a user to browse your information, you need a format file that displays the database contents in a table. If you want users to be able to edit the database, you can add the code to let them choose a record from the table.

Tables themselves are regular HTML code, but by inserting CDML's replacement tags you can build a table that pulls its information from the database and displays it "on the fly."

For this example, we'll create a format file that displays ten records at a time, with links to the next and previous pages. This file will display the Last Name, First Name, City and State fields in a table, with a link to a separate format file to edit each record. In order to make the display neat, we will use a Table to show the data.

To create a browse format file:

1. Open your text editor and follow the instructions in "To create a basic Web page" on page 314.

    Don't enter the header data as you did in previous format files. This format file will be called from the home page with a tag.

2. To set up the parameters of your table format, add these lines right after the <BODY> tag:

    ```
    <TABLE border=1 align=center
    cellpadding=3>
    <P>
    <TH>Last Name</TH>
    <TH>First Name</TH>
    <TH>City</TH>
    <TH>State</TH></P>
    ```

    This code creates the headings and format for a multi-column table with a narrow border around it. The table is centered on the Web page. You can customize the look of the table in a text editor or Web page layout program (**Figure 15.54**).

Figure 15.54 Basic table formatting is set in the <TABLE> HTML tag.

3. Next, enter this line:

```
[FMP-record]
```

The [FMP-record] tag tells FileMaker to repeat everything that follows it for all records until it sees a [/FMP-record] tag.

4. Add the following lines of HTML code and CDML replacement tags, which set up placeholders for each of the fields in the table:

```
<TR>
<TD>[FMP-FIELD:LastName]</TD>
<TD>[FMP-FIELD:FirstName]</TD>
<TD>[FMP-FIELD:City]</TD>
<TD>[FMP-FIELD:State]</TD>
```

5. The next line of code creates a link to the database to edit a record. It tells FileMaker to display the data using the indicated layout and format file. In this example, the format file is findedit.htm and the layout is called webform.

```
<TD><A HREF=
"[FMP-linkrecid: layout=webform,
format=findedit.htm]">Edit</A>
```

6. Adding the following HTML and CDML tags closes all the table tags and ends the [FMP-record] repetition.

```
</TR>
[/FMP-Record]
</table>
```

7. Insert these last code lines after the end of the table (**Figure 15.55**):

```
<P>[FMP-linkprevious]
BACK[/FMP-linkprevious]
<P>[FMP-linknext]
NEXT[/FMP-linknext]
```

The [FMP-linkprevious] tags tell FileMaker to create a link to the previous page. The text link won't appear on the first page. Conversely, the [FMP-linknext] tags link FileMaker to the next page. The NEXT link doesn't appear on the last page.

8. Save the format file to your Web folder. In this example, we've called this format file browse.htm.

9. Next, we'll add a link from your home page to the browse format file. In your text editor, open your default Web page.

continues on next page

Figure 15.55 Scroll through the database in the browser by using the BACK and NEXT links.

10. Add this complex code line to the link choices:

```
<P><a href="FMPro?-db=
Webguest.fp5&-Lay=webform&-Format=
browse.htm&-Error=err.htm&-SortField=
LastName&-SortOrder=Ascend&-Max=
10&-FindAll">Browse</a>
our records</P>
```

In this example, the tag tells FileMaker to use the browse.htm format file to display all records (-FindAll) from the database Webguest.fp5, ten at a time (-Max=10), sorted by Last Name (-SortField=LastName) in ascending order (-SortOrder=Ascend).

11. Save your default page in the Web folder. If users choose the Browse option from the Web page (**Figure 15.56**), they'll see the first ten records of the database sorted by the Last Name field. There will be links to previous and next pages at the bottom (**Figure 15.57**), as well as an Edit link so they can update their information.

Figure 15.56 The Web page can contain links to each of your format page actions.

✔ Tip

- You're not limited to plain-vanilla design with CDML. If you're comfortable with Web page creation, you can replace the BACK and NEXT text links with graphic buttons or navigation bars.

Figure 15.57 The FileMaker database looks like a regular Web table, but pulls its information directly from the published file.

Figure 15.58 Enter the name of the database (or All Databases) for which you want to set restrictions.

— Master password

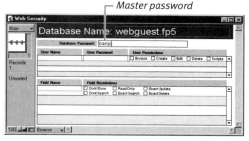

Figure 15.59 The master password grants full access to the database.

— User password

Figure 15.60 Each user can have a different password and access.

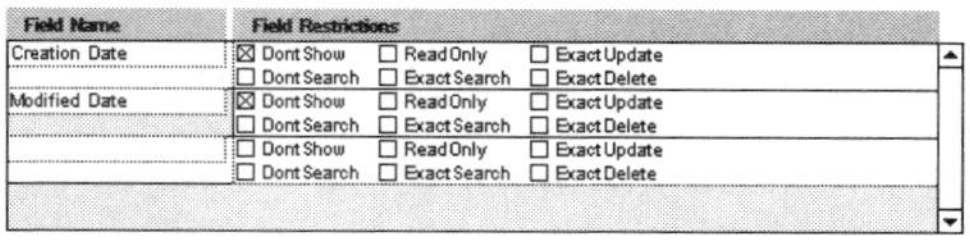

Figure 15.61 You can set restrictions for each field in the database.

Using the Web Security Database

A FileMaker database published with Custom Web Publishing can use the password settings that have already been set in the database. However, if you want more detailed control over access, you can use the Web Security database. The Web Security database doesn't work with Instant Web Publishing, only with Custom Web Publishing.

To use the Web Security database:

1. In the folder that holds your FileMaker Pro 5 application, open the Web Security folder, then the Databases folder inside it. Double-click Web Security.fp5. Choose Records > New Record (Ctrl+N/ Command-N). A new blank record will appear.

2. Click the Database Name text field and type the name of your published database (**Figure 15.58**). If you want to apply the security settings to all published databases, enter All Databases.

3. Click the Database Password field. Type the master password for the published database (**Figure 15.59**).

4. If you want to set permissions and passwords for certain users, type the name under User Name and enter a password for that user in the User Password field. Click the actions you want that user to have access to (**Figure 15.60**). To apply the setting to everyone, type All Users in the User name field.

5. To restrict access to certain fields, type the field name you want to restrict in the Field Name field. Click the check boxes next to the field names to set the restrictions for each field (**Figure 15.61**).

continues on next page

6. Choose Edit > Preferences > Application.

7. Click the Plug-Ins tab.

8. In the Plug-Ins list, double-click the Web Companion.

9. In the Web Companion Configuration dialog box's Security section, click the Web Security Database radio button (**Figure 15.62**). Click OK, then OK again.

When users access the database, the password they enter determines which actions they can perform and which fields they can access.

✔ Tip

■ The settings in the Web Security database do not override settings made in the database itself. So if an action is restricted in the passwords/groups settings, it won't be available even if you didn't restrict it in the Web Security database.

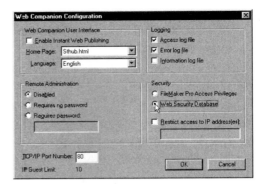

Figure 15.62 Enable the Web Security Database to use its settings instead of the built-in password settings of the database.

XML and JDBC

In addition to using CDML to access a FileMaker database on the Web, FileMaker now supports both XML and JDBC. This is wonderful news for the future, because unlike CDML, which is a proprietary standard (it only works with FileMaker), XML and Java are both open standards that many companies support or have committed to support in the near future. FileMaker Inc. has made it clear that they consider XML to be the future of the product. Its flexibility and power make it a very promising environment for publishing data.

Neither of these technologies is something you'd pick up overnight. For the average FileMaker Pro user, JDBC is inaccessible in the short term unless you are already a programmer. It is a bona fide language much closer to C++ than HTML. Although XML is somewhat more approachable, it's more complex than CDML because it's both extensible and object-oriented. In addition (at the time of this writing) XML is also only supported by one browser: Microsoft's Internet Explorer 5.0. Unless you are working in an environment where you can dictate which browser people
will use to access your database, these are serious stumbling blocks. Until support for XML is more common, we think you're better off concentrating on CDML with HTML.

✔ Tip

- Microsoft Internet Explorer 5 is currently the only browser that supports XML. Explorer 4 will display data with XML but does not allow users to edit the data.

The Future of XML

Those of you who are interested in creating connectivity between FileMaker and other databases should stay tuned in to XML developments. Not only is it great for moving data to the Web, but it's also optimal for transferring data between different database applications. In the not-too-distant future, it may surpass ODBC for this purpose.

FM Developer's Edition

If you are doing serious Web design or advanced database programming with FileMaker, you should consider purchasing the Developer's edition. In addition to a full copy of FileMaker 5, the Developer's Edition includes:

◆ A utility program that automates creating CDML code.

◆ Extensive documentation for Web publishing including CDML, XML, and JDBC.

◆ Some nifty utilities for renaming files and references.

◆ An application that can make your FileMaker databases into stand-alone programs (so they can be run on computers that don't have FileMaker installed).

◆ Lots of example files demonstrating advanced programming techniques.

FileMaker and Third-Party Software

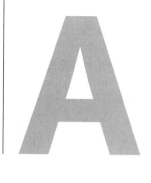

FileMaker gives you a variety of tools to construct interfaces, manipulate data and serve databases over the Web. But, like any off-the-shelf program, there's a limit to what it can do—you don't want it to become so enormous it would overwhelm your hard drive, and so complicated that it would stop being the best choice for database users who also want to have a life. Like many savvy software developers, the folks at FileMaker have found a way to keep FileMaker easy to understand while meeting specialized user needs. They've built into the program the ability to incorporate a wide variety of plug-ins, as well as making it easy for other developers to create external programs that work seamlessly with FileMaker to make it a true database powerhouse.

Web Integration

Blue World Communications

`http://www.blueworld.com`

Lasso

Macintosh, Windows

List Price: $649

Lasso is an add-on that goes well beyond Custom Web Publishing in providing a professional Internet database. Lasso offers Secure Sockets Layer support, which closes some of FileMaker's security holes to provide secure Web transactions for online commerce, integration with Web servers other than FileMaker Server and more markup tags than FileMaker's CDML.

WebFM

`http://www.Webfm.com`

WebFM

Macintosh only

List Price: $395

WebFM is a FileMaker add-on that allows database access through Web servers like WebStar and WebTen. As with Lasso, Web FM uses custom markup tags with greater capabilities than CDML.

PictFM

Macintosh only

List Price: $195

PictFM is an add-on that converts graphics stored in a FileMaker database into Web-compliant JPEG files on the fly. PictFM makes it simple to store graphic images in a FileMaker database and still make them available for viewing in Web pages.

Note: WebFM and PictFM are currently available only for FileMaker 4.0.

Fax and Email

Data Designs

`http://www.datadesigns.com`

FaxTool

Macintosh, Windows

List Price: $199.95

FaxTool is a FileMaker add-on that employs FaxSTF (Macintosh) or WinFax Pro (Windows) to send faxes directly from a FileMaker database.

Datamail Corp.

`http://www.datamailcorp.com/`

dbMailer

Macintosh, Windows

List Price: $30

dBMailer turns FileMaker Pro into a full-fledged email program. It allows you to implement email without the use of an external email application.

Plug-Ins and Utilities

New Millennium

`http://www.newmillennium.com`

Dialog Magic

Macintosh, Windows

List Price: $79.95

The Dialog Magic plug-in allows you to easily script imports and exports, change all of the passwords in a series of FileMaker databases, script data entry with dialog boxes and perform many other scripting tasks that usually require tedious step-by-step work.

Secure FM

Macintosh, Windows

List Price: $99 (five-user license)

FileMaker is a fairly imprecise tool for securing database information. The Secure FM plug-in gives you precise control over the FileMaker interface itself. For example, you can determine which menus a user has access to, and disable menu commands and specific dialog boxes.

Troi

`http://www.troi.com/`

Troi is the best known of the companies that make FileMaker plug-ins. They offer a wide variety of add-ons that can alter and extend the FileMaker interface. Check out Troi's Web site for their full range of goodies.

Dialog Plug-in

Macintosh, Windows

List Price: $20

Dialog Plug-in is a user-interface control. With it, you can create custom message boxes with variable text, dialog boxes with up to four buttons, flash message boxes, and progress bars for long operations. Users can even input data in dialog boxes.

File Plug-in

Macintosh, Windows

List Price: $39

File Plug-in is a file-management utility. It allows you to create and move and delete files and folders on your hard drive, as well as insert and extract text from external files.

Coding Plug-in

Macintosh, Windows

List Price: $39

Coding Plug-in adds industrial-strength data encryption to your FileMaker files and exported and imported text. Using DES encryption technology, this plug-in provides much stronger security for your databases.

Graphic Plug-in

Macintosh, Windows

List Price: $49

Graphic Plug-in is a plug-in that gives you powerful graphic functions like thumbnail creation, screen captures and the ability to create container fields in any RGB color.

Waves in Motion

`http://wmotion.com`

Analyzer

Macintosh only

List Price: $239

Analyzer is a developer's utility that creates a FileMaker database listing all of the constituent parts of an entire FileMaker solution. After running Analyzer, you have a complete database of fields, layouts, relationships, value lists, passwords and buttons from all of the databases. Analyzer is an invaluable tool when you are trying to get a handle on large multi-file systems.

cc Authorize

Macintosh, Windows

List Price: $200

The cc Authorize add-on makes it possible to integrate credit card authorization (through third-party systems) into a FileMaker database. It is also available as a stand-alone application.

Azium Strings Functions

Macintosh, Windows

List Price: $49

Azium Strings Functions provides you with new functions to control character strings. It can convert a textstring into a desired format, extract an item from a list within a text string, distinguish between upper- and lower-case and extract sub-strings without having to create complex calculations.

DocuScript 2.0
Macintosh only
List Price: $79

DocuScript 2.0 can troubleshoot and analyze your scripts. It can search through all your scripts and find all scripts that reference a certain layout, relationship or field.

Interface Design

Cinco Group
http://www.cincogroup.com

Theme Creator
Macintosh, Windows
List Price: $99.95

Theme Creator makes layout themes, automating and enhancing the formatting of FileMaker layouts. Theme Creator expands upon the Layout Assistant in FileMaker Pro 5 enabling you to build, modify, save, and share your themes.

Krische Data Systems
http://www.krischesystems.com

1000 Buttons Series (vol. 1–5)
Macintosh, Windows
List Price: $5

This collection of buttons and graphics is a great help for developers who want a professional-looking interface but don't want to take the time (or don't have the artistic flair) to design new buttons themselves.

Handheld Devices

FileMaker Inc.

FileMaker Mobile
Macintosh, Windows
List Price: $99

FileMaker Mobile is a companion to FileMaker Pro 5 that will allow a user to transfer and synchronize data between FileMaker Pro databases on Windows and Mac OS systems and Palm-powered handhelds.

A user simply selects and loads the FileMaker data they require from their desktop computer to the Palm OS handheld. Later, the data on the handheld may be re-synched via the Palm HotSync® technology with the FileMaker Pro database on the desktop computer.

Land-J Technologies
http://www.land-j.com/jfile.html

JFile and FM-Synch
Macintosh only
List Price: $38

Wouldn't it be nice if you could run FileMaker on your Palm Pilot? Alas, at the moment there is no Palm version of FileMaker. But there is JFile, a database application that does run on a Palm Pilot. FM-Synch is a Palm conduit that synchronizes records between selected FileMaker files and JFile databases on the Palm. So you can add, edit and delete records on either the Palm or your desktop computer and have all the changes appear in both databases after you synch your Palm.

FileMaker
Resources

Books

Many fine books on FileMaker are available. Here are just a few:

Database Publishing on the Web with Filemaker Pro (Peachpit Press)
Maria Langer

Filemaker Pro and the World Wide Web (FileMaker Press)
Jesse Feiler

Although both of these books cover earlier versions of FileMaker, they are excellent resources for learning CDML and other methods of FileMaker data publishing.

Scriptology: Filemaker Pro Demystified (ISO Publishing)
Matt Petrowsky & John Mark Osborne

Scriptology is *the* encyclopaedia of FileMaker. It covers in detail all aspects of scripting and formula building.

For more on XML, we recommend:

XML for the World Wide Web: Visual QuickStart Guide (Peachpit Press)
Elizabeth Castro

Web Pages

FileMaker Inc.

`http://www.filemaker.com`

FileMaker has always provided exemplary support for its products. Its Web pages provide access to sample files, FileMaker news, product updates, links to other Web sites and lots more. If you're looking for FileMaker resources online, this should be your first stop.

ISOFileMaker World

`http://www.filemakerworld.com/`

FileMaker World is a comprehensive Web site for FileMaker. It has links to many other FileMaker related sites, downloadable sample files, job listings, and other subjects pertaining to all aspects of FileMaker.

FMPro.org

`http://www.fmpro.org/`

Like FileMaker World, FMPro offers an extensive array of links to other FileMaker sites, sample files, tips and tricks, job opportunities, information about commercial applications built with FileMaker and many other resources.

Mailing Lists

http://www.blueworld.com/blueworld/
lists/filemaker.html

Blueworld (of Lasso fame) runs a top-notch listserv where FileMaker users and developers swap tricks and tips, post queries and help other users solve problems. This is a fairly high-volume list (which is good), so be prepared for lots of email. A daily digest is also available.

Usenet

comp.databases.filemaker

The FileMaker newsgroup is a forum where questions, answers and comments are posted. Although Usenet has been somewhat overshadowed by email lists, this group can be useful resource.

Publications

FileMaker Pro Advisor

http://www.advisor.com

This is the only currently available magazine that specializes in FileMaker Pro. *FileMaker Pro Advisor* offers excellent articles on FileMaker development, a great tips column and stories about how FileMaker is used in a variety of business applications.

ISO FileMaker Magazine

http://www.filemakermagazine.com

ISO FileMaker Magazine is a monthly maagazine distributed as a downloadable FileMaker database. It contains useful articles, tips and tricks, and FileMaker news.

User Groups

There are many local user groups that specialize in FileMaker. User groups are a great way to meet others who are involved in FileMaker use and development.

A current list of user groups is available at http://www.filemaker.com/support/usergroups.html.

FileMaker Solutions Alliance

If you are a professional FileMaker developer, either as an independent contractor or as part of your regular job, FSA is FileMaker Inc's resource for you. FileMaker provides a private section on its Web site for FSA members offering access to news and other resources not available to the public. The annual FileMaker Directory and Resource Guide (included with every copy of FileMaker) lists FSA members by specialty and geographic region. FSA also runs a yearly conference for its members that presents seminars in advanced FileMaker development.

FileMaker Hosting

If you want to host your FileMaker databases online but don't have high-speed Internet access, there are companies that will host your files for you.

FMPhost.net

http://www.fmphost.net

World Wide Host

http://www.worldwidehost.com

ASYS

http://www.oasysglobal.net

Macmacs

http://www.madmacs.net

These companies offer different hosting packages, as well as in-house FileMaker experts to help you get your databases up and running on the Internet.

INDEX

INDEX

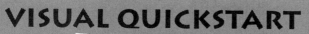